The Book of DOLL MAKING

The Book of DOLL MAKING

A comprehensive project
book and reference to making traditional
and innovative dolls

Alicia Merrett

CHARTWELL
BOOKS, INC

DEDICATION

To my daughters, Juley and Selena, for providing inspiration,
and for playing with dolls; to my husband Steve, for his
unfailing support over the years; to my late mother, Dorita
Kaner, who taught me not only to sew but also to create; and
to my Aunt Elena, for being herself.

A QUINTET BOOK

Published by Chartwell Books
A Division of Book Sales, Inc.
114, Northfield Avenue
Edison, New Jersey 08837

This edition produced for sale in the U.S.A., its
territories and dependencies only.

ISBN 0-7858-0887-6

This book was designed and produced by
Quintet Publishing Limited
6 Blundell Street
London N7 9BH

Creative Director: Richard Dewing
Art Director: Silke Braun
Project Editor: Clare Hubbard
Editor: Dorothea Hall
Photographer: Ferguson Hill
Illustrator: Nicola Gregory

Typeset in Great Britain by
Central Southern Typesetters, Eastbourne
Manufactured in Singapore by Bright Arts (Singapore) Pte Ltd
Printed in China by Leefung-Asco Printers Ltd

ACKNOWLEDGMENTS
The Traditional Doll and the Witch were first published in
Crafts Beautiful magazine and the Pierrot was first published
in *Popular Crafts* magazine.

Contents

Part I
Rag Dolls

Part II
Fantasy Dolls

Part III
Special Dolls

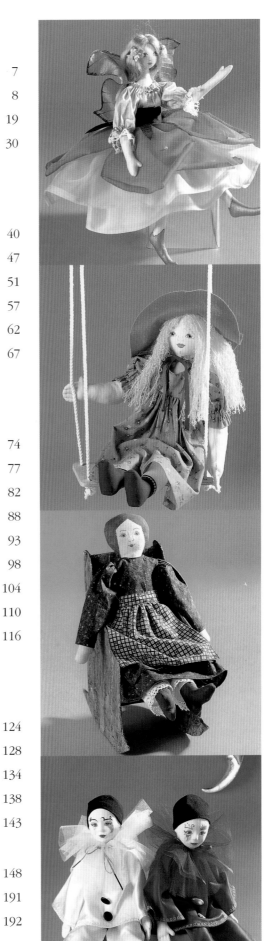

Dolls with shaped mask faces look expressive and realistic.

Doll Making—A Creative Art

What is a doll? The first reply that comes to mind is that it is a toy, a plaything. However, it can mean different things to different people. The anthropologist may say it is a cultural artefact, while a collector will see it as a collectors' piece. We can all agree that a doll is a representation of the human form—a manifestation of the inclination of humans to make images of themselves.

People across the world have been making dolls since the dawn of time. Many have not survived because they were made from perishable materials. The contemporary commercial playdoll is now made from modern, safe, and unbreakable materials, suitable for children to play with. Collectors' dolls are often made of porcelain or wax.

The humble rag doll, born centuries ago, and reborn many times, still has its secure place in the affection of both the child and the adult.

Fabric dolls, in their most recent incarnation, also appeal to grown ups and collectors. A whole creative area, spanning the crafts and the arts, has grown as people use their imagination to express themselves in a representation of the human shape. The artist dollmaker is born.

A few oddments of fabric, a ball of yarn, a touch of paint, or maybe a little embroidery are all you need to begin the magical process of creating a doll—a being with its own personality.

In this book I have tried to present doll-making projects to suit everyone—from the beginner to the budding artist. There are rag dolls for children and cloth dolls for collectors; but with some thought for safety, many are suitable for both. There is also a section on beginning to design your own dolls.

So why not start today, using your imaginative powers to craft your own creation—and feel the magic of doll making.

Rag doll made by Art Fabric Mills, New York, 1900.

Note

Each doll has a level of difficulty rating to help you choose the right project for your skill level.

★ Very easy, suitable for beginners

★★ Fairly easy, doll has detailed parts

★★★ Intermediate

★★★★ Advanced

Getting Started

Tools and Equipment

The majority of the tools and equipment necessary for doll making are found around the house: needles, pins, threads, scissors, pencils and pens, stuffings, sticks, and glues. A few of the pieces are specialized, and as they are very useful, it may be worth making an effort to buy them if you are going to make more than the occasional doll.

Sewing Tools

Selection of needles: sharp sewing needles, crewel embroidery needles with larger eyes, extra-fine needles for soft-sculpting faces, extra-long needles for button-jointing. Each needle has its own specific job to perform (1).

Color-headed pins are the safest type of pin to use as they do not get lost amongst the work (2).

Safety pins, for threading elastic through narrow casings (3).

Seam ripper, for removing unwanted stitches (4).

Threads

Hand-quilting thread, slightly thicker and stronger, recommended for soft-sculpting dolls' faces (1).

Cotton and polyester sewing thread (2).

Extra strong carpet thread, recommended for button-jointing of dolls' limbs (3).

Hand-embroidery threads, for embroidering faces and clothes (4).

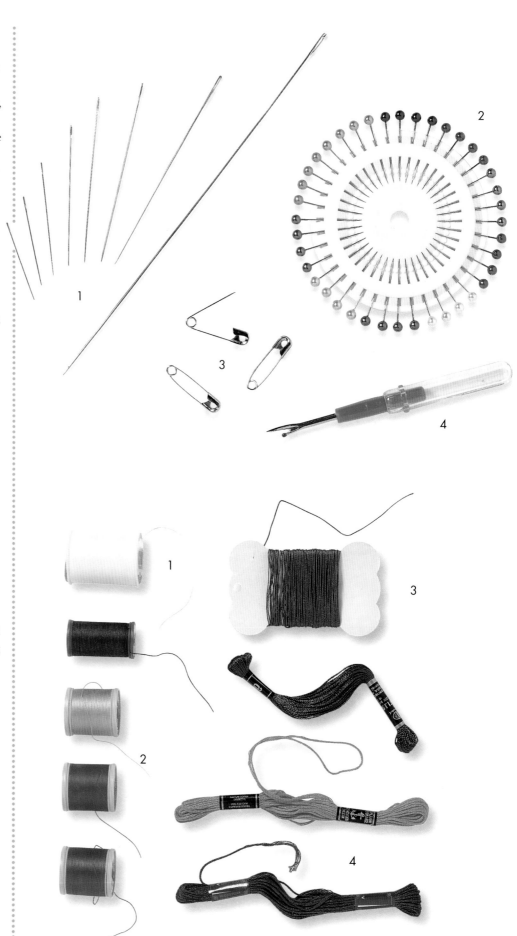

Cutting Tools

Small sharp pointed scissors, for embroidery and jobs in tight areas (1).

Dressmaking scissors, for cutting fabric (2).

Pinking shears, for the neat finishing of raw edges (3).

All-purpose household scissors, best reserved for cutting paper, so as not to dull the edge of fabric scissors (4).

Rotary cutter, very useful for cutting straight edges, for example, a skirt. Use on a self-healing cutting mat (5).

Turning and Stuffing Tools

Surgical forceps or hemostats: this specialized tool is now widely available from embroidery and fabric suppliers. It comes in various sizes and with straight or curved ends. The jaws lock tight when closed. It is invaluable for grabbing fabric seams when turning pieces right side out, and for pushing stuffing right to the end of long narrow pieces (1).

Different types of stuffing sticks: you can buy specially made wooden and metal sticks, however chopsticks and wooden dowels with the ends rounded by sanding can also be used (2).

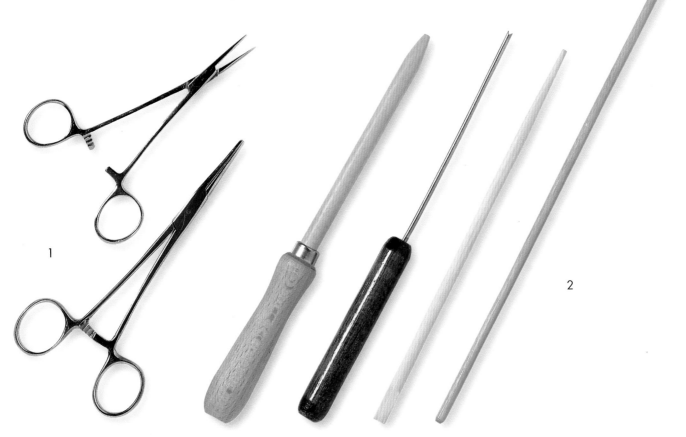

Markers

Color pencils for coloring faces, and a waterproof drawing pen for drawing face outlines (1).

Colored fabric crayons for coloring faces (2).

Markers, for marking patterns on fabric; silver and white pencils for marking dark fabrics; air-vanishing pen; ball-point pen (3).

Painting Tools

Acrylic fabric paints in basic colors (1).

Acrylic fabric paints: gold metallic, clear glitter, and colored glitter (2).

Fabric medium. Use to dilute paints instead of water, to avoid the paint running in the fabric (3).

Fine pointed brushes (4).

Materials

Lots of different materials are useful for dollmaking and below is a selection of the most popular ones. Many do not need to be bought, as they may be found around the house—leftover pieces of fabric or even recycled children's clothes. Be imaginative and discover other materials to make your dolls with.

Fabrics for Dolls' Bodies

Unbleached muslin (most commonly used to make the body), tea-dyed muslin (for old-looking dolls), brown and pink woven cottons (for different flesh tones) (1).

A variety of stretch fabrics: double and single knit, jersey, and stretch fabric with Lycra™ (2).

Linings for dolls' bodies: soft open-weave fabric for head layer on masks; batiste for body lining. Linings strengthen fine fabrics and stop stretchy ones from distorting (3).

Iron-on lining, woven and non-woven (4).

Fabrics for Costuming Dolls

Cotton fabrics in plain colors, stripes, checks, and prints (1).

Fine gloving leather and felt for shoes and boots (2).

Organza, for fairy's wings and other fantasy costuming (3).

Velvet, silk, satin, and netting for fantasy or character costumes such as Santa, Jojo the Clown, and Pierrot (4).

Trimmings

Lace edgings: nylon lace, cotton lace, and broderie anglaise (1).

Decorative edgings and ribbons: gold edging, zigzag trimming, narrow gold ribbon, narrow satin ribbon, medium satin ribbon, tartan ribbon (2).

Decorations and Accessories

Small artificial flowers (1).

Buttons: used for decoration and for button jointing (2).

Wooden beads with ¼ inch holes for doll jointing (3).

Press studs, plastic and metal, for fastening clothes (4).

Small beads, for embellishment purposes (5).

Decorative star, one of the many appliqués available in haberdasheries (6).

Doll spectacles (7).

Miscellaneous Items

Velcro™ fastening strips (1).

Chenille stems for making finger armature (2).

Narrow elastic, available in different widths (3).

Awl—used for making holes in fabrics by separating rather than breaking the threads. Very useful for making holes for fitting plastic joints (4).

Plastic joints (5).

BELOW *Decorations and accessories can enhance the look of the doll.*

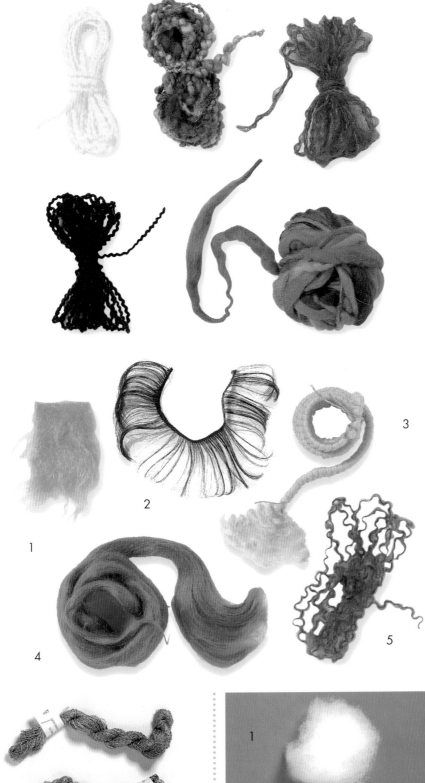

Hairmaking Materials

Knitting Wools
A variety of knitting wools can be used for dolls' hairmaking: acrylic and wool boucle, mohair, variegated spaced-dyed wools (left).

Other Hairmaking Materials
Long fiber fur fabric (1).

Wefted "real" hair, for making into wigs (2).

Crepe mohair (3).

Spun straight wool (4).

Wavy mohair, especially made for dolls wigging (5).

Fantasy Threads
Different types of fantasy embroidery threads that can be used for making hair: two types of rayon boucle, chenille, and fine viscose ribbon (6).

Stuffings

Many stuffing materials have been used in the past, but today's safety regulations mean that the only really clean and safe stuffing one should use is polyester filling, a man-made fiber which comes in different qualities, heavier or bouncier.

Types of Stuffing
Bouncy polyester stuffing, suitable for cuddly-type dolls, and larger ones (1).

Flat and heavy polyester stuffing, suitable for firmly-stuffed dolls, especially small ones (2).

Wadding: polyester sheets used for quilted areas (like the Mermaid's tail (see page 96), and also for wrapping chenille stems for fingers (3).

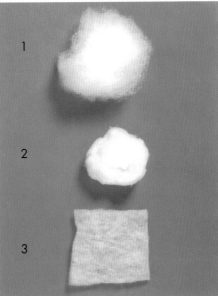

Techniques

Turning Through

Blunt sticks (or stuffing sticks), such as lengths of ½ inch dowel are easy to find or acquire. They are used to help turn to the right side all the narrower sections of the doll, such as arms and legs, prior to stuffing. It is important that sharp instruments like scissors are never used, because they may accidentally cut through the fabric or the stitching.

In my experience, the best tools for the job are surgery forceps or hemostats, which are becoming easier to find, see page 9. These instruments look a bit like blunt scissors, but have "grabbing" ends and a locking device which allows the fabric inside the stitched section to be held securely, and gently pulled through to the right side. The same tools can be used for easing seams right side out, and smoothing them for a neat finish.

Small forceps, fine blunt sticks, or knitting needles will help you to turn narrow tubes, such as fingers.

The Art of Stuffing

It is very important to stuff the doll quite thoroughly. The stuffing should be well packed, first in those areas such as the feet, which are furthest away, before proceeding with the rest of the body. Small areas require small pieces of stuffing, while large areas require bigger handfuls of stuffing. Think of the doll as a ball and press the stuffing against the outside skin before filling the center. Avoid lumps by pushing the filling well down with your hands or a suitable tool. Use your hands for shaping and modeling the different parts until the desired look is achieved.

Dolls' hands should be kept relatively flat, while feet, ankles, heads, necks, and shoulders must be very firm and rounded. All creases can be smoothed out by adding stuffing in the right places and pushing it in firmly. Bodies can be filled more or less firmly depending on the type of doll required, its size, and the material it is made of. It is amazing how much stuffing a doll can take. Remember that fillings settle down with time, so it is best to put more stuffing in than less.

Neatening Techniques

These are used to make the fabric lie flat, stop it unraveling, and generally achieve a better finish for your work.

Trimming corners (Figure 1)
Snipping curved seam allowances (Figure 2)
Pressing seams open
Fray-stopping seam edges

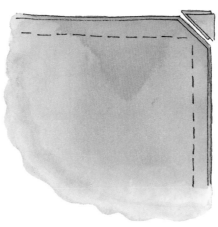

Figure 1

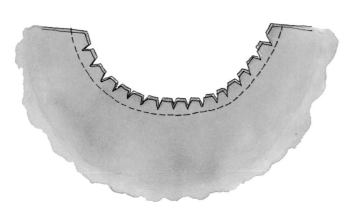

Figure 2

Dictionary of Stitches

Machine Stitches

Straight stitch (Figure 1)
Zig zag stitch (Figure 2)
Machine embroidery stitches (Figure 3)
Quilting (Figure 4)

Figure 1

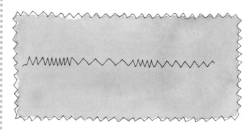

Figure 2

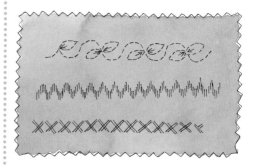

Figure 3

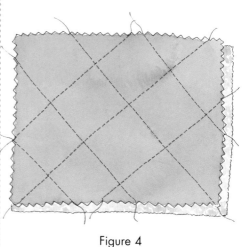

Figure 4

Hand Stitches
Back stitch (Figure 5)
Gathering stitch (Figure 6)
Ladder stitch (Figure 7)

Embroidery Stitches
Stem stitch (Figure 8)
Satin stitch (Figure 9)
Buttonhole stitch (Figure 10)
French knots (Figure 11)
Bullion stitch (Figure 12)
Turkey stitch (Figure 13)

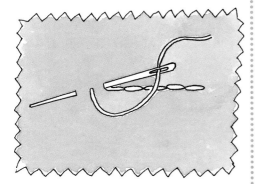

Figure 5

Figure 8

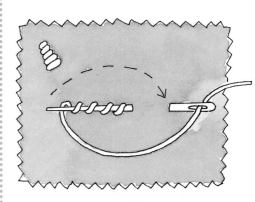

Figure 11

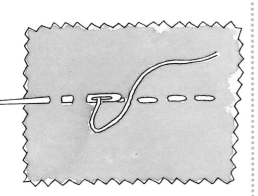

Figure 6

Figure 9

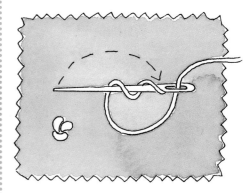

Figure 12

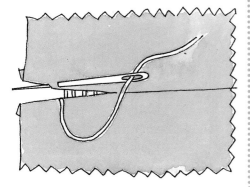

Figure 7

Figure 10

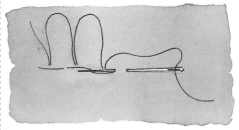

Figure 13

Preparing and Using Patterns and Templates

Understanding Patterns and Templates

Patterns are, according to the Oxford English Dictionary, "models from which things are to be made." For the purposes of doll making, "pattern" has two meanings: firstly, it is a generic word for all the "paper models" from which the dolls and their clothes are made, and secondly it is used specifically for those "paper models" which include seam allowances. These have an outer solid cutting line, and an inner dotted stitching line, usually placed ¼ inch away from the first (Figure 1).

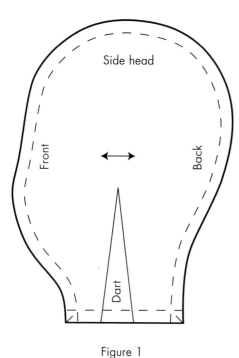

Figure 1

Templates are defined as a "guide to cutting." In this book, "template" means those "paper models" which do not include seam allowances, that is to say, where the drawn outline is the stitching line (Figure 2).

A combined pattern/template is sometimes used in this book, for example, where one side includes the seam allowance and the other does not, because that side of the fabric has to be stitched before cutting (Figure 3).

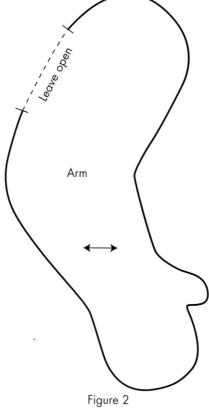

Figure 2

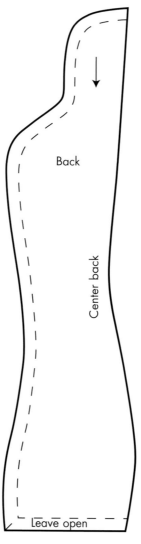

Figure 3

Preparing Patterns

When patterns are given full size, they can be copied either by photocopying, or by hand using tracing paper, and then they should be carefully cut out and labeled. Patterns that are going to be reused are best glued to, or made from thin card. Remember to use paper scissors for cutting out.

When patterns are given at a reduced size, they will need to be enlarged. This can be done by using one of the following methods.

Enlarging with a photocopier
This is the easiest and quickest way. If patterns have been reduced to half size, the photocopying machine needs to be set to enlarge by 200 percent. If the reduction rate is different, there will usually be instructions given as to the setting required.

Enlarging with the grid method
This is more laborious, but it is necessary when a photocopier is not available. This example details how to enlarge a pattern if it has been shown at half size.

1 Trace two grids on large sheets of tracing paper, the first one with ½ inch squares, and the second one with 1 inch squares.

2 Place the smaller grid on top of the pattern piece to be enlarged. Trace the pattern onto the grid.

3 Now mark the outline of the pattern on the larger grid, first marking the points where the pattern lines cross the grid lines. Then join up these points with pencil, following their curves and straight contours. Transfer all the markings indicating openings, joints, facial features, and so on.

How to Use Templates and Patterns

Half Patterns and Templates

Sometimes with symmetrical shapes, only half the pattern is given, and either a complete one has to be made before marking and cutting the fabric, or the half pattern can simply be placed on the fold of the fabric before cutting out, depending on the particular instructions. To make a complete pattern, either trace the half pattern twice on paper, reversing one of them, cut out, and join them together along the center with adhesive tape, or fold tracing paper and place the fold to the center, draw one side and cut out the two layers of paper, open up to obtain the whole pattern (Figure 1).

Pattern Layouts

For economic use of fabric, it is best to fit all the pattern pieces onto the fabric (following the correct grain) before starting to mark or cut out. When using templates, always allow sufficient space between pieces for seam allowances.

Fabric Grain and Nap

Items made from fabric are usually cut on the straight grain (with the warp, nap, or pile running from north to south) because fabrics hang better this way. Each paper pattern piece is marked with an arrow, which indicates the straight grain and should be placed on the fabric so that both straight grains match, unless the bias grain is specified. This runs diagonally across the fabric and is more stretchy than the straight grain.

With most stretch fabric, it is the width that usually gives the most stretch, except for Lycra™, which stretches equally in both directions. To indicate the direction with the most stretch, the pattern is marked with a horizontal double-headed arrow.

Hints and Tips

Marking fabric Most fabrics can be marked either with a soft pencil, ball-point pen, or air-vanishing pen. For dark fabrics, white or silver-colored pencils can be used.

Using patterns The outer (cutting) line is first traced onto the fabric with a suitable marker, and then any information marks such as openings, joint points, and so on are transferred, and the fabric is cut out along the cutting line (Figure 2). The appropriate pieces are then stitched together ¼ inch inside the edge, on the stitching line (Figure 3), following the instructions for the particular doll.

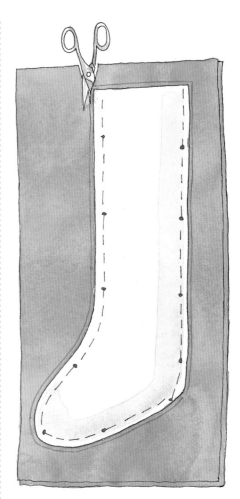

Figure 2

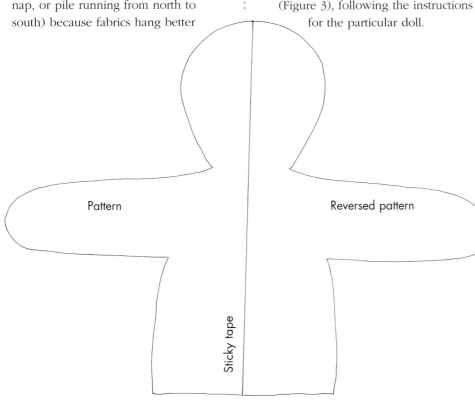

Pattern   Reversed pattern

Sticky tape

Figure 1

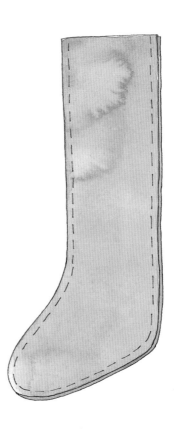

Figure 3

Using templates The outlines are traced onto the fabric, any information marks transferred, and then the appropriate pieces of fabric are stitched together on the marked line (Figure 1). The pieces are only then cut out, adding ¼ inch seam allowance (Figure 2).

You will see that many pattern pieces are given as templates, because I have found it a lot easier to stitch first and cut

out afterward, rather than try and hold together small, fiddly pieces in the sewing machine (Figure 3).

To prevent cutting out pattern pieces without seam allowances, do not cut any fabric before you have double-checked whether you are working with a template or a pattern. Before you begin to make your dolls, always read the particular instructions through very carefully.

Reversing patterns Often pattern pieces have to be reversed to give a second one as a mirror image, perhaps for the right and left sides of the doll and the costume. This happens automatically when patterns are cut from double fabric (Figure 4).

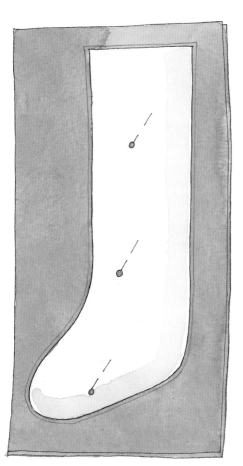

Figure 1

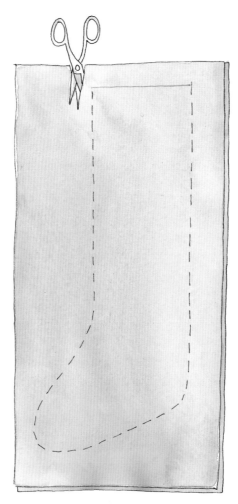

Figure 2

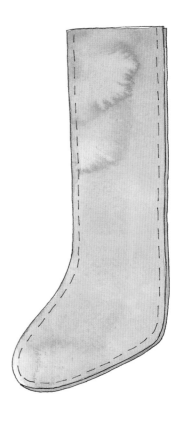

Figure 3

Figure 4

Elements of the Doll

A doll is a representation of a human being; it has a head, a body, two arms, and two legs. In making a doll we keep roughly to the proportions of the human figure. It does not have to be strictly realistic, in fact, dolls' heads are generally larger in proportion to the body than human heads are, but other parts of the body should be in harmony with each other. We also have to keep in mind that proportions vary with age and gender. Children and adults, for example, have quite different physical characteristics.

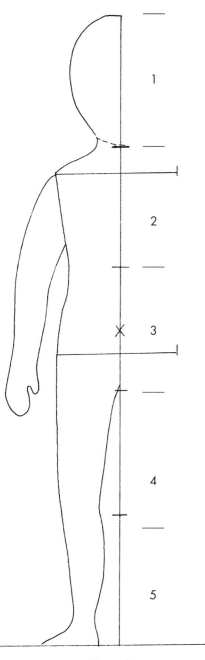

Figure 1

Proportions vary also between people of the same age and gender—they can be tall or short, slim or full-figured, broad-shouldered, or pear-shaped. So there is not a single formula to establish proportions for a doll. When designing a doll, one should refer to photographs of children or people of the same age and gender as the desired doll, and study their proportions. All this information can then be adapted to make the doll of your choice, which may have a larger head, or longer legs, depending on what you want it to look like.

Designing a Doll

This method of designing a doll is based on the visual artists' method of using the length of the head as a way of measuring the body and calculating proportions. The following example will illustrate the method which you can then use to design dolls of other ages and types (Figure 1).

Choose a photograph or picture from a book or magazine of the type of doll you would like to make—child, teenager, or adult, standing upright. Alternatively you can measure a real person. Measure the total height, A, and the length of the head from the top to the chin, B. Then divide A by B and this will tell you how many "heads" tall the person is. This number will also be your guideline for the doll.

Drawing the Basic Shape

1 In this example we will draw a doll about 17½ inches high or five heads tall: these are the proportions of a child three to four years old. The head measurement, from top to chin, should be 3½ inches (the height divided by 5). On a piece of tracing paper and using a ruler and pencil, draw a vertical line in the center, 17½ inches long, and then divide it into five sections each 3½ inches long. This line is the vertical center of the body. For reference purposes, number the sections 1 to 5, starting at the head.

2 To achieve symmetry, work on one half of the body first, fold the paper along the center line, and trace the other half. The head will be an oval filling the first section, and the neck will extend a little into the second section. Draw a line at right angles to the center line, 3½ inches across (the "head" length) placing it just below the neck, and evenly spaced on the central line. Use this width as a guide to shape the shoulders.

3 Mark the middle of the body, as shown, halfway down the third section: in a child of this age, the middle is approximately level with the navel. Mark the crotch two thirds of the way down the same section. Draw another 3½ inch line at right angles to the center line, a little above the crotch point, as a guide for shaping the hips.

4 To shape the body, mark the position of the waist which should be approximately level with the end of the second section.

5 The next stage is to draw the legs. Place the knee two thirds of the way down the fourth section. Draw the sole of the foot on the base line, which is a line placed at right angles to the end of the fifth section.

6 Complete by drawing in the arms. The tip of the hand in a small child should reach just below the crotch, and the elbows should be in line with the waist.

7 Fold the paper in half along the central line, and trace the second side of the doll. This is our basic doll shape. Do not cut it out, but keep this sketch for future reference.

Making the Body Patterns

1 Begin by placing a sheet of tracing paper on top of the original drawing. For a simple five-piece pattern, where the head and body are joined together, trace around the body and head as one piece, adding about ¼ to ½ inch around the edge. This addition is to allow for the roundness of the body and *not* the seam allowance.

2 Move the paper along and, quite separately from the body and head piece, trace the arm and leg, slightly increasing the size as before.

3 These are the basic pattern shapes, which can be used as templates, where the seam allowances are cut after stitching, or convert them into patterns by adding an integral seam allowance of ¼ inch (Figure 1). See Understanding Patterns and Templates on page 16.

4 To be absolutely sure that the pattern is to your liking, make a trial doll using the fabric you will use for the finished doll. Patterns usually need adjusting and refining, and it may take two or more

tries to get the shape of your doll exactly right.

5 From the same original sketch, a number of doll patterns can be developed by subdividing the parts into more sections, such as at the elbow and knee joints—when joined together they tend to give the doll a better shape and volume. The main types are explained in the next section. Different body and head shapes can be achieved by the addition of darts and gussets, which shape the doll by removing or adding volume in appropriate places. There are many variations of these, and the dolls in the project chapters illustrate many types of body and head shapes (Figure 2).

Types of Jointing for Dolls' Limbs

An important variation in dolls' shapes is achieved through the jointing used to link the limbs to the body. There are many variations of these, such as different types of stitching, using buttons and beads, and special plastic joints.

Jointing the dolls' limbs by stitching them to the body at the shoulders and hips only. The actual arms and legs are stuffed firmly, so they are fairly stiff (Figure 1).

Hinging shoulders, legs, elbows, and knees by stitching across with a flat seam. This extra flexibility of elbows and knees can also be achieved by doing a gathering stitch instead of a flat one, or alternatively threading the arms and legs through large-holed beads (Figure 2).

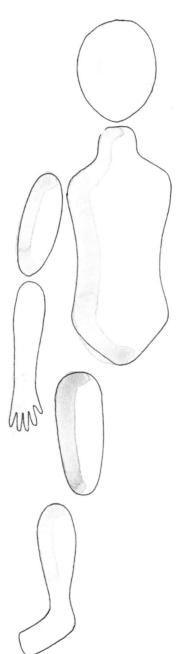

Figure 1

Figure 2

Figure 1

Figure 2

Figure 3

Figure 4

More flexibility, and better movement of limbs can be achieved by jointing the doll with extra-thick thread, held in place with the help of buttons on the outside of the joint. There are several types, explained later on in more detail, but the general effect is extreme poseability (Figure 3).

The most realistic way of jointing a doll is to use the plastic safety joints designed for teddy bears, which are discs hidden inside the limbs and body, and joined through a stem secured with a washer (Figure 4).

Assembling a Button Joint

Arms to shoulders and legs to hips

1 Mark the corresponding jointing points on the limbs and the body, as indicated on the original pattern.

2 Use a very thick thread—one made from a rough-finished natural fiber which will knot well. Linen carpet thread is the best, smooth, slippery nylon thread is useless. Thread a long needle, which should be a minimum of 3½ inches long. The thread should be long enough to be threaded doubled through the relevant body parts, plus 5 inches. Do not knot the ends.

3 Insert the needle just once through the marked points, going first through one limb, then the body, and the other limb, and bring it out at the other side. Cut the thread off near the eye of the needle, making sure tails of 2½ inches are left at each end.

4 Thread each pair of tails through two holes of a button; if the buttons have four holes, use two placed diagonally opposite each other. Make a knot on one button to hold it in place; then pull the threads from the other side, making sure you pull evenly so that all parts are equally squashed. Make a knot on the second side (Figure 1).

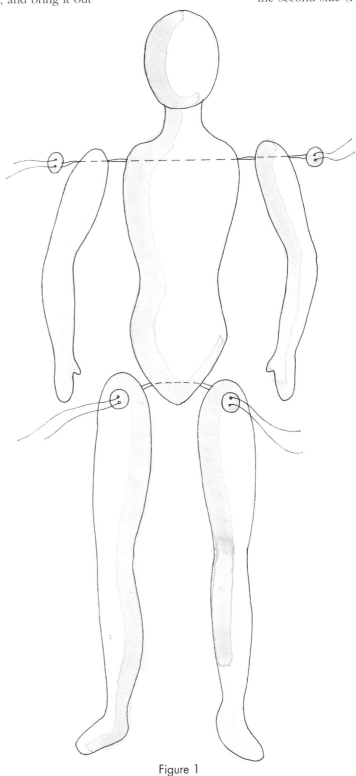

Figure 1

5 When the joint is tight enough (it should feel fairly stiff, not loose), make two more knots on each side, but do not cut the tails off yet. Take the tails under each button, twist them round several times, and make further knots underneath. Only then cut the tails off, leaving short ends hidden under the buttons. A spot of clear glue will hold them more firmly in place.

6 Alternatively, the ends of the thread can be hidden inside the body or between the body and the limbs. Other variations involve self-cover buttons with loop shanks. These can be used either in the way explained above, or inside the limb, more in the manner of the plastic joint (explained later as the teddy bear type joint). In this case, the thread goes through the body and the shanks, and after pulling tight it is knotted securely around the shanks.

Elbow and knee joints

Two types of elbow and knee joints have been used for the dolls in this book.

1 The simplest method is where the upper and lower parts of the limbs are put together alongside each other, with the lower arm overlapping the upper arm, and buttons are then attached as described above (Figure 1). See Hepzibah the Witch doll on page 77.

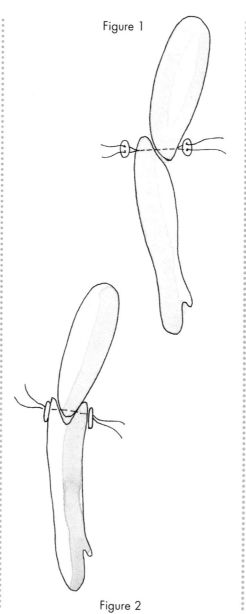

Figure 1

Figure 2

2 The more elaborate method has tabbed ends on one section of the limb, and the rounded end of the other section is placed between the two tabs, as seen in Clarissa Bow, the Fantasy Flapper on page 116. Buttons are then securely knotted on the outside, as described above (Figure 2).

Assembling a "Teddy Bear" Type Joint

1 This is a three-part plastic joint that consists of a circle with an attached stem, which is placed inside the limb (or even the neck in some cases), with the stem protruding through a hole in the fabric (Figure 1). A second plastic circle with a hole in the center goes inside the body, behind the corresponding joint position.

2 The stem is then placed into the body through the appropriate hole in the fabric, the second circle is slipped onto it, and finally a metal or plastic washer secures the whole joint together (Figure 2). To make it firm, a cotton reel, preferably the old wooden type, can be placed on the joint, and the assembly gently hammered down (Figure 3).

A "teddy bear" joint.

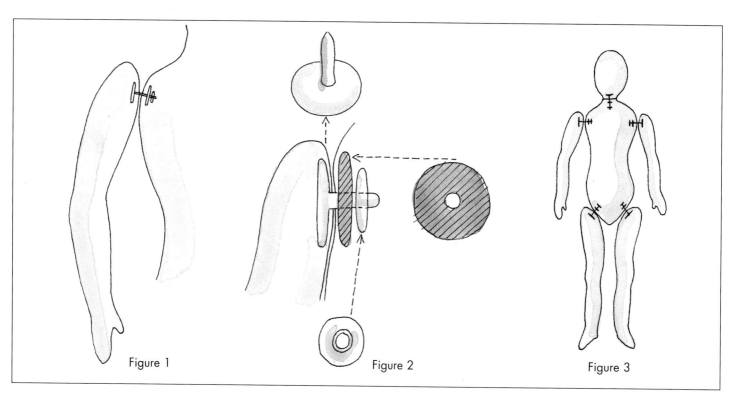

Figure 1

Figure 2

Figure 3

Making Faces

The face is the most important feature of the doll and it is essential to spend time getting it right. Heads should be firmly stuffed and well-shaped.

Hand-drawing and painting the features is the easiest way to make a face. This can be kept to very simple lines, dots, and dashes, or it can be done in a rather more elaborate way to achieve a life-like expression.

When designing a doll's face from scratch, the best way is to draw it on paper first, and when you have achieved your desired face, use this as a guide for the real thing. Begin by considering the type of doll you would like to make, because features are placed in different positions in the face according to age, gender, and style.

On paper, outline your chosen face shape, and draw a vertical line through the center of the face, and a horizontal line, also in the center. On the lower half of the face, add a horizontal quarter line, and an eighth line within the lower quarter. These are the reference lines for placing the features. Now draw the features according to the following principles (Figure 1).

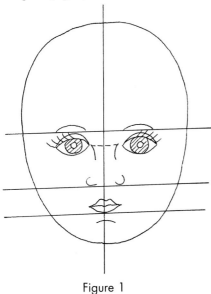

Figure 1

1 The eyes are positioned approximately on the horizontal center line; below it in babies and young children, on it in older children, on it or just above it in adults. The separation between the eyes is approximately one eye's width. The eyebrows are only slightly above the eyes.

2 The lower edge of the nose is halfway between the eyes and the chin on all faces.

3 The mouth fits just below the nose touching the eighth line.

These proportions should be followed for more realistic types of dolls, or they can be exaggerated for character dolls, as shown below (Figure 2).

Once you have decided on the features, transfer them to the face fabric by tracing against a window, placing the drawing under the fabric. When you are confident enough, you will be able to draw them directly onto fabric.

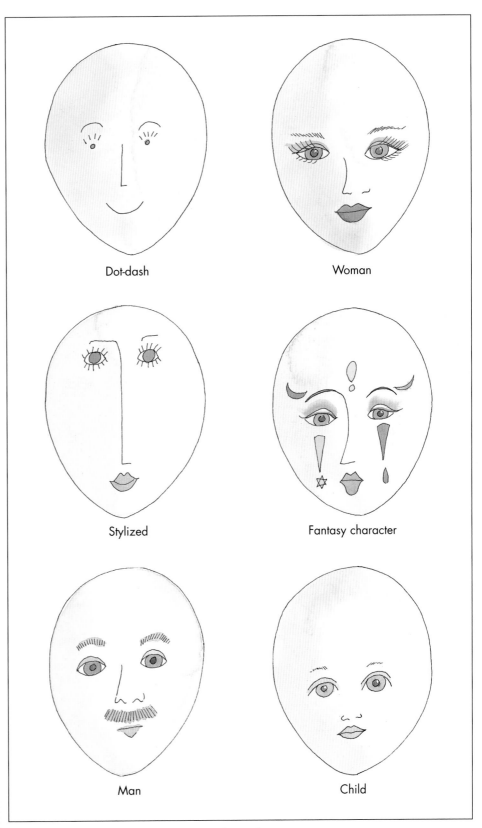

Dot-dash

Woman

Stylized

Fantasy character

Man

Child

Figure 2

Painting a Cloth Doll's Face

A very important element in painting a realistic, expressive doll's face is to base it on observations of real faces, and to use photographs as reference. Practice drawing and painting on fabric before tackling the doll, as this is different from painting on paper. Be prepared to discard a few faces before you make one you really like; for this reason, it is better to paint the face *before* attaching it to the body. Sometimes the face is best painted flat, and then assembled and stuffed, while at other times, it is best to do it after stuffing.

A number of painting and drawing materials are suitable for painting on fabric but I will refer here principally to acrylic fabric paints, which are applied with good quality, fine paint brushes. It is best to thin paints with acrylic fabric medium—not water, otherwise the paint may run and ruin the doll.

If you prefer not to use a brush, there are plenty of other suitable materials such as waterproof fabric pens, watercolor pencils, crayons, pastels, and others. Metallic paints and glitter paints are also very useful for fantasy dolls, like the Pierrot (see page 138).

When using paints, make sure the first layer of paint is really dry before painting on the next one, unless you want to blend the colors. When using pencils or crayons, colors can be blended simply by applying different colors on top of each other.

1 Referring to your photograph, lightly draw the shape of the eyes and mouth with pencil. Notice that the middle line of the mouth should follow the contour of the upper lip. The nose can be suggested with carefully shaped

Figure 1

squiggles for the nostrils and/or a short line for the bridge. Do not draw them too big and remember that the pencil lines should not be visible after painting (Figure 1).

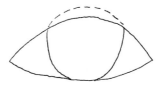

Figure 2

2 Drawing the iris. As a rule, the bigger the iris, the friendlier the doll will look. Children's irises are particularly large, and generally small irises in a large white area give a frightened or angry look. The top eyelid normally covers the top edge of the iris, so we do not see them as being completely round, but more like a "u" shape, completed by an "imaginary line" hidden by the eyelid. To preserve the "friendly look," the bottom edge of the iris should touch the edge of the eye (Figure 2).

3 Choose a color for the iris from brown, blue, gray, green, or violet. Paints can be mixed with white to make lighter shades, or with black or gray to darken them or to tone down bright colors. With pencils and crayons, apply successive layers of colors to achieve the required effect.

4 To give more expression to the eyes, shade them with darker and lighter variations of the main eye color, by blending white, gray, black, or brown,

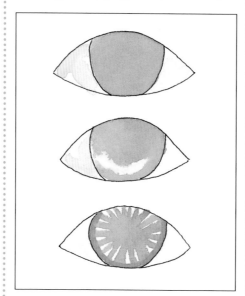

Figure 3

as appropriate, with the original color. You can also lighten the heavy solid color of an iris with a brushstroke of lighter eye-color applied to the bottom quarter of the eye; or, if the iris is already very light, darken the top quarter. Alternatively, lighten or darken the solid color with lines radiating from the center. You can also draw a darker edge around the iris of light-colored eyes (Figure 3).

5 With a darker shade of brown paint, or a brown waterproof drawing pen, paint or draw a slightly heavier line along the top edge of the eye, to indicate the eyelash line. Use black only if the doll is supposed to wear mascara. With a peach color, paint a line to indicate the eyelids, just above the eyelash line. If the doll requires it, paint or draw individual eyelashes with a fine pen or brush.

Paint the pupil, which is a black dot in the center of the iris. Remember that the larger the pupil and iris are in respect to the white of the eye, the friendlier the look of the doll. Paint one or two white dots on the top quarter edge of the pupil for the highlights. This always seems to breathe life into the doll. A small white crescent shape can also be painted on the opposite lower corner. Look at real people's eyes to understand the way highlights work; they are reflections of the surrounding light, and vary a lot (Figure 4).

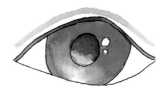

Figure 4

6 Paint or draw the eyebrows with lighter or darker brown, according to the general coloring of the doll; the more lifelike way is to paint them with small inclined strokes, simulating hairs. Do not place them too high up, or the doll will have a startled look (Figure 5).

Figure 5

7 The natural color of the lips is not a bright red or pink, but a peachy fleshtone; this is important when making child dolls. Adult dolls can have their lips painted in any "lipstick" color desired. The upper lip is often darker than the bottom one because of the way the light falls on it. First paint a solid color, but then either darken the top or lighten the center of the bottom lip. Little fanning lines can also be used to break the solid color; or sometimes the lips can be given a darker edge. Draw the middle line of the mouth with a darker shade of lip color, or a light brown (Figure 6).

Figure 6

8 As previously suggested, the nose can be indicated with different types of lines, long to represent the whole nose, or small round shapes to indicate the nostrils. Dolls with masks, however, do not need any nose indications.

9 When the paint is thoroughly dry, and you are satisfied with the look of the doll, you can paint a thin layer of acrylic gloss medium/varnish on the eyes and mouth. It will look milky when wet, but it dries clear and fulfils both the functions of protecting the paint, and

Figure 7

Figure 8

giving a shine to the eyes. If using other materials such as pencils or crayons, you may need to apply an artists' spray fixative, but test first on a spare piece of fabric, as different materials react in different ways (Figure 7).

10 When painting a fantasy or carnival character, such as Pierrot (see page 138), experiment first with different colors and shapes, and the variety of effects you can get with metallic paints, glitter paints, glues, and so on (Figure 8).

Embroidering a Cloth Doll's Face

The same types of face can also be achieved with embroidery, but this method is more laborious. The information given for painting a face, such as drawing shapes and the color suggestions for eyes, lips, and so on, can also be used as guidelines for embroidery. Draw the face on a piece of fabric big enough to fit in an embroidery hoop, and then embroider all the features before cutting, assembling, and stuffing (Figure 1).

Suitable stitches for embroidering faces are satin stitch, stem stitch, buttonhole/blanket stitch, and turkey stitch (for eyelashes). Details for working

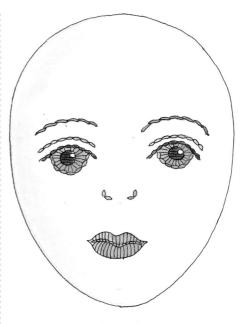

Figure 1

them are given on page 14 in the Dictionary of Stitches.

Clarissa Bow, the Fantasy Flapper on page 116 has a fully embroidered face which includes eyelashes, eyelids, eyebrows, nose, and mouth. The specific stitch details for working them are included in the instructions for making the doll. Other dolls such as Beth the Traditional Doll on page 51 also look good with embroidered faces.

Needle-sculpted and Soft-sculpted Faces

These techniques require a fair amount of practice to get good results, and many variations are possible. Details for sculpting specific faces are given with the relevant doll-making instructions later in the book. But before you embark on the real thing, it is a good idea to practice the techniques following these general principles.

1 Make a head shape using stockinette or other stretch material. Stuff thoroughly with high-bulk filling. Nose and cheek bulk can be increased by placing small balls of filling, wadding, or clay shapes in the relevant areas, such as the nose. Profile shapes are particularly appropriate for this technique.

2 Use a fine, long needle, and strong but fine thread—such as hand-quilting thread. Use it singly, as double threads tend to twist. Anchor the end by taking several stitches at invisible starting points, like the top or the back of the head.

3 Shape the features by molding the stuffed head with your hands, and use the point of the needle to shift stuffing around if required. Secure the shapes in place by taking very tiny stitches, about 1/16 inch. Go back and forth at least twice for each stitch, to secure the shape in place. Some larger stitches are taken through to the outside of the head, as for some mouths, eyes, and nostrils.

4 Begin by forming the nose, starting just above the nostrils, which are the widest section, and decreasing the width upward—the top of the bridge of the nose is level with the eyes (Figure 1).

5 Sink the eye and mouth corners, with stitches going to the back or top, and

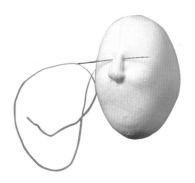

Figure 1

Figure 2

link them to each other to form cheeks. Use the tip of the needle to pull stuffing further up into the features, or to move it from one area to another (Figure 2).

6 Creases and folds of all sorts can be achieved with these techniques, to obtain older looking characters.

Other Techniques

Trapunto This is a method where small amounts of stuffing and wool are placed in shapes and channels stitched between two layers of fabric, as shown on the head front of the Mermaid on page 93.

Appliqué Additional pieces of fabric can be stitched on, or fused to the face fabric to indicate the features.

Mask heads A separate mask is made which is then covered in fabric and attached to the doll's body. Detailed

instructions for making masks are given on pages 30–37, see also Lara on page 128.

Separate Ears and Noses

Separate "button" noses, made by stuffing gathered circles of fabric, and individually stitched ears, can be added to suitable dolls for special expressions (Figure 3).

Hair

Hair frames the face and it is very important to the overall look of dolls. Many different fibers and materials can be used, as listed on page 13.

Yarn Hairstyles

1 Lengths of knitting wool, tapestry yarn, and embroidery threads, held together by machine stitching, are the most usual way of making dolls' hair. A piece of stiff card is used to wind the yarn around (Figure 1). Measurements are taken on the doll's head from one side to the other, and from back to front, or across the head, according to the type of hair style required. This will give you the length of the hair and the width

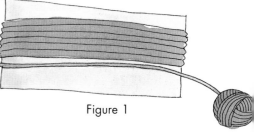

Figure 1

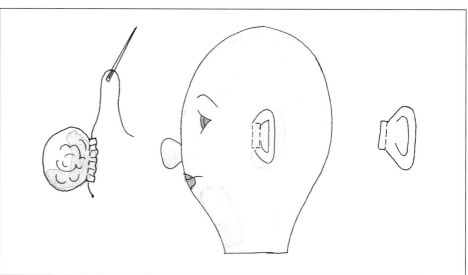

Figure 3

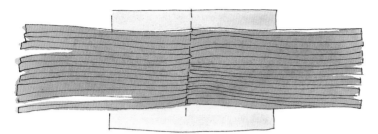

Figure 2

Figure 4

(number of yarn strands) required. The card is cut to the correct length, but a bit wider than required to facilitate handling. Then the yarn is wound around as many times as required to obtain the correct width.

2 When enough yarn has been wound around carefully remove the yarn from the card and place it on a piece of paper where a line of the correct width measurement has been drawn. The yarn should cover the line. For center partings, place the center of the yarn on the line, and carefully machine stitch across twice, working slowly so as to avoid the yarn bunching (Figure 2).

3 Tear off the paper. Attach the hair to the doll, stitching from the forehead to the back of the neck, along the center of the head, using back stitch. If desired, plaits and bunches can be made to style the hair (Figure 3).

4 Other variations include stitching the yarn closer to one end so that the shorter length makes a fringe (Figure 4). This is attached across the top of the head (Figure 5).

Figure 3

Figure 5

5 For more elaborate hairstyles with greater fullness, "wefts" of yarn can be made by stitching down the center on long, but thin lengths of yarn (Figure 6). These are then folded in half along the stitched line, and attached to the head in rows across, starting at the back and working upward. How many pieces are used depends on the size of the doll's head and the thickness of the yarn. The top is finished with a section of center parting or "fringe-stitched" yarn (Figure 7).

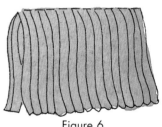

Figure 6

Figure 7

6 Ponytails or Edwardian hairstyles can also be made with long lengths of this center-stitched yarn. It is folded along the stitch line, and attached all around the doll's head at the hairline. The yarn is then pulled up toward the crown of the head, and made into a ponytail or bun (Figure 8).

7 Short, thick hairstyles can be made from looped yarn. Begin by folding typing paper lengthwise in four so that it is only about 2 inches wide. You will need several lengths to cover the head. Wind the yarn tightly around the paper and machine stitch through the paper and yarn lengthwise along the center of the strip. Tear off the paper, and attach the looped yarn to the doll's head,

working in a spiral, starting at the hairline and finishing on the top of the head. The loops can be left as they are for a curly hairstyle, cut for a more wild look, or trimmed for a tidy style. Longer or shorter loops can be made, depending on the doll and the style required (Figures 9 and 10).

8 Curly yarn can be obtained by either unraveling a knitted garment or by wrapping yarn tightly around a dowel or pencil; secure the ends, dampen the yarn, and let dry thoroughly before removing from the dowel. The curls can be attached to the head directly, used with other types of yarn styles, as bangs, for example, or made into wefts as previously explained (Figure 11).

Figure 11

Hairstyles using other Fibers

There are a number of natural and artificial fibers and yarns which are suitable for making dolls' hair; some are specifically marketed for this purpose. These fibers can be attached directly to the doll's head, or stitched on paper and then attached to the head in exactly the same way as for yarn hair. Mohair, curly crepe, roving and unspun wool, silk, flax, and hemp, are all suitable fibers.

Some of them come already bunched up and stick to each other, so they do not need stitching. Instead, they can be twisted into different shapes and attached directly to the doll's head. They can also be glued instead of stitched (Figure 1).

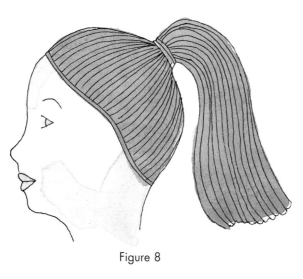

Figure 8

Figure 9

Figure 10

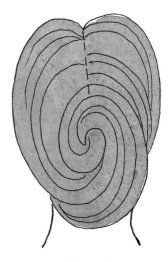

Figure 1

Fur Fabric Wigs Fur fabrics make good short hair. Shapes are cut and darted to fit the head. Chima, the African Boy (see page 134) and the Baby Doll (see page 124) have specific patterns for fur fabric wigs (Figure 2).

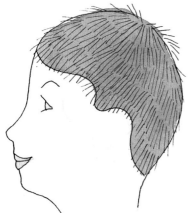

Figure 2

Fantasy Hair All sorts of materials can be used for fantasy hair. This is the occasion when you can just follow your own imagination—using torn and cut fabrics, ribbons, straw, raffia, and so on to great effect.

Beards Beards can be made from yarn or any of the other fibers mentioned above. They can even be made from long-pile fur fabric, either glued or stitched to the face (Figure 3).

Figure 3

"Real" Hair The mask dolls, as they are more realistic, look better with "real" hair wigs. This type of "real" hair is often produced from man-made fibers, but it looks and feels similar to real hair. Porcelain doll suppliers usually stock ready-made doll wigs of this type, and sometimes they sell lengths of wefted hair that can be made into a wig. Alternatively wefts from adult wigs can be carefully unpicked and made into a doll's wig (Figure 4).

Figure 4

Making a Doll's Wig

Wigs have a fabric base to which the wefts of hair are attached. The base serves to hold the wig together, and also to prevent light-colored skull fabric from showing through the fine wefted hair.

1 To make a "skull cap" from felt, cut a square about 1 inch bigger all round than the head it is going to cover. Wet the felt with water and squeeze it thoroughly to leave it just damp. Shape it by draping it around a tennis ball, or any other suitably sized ball, or an orange covered with plastic wrap. Secure it with an elastic band placed two thirds of the way down the ball and let it dry. Remove from the ball and trim the surplus felt along the line left by the elastic band. Place it on the doll's head, approximately following the hairline. Trim to shape if required (Figure 1).

2 Prepare the wefts of hair by unpicking them from a wig if necessary. Pin and stitch them to the skull cap by stitching first one row of weft all around the head, on the edge of the skull cap. Then stitch two rows of weft at the back of the head, from one side to the other,

Figure 1

and one or two short rows at the front of the wig, from one side to the other, to make a good thick area of front hair (fringe). Then attach the rest of the weft either in concentric circles or a spiral until you reach the top of the head. The rows in the front area should be closer together than those in the back area. Leave a small circle of felt about ¼ inch showing in the middle. Cut a very small hole through the center. Then take a 3 inch length of weft and roll it tightly. Push the weft end of the rolled hair into the hole. Open up the weft into a circle inside the cap, and check that the hair on the outside is evenly spread on top of the other hair, giving a good finish to the wig. When you are satisfied, neatly stitch the weft to the inside of the felt cap to hold it in place (Figure 2).

3 To attach the wig to the head, backstitch it along the edge and then, using a long needle, take several stitches through the head for security.

4 This type of wig can also be made with wefts of mohair or other suitable fibers. Stitch lengths of mohair to make them into wefts, as explained above for yarn hair, and then stitch them to the skull cap as for real hair.

Figure 2

Making Shaped Face Masks

One way of giving the face of your doll a very special quality is to make a shaped mask for the face, which is then covered with stretch fabric, painted, and attached to the doll's body. You will need a suitable model of a head to work from. Plastic or porcelain dolls' heads can be adapted for this purpose, or a specially made model can be created by the dollmaker, which would, of course, produce a truly original doll.

Types of Mask

Buckram or papier mâché masks
These masks are made directly from a face model. The Pierrot doll on page 138 is made with this type of mask, using stretch fabric over a buckram mask.

Latex face mask A plaster mold is first made from the face of the model head. The mold acts as a vessel into which the liquid latex is poured. Lara and her Friends on page 128 are made with masks like these.

Whole latex head For this head, a two-piece plaster mold is required, like those used for making porcelain dolls' heads. The Baby Doll and the African Boy doll on pages 124 and 134 have this type of head.

In all cases, when the mask is completed stretch fabric is then glued to the mask, and the face painted on it.

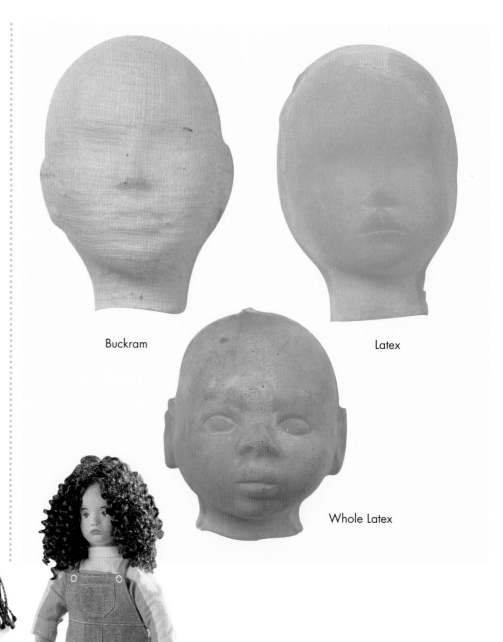

Buckram

Latex

Whole Latex

Dolls made with shaped face masks have a much more realistic look than dolls with flat fabric heads; they resemble porcelain or plastic dolls. This is further emphasized by painting the stretch fabric, which covers the mask, with great attention to fine detail, and by finishing them with "real hair" wigs and more elaborate clothing.

Suitable Model Heads

A model head can be an existing plastic or porcelain doll's head. The size required depends on the body pattern used, but a face 3½ to 4 inches long, measured from the top of the head to the chin, is a good starting point. This should make a doll about 18 to 20 inches tall.

Plastic doll's head First remove any inserted hair from the front half of the head. Eyelashes should also be removed, and the eyes securely closed with glue or small pieces of tape.

Porcelain doll's head Choose one with a flange neck and painted eyes. Other types may need sections building up with self-hardening clay and the eye holes carefully blocked.

Original head The third alternative, and the most creative, is to make your own original head model in clay.

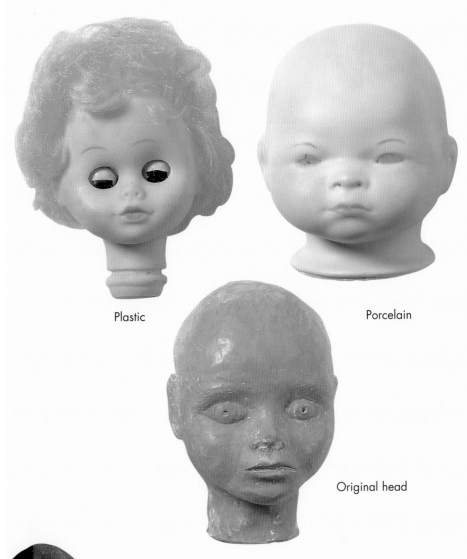

Plastic

Porcelain

Original head

The shape of the model head, in conjunction with the painting of the face, determines the final look of the doll. To make a more adult-looking doll, such as Pierrot, we need a model face quite different from that required to make a young-looking baby doll. Fantasy characters can have much more freely and creatively painted faces.

Modeling a Clay Head

You will need modeling clay, either the traditional ceramic type, or any of the modern self-hardening varieties. For modeling tools, use toothpicks, spoons, ends of brushes, and fingers. You will also need a selection of photographs showing the full face and the profile of children or adults, depending on the doll you wish to make, to use as reference.

1 To make a mask for an 18 to 20 inch doll, make the following shapes from clay:

❖ An egg-shaped ball of clay, approximately 3½ inches across by 2½ inches wide

❖ A half-egg shape, as if it were cut lengthwise, about 3 inches by 2½ inches

❖ A cylinder of clay, about 1¼ inches diameter by 1½ inches long. Press or cut to slant one end.

2 Join all three pieces, smoothing the joins to form a solid, nicely rounded shape which resembles a head on its neck (Figure 1).

3 Lightly mark the center of the face with a vertical line, using a toothpick. Find the halfway point and mark a horizontal line.

4 Using your thumbs, press two hollows for the eyes. These should be just below the horizontal line for a young child, on the line for a grown-up, and above for an older person.

5 Make a small triangular, pear shape for the nose and press onto the face. Smooth all sides to blend in. With a rounded stick, make two shallow indentations for the nostrils (Figure 2).

6 Make a trapezoid (a plane figure with four sides, only two of which are parallel) shape and apply below the nose for the upper lip. Make a small sausage shape and apply for the bottom lip. Smooth the edges to blend in with the face. Define the line between the top and bottom lips with the help of a toothpick (Figure 3).

7 Make small balls of clay and use to round the cheeks and chin until the

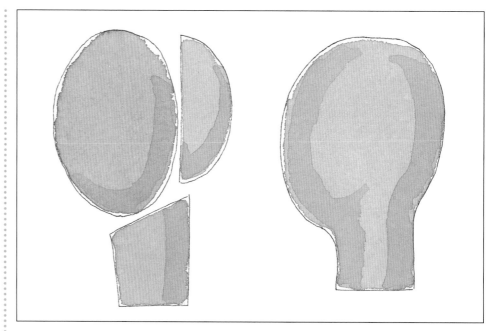

Figure 1

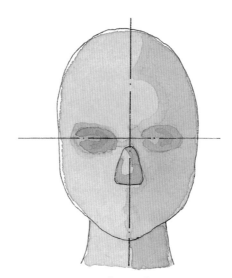

Figure 2

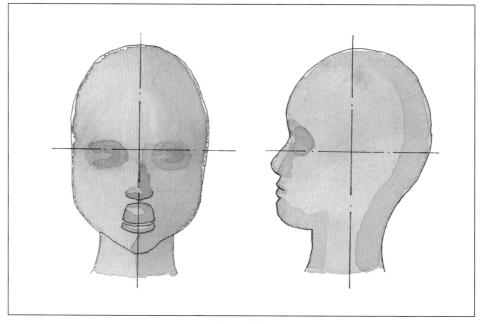

Figure 3

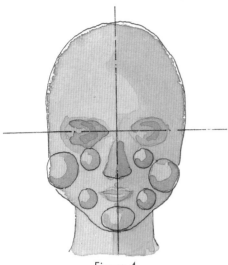

Figure 4

right effect is achieved. Refer to your photographs from time to time for guidance.

8 Look at the face from all sides, and upside down—round the sides and the cheeks to avoid the face looking flat. Add more sausages or balls of clay if needed. The eyes can either be left flat, or made rounder by adding a small ball of clay (Figure 4).

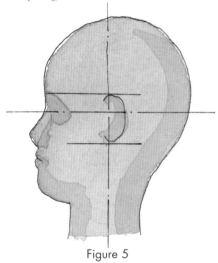

Figure 5

9 For ears, make a small oval ball about 1 x ½ inch. Cut lengthwise in half. Flatten one long edge of each piece and apply to the sides of the head, halfway between the face and the back, and extending from the eyes to the bottom of the nose (Figure 5).

Note that ears are recommended for the Pierrot doll, which has a buckram or papier mâché mask, but they are not recommended for child dolls with front latex masks, as it is much more difficult to make front mask molds when the head has ears.

Face Masks

Making Buckram and Papier-Mâché Masks

These are quick and easy to make, and will withstand a fair amount of use, but they should not be allowed to get wet, or be pressed in too much, or they will lose their shape.

1 Place the model head on an upturned jar lid or other suitable support, face side up. Smear it with a "barrier" substance such as petroleum jelly, sculptor's soap, or washing-up detergent. This will prevent the mask from sticking firmly to the mold.

2 For a buckram mask, cut a piece of buckram big enough to cover the front and sides of the face plus 1 inch all around. Pour hot water into a container, and dip the buckram in it for just a couple of seconds. Remove and gently squeeze out the surplus water. Place the buckram on the face, making sure that it covers the ears (if the model has them), and then smooth it down until it takes the shape of the face. This may take a few minutes.

2a For a papier-mâché mask, tear (don't cut) pieces of paper into strips and then into smaller pieces. Suitable paper is newsprint, tissue paper, or brown paper. For the first layer, dip the pieces in water and completely cover the face with them. The next layer of paper should be dipped in white craft glue. If the glue is too thick, add a few drops of water to slightly dilute it. Use three or more layers of paper-and-glue, smoothing the top layer thoroughly with the fingers and a coat of glue.

3 Leave the mask to dry on the head, undisturbed, for 24 hours. Then remove it by easing the edges away from the mold (use a round-ended table knife to help if necessary). Trim the unwanted edges with scissors or a craft knife, making sure you keep a good shape around the ears (if the mask has them) (Figure 1).

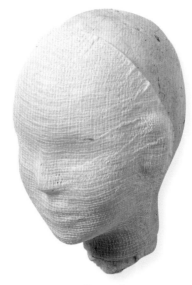

Figure 1

Making Molds for Latex Face Masks

Method 1 Quick Plaster-Bandage Mold
Plaster bandage is available in several widths from 2 to 8 inches and can be bought from drugstores or from modeling craft stores. Two or three masks can be made with this type of mold before it deteriorates (Figure 2).

Figure 2

1 Support the head model firmly with small pieces of wood or Plasticine™. Note that barrier substances *should not* be used. Cut lengths of plaster bandage long enough to cover the head from the top to the neck, plus 1 inch. If the bandage is not wide enough, cut as many lengths as are required to cover the width of the head, and sufficient to make three layers.

2 For the first layer, place pieces of bandage in a bowl of cold water for just two seconds. Remove them and quickly place them on the head, working to cover the shapes of all the features, the forehead, and neck, and the sides of the face up to the ears. Smooth well with your fingers.

3 When nearly dry, repeat the process, adding a second and then a third layer. Leave to dry undisturbed for 15 minutes. Then gently pull the head away from the mold, before it gets too stiff. Leave to dry completely for two to three days before pouring in latex to make a mask.

Method 2 Plaster of Paris Mold

This is a more durable mold, from which a dozen or more masks can be made (Figure 3).

1 Protect your work table with a plastic sheet. Using a toothpick, draw a line around the sides of the head to mark where the mold edges will be. Place the head on the table with the face looking upward, and support it with clay so that it cannot roll over.

Figure 3

2 Build a "wall" of clay around the head, about 2 inches wide, and at right angles to the marked line. Join it securely to the head. Build up any undercuts with clay so that no areas protrude inward (even in the case of plastic or porcelain heads), or it will be very difficult to remove the head from the mold. **Do not use any "barrier" agents on the head, or the latex will not set later on.**

3 Put water in a bucket, three quarters of the volume recommended to make a mold about ¾ inch thick above the nose. Then, using a jug, sprinkle plaster into the water until it forms peaks which do not sink immediately. Let it soak for a short while, then stir.

4 When it starts to thicken, literally throw plaster in handfuls onto the head, making sure it is well covered and that no bubbles have formed. Keep throwing plaster onto the head as it becomes thicker, until the plaster is at least ¾ inch thick all round the face. Smooth the surface, making a flatter area at the top. Leave to set.

5 Now remove the head very carefully, rocking it from side to side and back and forth if necessary. Plastic heads can be "squeezed" out of the mold, and soft clay heads are also relatively easy to remove, although they may be damaged in the process. Porcelain heads and hard clay heads are the most difficult, therefore they are the least recommended for this method.

6 Leave the plaster mold to dry thoroughly for a week or two before pouring latex into it, because if the plaster is still damp, the latex will not set properly.

Pouring the Liquid Latex

Liquid latex can be obtained from sculptors' materials suppliers, or craft stores. For an average size mask, you will need at least 1 pint. It is, however, reusable.

1 Work in a well-ventilated area. Put the mold on a firm, level surface, so that it cannot fall over, and support it if necessary. Carefully pour the liquid latex into the mold until it reaches the top.

2 Leave the latex undisturbed until a film of about ⅛ inch has formed on the surface; this may take between 20 minutes and 2 hours, depending on the latex and the mold. Then carefully pour it out into a plastic, metal, or glass container with a screw-on lid, for reuse.

3 Leave the latex until completely dry; it will take several hours or overnight. Peel the latex mask away from the mold, and trim any thicker or uneven edges of the head and neck. Leave until its milky look becomes yellowish brown before using (Figure 1).

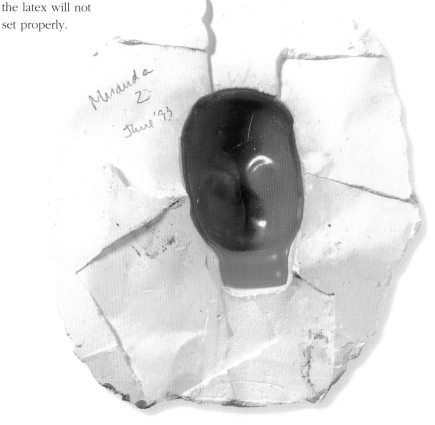

Figure 1

Covering the Face Mask with Fabric

Use this technique for covering buckram, papier mâché, or latex masks.

1 Cut out the face covering from stockinette or stretch fabric, with the maximum stretch of the fabric placed widthwise on the face. If the fabric is rather thin, use two layers: either two layers of stockinette, or one of soft, open-weave fabric (cut on the cross) placed underneath the stockinette.

2 Spread an even thin coat of white craft glue all over the mask using a medium size brush. Place the fabric centrally over the face, making sure there is about 1 inch of fabric below the neck, and about 2 inches above the forehead (Figure 1).

3 Smooth down carefully so that the fabric goes well into the hollows of the features, and then stretch it on the sides and neck to eliminate creases. Do not press hard—stroke the fabric gently, so that the glue does not seep through. If using two layers, leave the first layer to dry for an hour and then apply the second layer in the same way. Let dry for about 2 hours before painting.

Attaching the Face Mask to the Doll's Body

1 Paint the face first, before attaching it to the body. For painting instructions, see page 24 for general guidelines, and refer to the individual doll instructions for specific details.

2 Turn under the loose fabric below the neck. Place the face mask on the front of the body, with the neck edge of the face against the lower neck of the body, and pin to hold it in place (Figure 1).

3 Stretch the folded edge of the neck fabric around the "inner head" to the back of the neck. Turn one of the back edges in, and overlap the other edge in the center back. Pin the back seam right up toward the top of the head, following the curve of the fabric, but leaving the top open, and stitch by hand. There should be some space left between the fabric cover and the inner head so be careful not to catch this when stitching (Figure 2).

4 Put extra stuffing in this space at the back of the head, to give it a good shape (Figure 3). Then tuck in the excess front fabric under the edge of the

Figure 1

mask at the top. If the excess is too bulky, trim it to about 1 inch over the top of the head. Now pull the back fabric upward and frontward to give a tight and well-shaped back of the head; tuck this fabric under the edge of the mask as well and hold it all in place with pins.

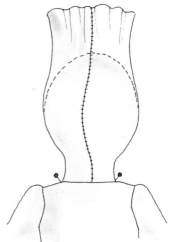

Figure 2

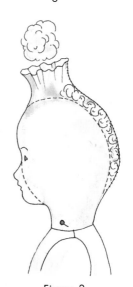

Figure 3

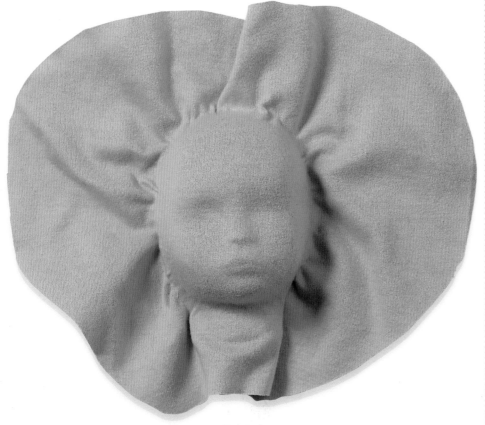

Figure 1

5 Stitch the seam along the edge of the mask, catching the fabric only, at right angles to the back seam. Lastly, stitch the neck edge of the mask to the inner head, using ladder stitch for an inconspicuous join (Figure 4).

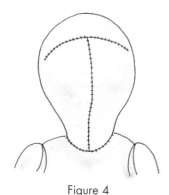

Figure 4

Making a Whole Head from Latex

1 You will need a commercial two-part plaster mold of the type used for casting a porcelain flange-neck doll head. To establish whether it is of the required size, open the mold and measure the head cavity from the highest point of the head to the level of the chin. This measurement should be the same as the head length required for the doll you are making (Figure 1).

2 Close the mold and secure it firmly with rubber bands. Pour the liquid latex into the mold almost to the top. Tap the mold firmly to release any air that may be trapped, and then leave it to stand until you can see a layer of latex forming, about ⅛ inch thick. Carefully pour back into the container all the liquid latex. Stand the mold upright with the hole uppermost, and leave it for at least 12 hours until it is set firmly.

3 When it is thoroughly dry, take the latex head out of the mold, and leave it until the color changes from cream to yellowish-brown. Trim the neck, about ½ inch below the chin, with strong, sharp scissors. Trim off any excess at the mold join line, as close to the head as possible. Nail clippers are quite good for this purpose, especially for neatening the join-line on the neck and around the edges of the ears. Ignore anything that will be hidden by the wig.

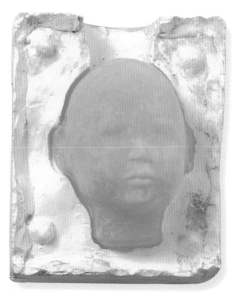

Figure 1

Covering the Latex Head with Fabric

1 Cut out the head covering in stockinette and mark the top and bottom of the center line with chalk or with a notch. Squeeze craft glue liberally onto the eyes, nose, nostrils, mouth, and under the jaw so that all the crevices are filled, then with a finger or a brush spread it over the face and neck until it is all lightly covered with glue.

2 With clean hands, place the head covering centrally over the face, with at least 1 inch overhang at the bottom of the neck. Press down the center forehead, nose, mouth, chin, and neck. Then gently smooth the fabric upward to the sides of the face, easing out any wrinkles. Press into the eyes and the crevices around the mouth and nose and under the chin several times to make sure they adhere well (Figure 2).

Figure 2

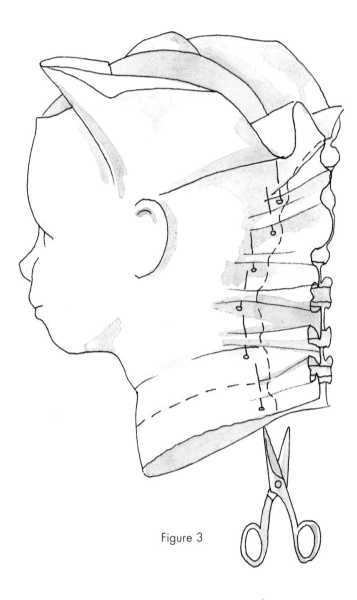

Figure 3

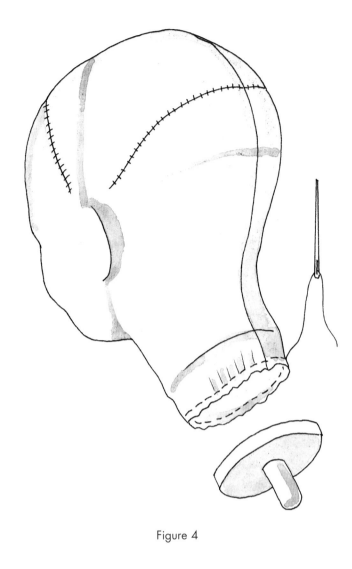

Figure 4

3 Pull the fabric to the back of the head and pin it, easing any surplus fabric into folds which will be hidden by the wig. Trim, leaving a ¼ inch seam allowance (Figure 3). Remove the pins and spread glue over the back of the head, neck, and lower head area, then stretch the fabric and press it in place, remembering to turn under the seam allowance along the back of the head. Trim the surplus fabric below the neck, leaving ½ inch for neatening.

4 Starting at the bottom, sew up the back head seam, using ladder stitch, so that the stitches do not show. Once you have reached the wig area, you can use any stitch you like, as it will not be seen. Where you have made tucks, stitch them down across the head (Figure 4).

5 When the head is covered and the glue dry, fit the neck joint. Take the disc with the central pin, and fit it into the neck base. Gather the edge of the overhanging fabric with strong thread, and pull it tightly around the disc. Fasten off securely and then cover liberally with glue, rubbing it into the gathers; let dry. Paint the face according to the instructions given with the individual doll (Figure 5).

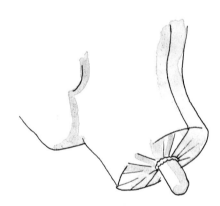

Figure 5

Part I

Rag Dolls

Cuddly and appealing, simple or more elaborate, traditional rag dolls, in their many shapes and sizes are perennial favorites of children and adults alike.

Basic Dolls
Sophie, Josh, and Molly

★

The basic doll is very simple to make yet it is extremely versatile. A "cookie cutter" shape for the head, body, and arms is rendered movable by stitching the joints at the shoulders and elbows. The legs are attached separately to achieve front-pointing feet, and they are also stitched at the knees and hips for poseability. An extension of the lower back body allows the doll to sit well. The doll can be made in muslin or flesh-colored woven cotton, and the face is drawn with easy-to-use fabric pens. Three dolls illustrate the wide variety and possibilities that are achievable with this pattern.

Making the Basic Doll

The templates and patterns for this doll are on pages 148–50. Trace or enlarge the pattern pieces as instructed.

Marking, Stitching, and Cutting

1 Fold your chosen doll fabric in half. Place the templates on the straight grain and trace one complete body and two legs on the double fabric, spacing them out so that seam allowances can be added. Mark the lower front body line; do not cut out yet.

2 If using light colored fabric, transfer the face onto the wrong side of the head by slipping the desired trace pattern (two faces are given opposite) under one layer of fabric, and tracing the shapes on the wrong side with a soft pencil, leaving clear dark lines that can be seen from the right side. If using dark colored fabric, the features will be transferred later.

3 Pin the two layers together, and machine stitch around the body, starting at one side of the body where it is marked with an X. Stitch upward along one side, around one arm and the

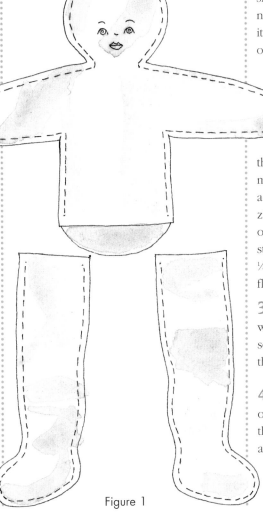

Figure 1

head, and continue around the other side, stopping at the other X point, and leaving the lower body unstitched for turning through.

4 Machine stitch around the legs, leaving the tops open.

5 Cut out the pieces, adding ¼ inch seams all round, but trim it down to ⅛ inch around the hand and thumb. On the front of the doll only, cut off the body fabric ¼ inch away from the lower front body line (Figure 1).

6 Snip into the curved seam allowances at the neck, underarms, thumbs, and ankles. Make sure you do not cut through the stitching. It is advisable to paint a small amount of fray stop solution on the edges of the snips to prevent the seams from bursting open when stuffing.

Turning, Stuffing, and Jointing

1 Turn all the pieces right side out. Using the paper templates as guides, mark the stitching lines for the elbows, shoulders, knees, and hips. If you have not traced the face from the inside, trace it now with dressmaker's carbon paper on the face area on the front body.

2 Stuff the feet, ankles, and lower parts of the legs very firmly, almost to the first knee stitch line. With the feet pointing forward, flatten the leg so that the front and back seams meet in the center of the leg. Stitch across the first line, preferably using a zipper foot in the sewing machine, in order to get nearer the stuffing. Then stitch along the second line, leaving the ¼ inch area between them completely flat and unstuffed.

3 Now stuff the upper legs, fill them well but not so firmly as the lower section. Stitch across about 1 inch from the top, as before, to hold the stuffing in.

4 Using well-teased but small amounts of stuffing, stuff the thumb firmly, then the hands (rather flatly) and the wrists and lower arm fairly firmly. Mark three lines to make the four fingers, and stitch them now either by machine or by hand.

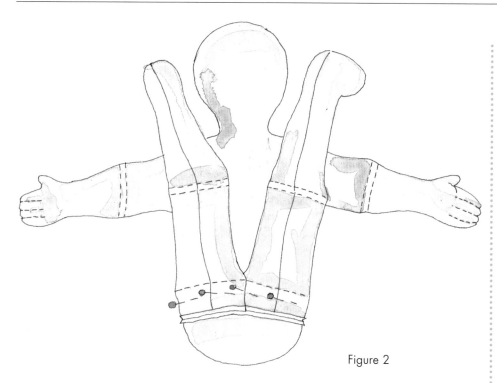

Figure 2

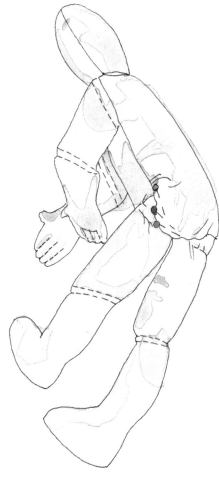

5 Stitch the elbows in the same way as the knees, except that the seams should stay on the edges. Stuff the upper arm more lightly, and then stitch twice from seam to seam for the shoulders.

6 Now stuff the head very firmly indeed, stretching the fabric with extra stuffing to eliminate any creases. Extend the firm stuffing down into the neck, but don't stuff the body yet.

7 Attach the legs to the front of the body by lining up the top of the legs with the edge of the front body line, with the feet pointing forward. Pin ¼ inch from the folded edge, tack, and machine stitch firmly in place (Figure 2).

8 Stuff the body very firmly, paying special attention to the shoulders. Bring the rounded back seat of the body forward over the lower part of the doll, turn under a ¼ inch hem, and hand stitch to the front body where the legs join (Figure 3).

Figure 3

The Face

1 If you are using light fabric and have traced the features on the wrong side, you will be able to see them well enough to trace them through onto the right side. If you are using darker fabric, you should have already transferred them with carbon paper.

2 Using a fine, brown waterproof fabric pen, trace the outlines of all the features on the right side of the stuffed doll.

3 With a soft, paintbrush-style fabric pen in blue, green, or brown, paint the irises of the eyes. Paint a black dot in the center for the pupils. Draw or paint the lips in red or peach. Finally put a small white dot of acrylic paint on each eye for the highlights. If you are using darker fabric, you may prefer to lightly paint the whites of the eyes as well, on the corners of the eyes.

An alternative face is given, which is more suitable for a boy doll. The mouth is traced with just one curved red line and two short strokes at the corners, and optional freckles can be made with a peach-colored soft fabric pen.

Making the Hair

Here we offer two styles and one variation. In every case, the yarn is first wound onto a piece of card, and then machine-stitched onto scrap paper, as explained on page 26. The dimensions are given for each style separately.

1 For the hairstyle with bunches, wind the yarn so that it is 16 inches long by 4 inches wide. Stitch across the middle, tear off the paper backing and place it on the doll with the stitching about ½ inch below the top seam of the head and reaching to the back of the neck. Pin and backstitch in place. Trim the hair to an equal length, and then make a fringe by cutting shorter some of the front strands. Tie each bunch with a length of yarn and, with a few stitches, secure to the sides of the head. Tie ribbon around each bunch and knot into bows.

2 For the boy's hairstyle, wind the yarn to measure 6 inches long and 6 inches wide. Stitch across, about 2½ inches from one looped end. Place on the doll, with the stitching across the top of the head. Pin so that it is even on both sides, and backstitch in place. Trim the fringe and the back of the hair to the correct length.

3 The black doll's hairstyle is a variation of the boy's. Wind yarn to measure 8 inches long and 6

inches wide, and then stitch in the same way, 2½ inches from one looped end, and attach it to the head along the top as before. Trim the fringe and the back of the hair to a longer length.

Making the Clothes

The dolls' wardrobe is very much a mix-and-match collection. Patterns can be combined in different ways to produce different items of clothing. For example, the pinafore skirt attached to the blouse or T-shirt makes a pretty dress. The vest can be worn on top of a T-shirt, a blouse, or a dress, and it is reversible, so it can be made to go with more than one outfit.

Basic Blouse

1 Fold the fabric in half and place the pattern pieces as follows: one front bodice and one neck facing on the fold, one back and one sleeve on double fabric, and cut them out. You will have one complete front bodice and one neck facing, two backs, and two sleeves.

2 Right sides together, place the two backs over the front, matching shoulder and side seams. Pin and stitch the shoulders.

3 Run a gathering stitch along the curved edge of the sleeves. Pull up the gathers to fit the bodice armholes, pin right sides together, and stitch in place.

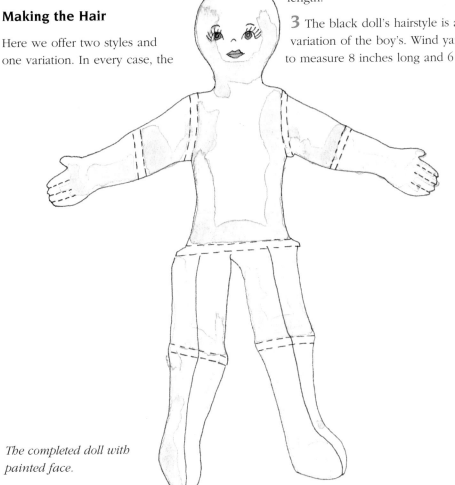

The completed doll with painted face.

> ### Helpful Tip
>
> These simple clothes patterns can be made into basic shorts, panties, pants, T-shirts, blouses, pinafores, and dresses. They can be mixed and matched to obtain a varied wardrobe. You may even prefer to make a vest and shorts for your girl doll. Basic footwear shapes can be made into felt shoes or boots. Different basic hairstyles complete the range of features which help to give character to the doll.

4 Fold backs over the front at the shoulders, right sides together, pin, and stitch the seams under the arms and sides (Figure 4).

5 Right sides together, place the neck facing onto the blouse neck, pin along the neck edge, and stitch. Turn the facing to the wrong side and stitch in place.

6 Make ½ inch casings on the lower edges of the sleeves. Measure two pieces of elastic around the doll's arms, and insert in the casings.

7 Hem both sides of the back opening, making sure the neck facing is neatly folded in place.

8 Hem the lower edge of the blouse. Attach two press studs on the back opening, one at the top and one in the middle, to finish.

Basic Shorts, Panties, or Pants

The pattern given for the shorts is exactly the same as for the pants, except that they are cut shorter at the knee, along the marked line. The method of making is the same for both.

1 Fold the fabric in half, pin the pattern in place, mark, and cut out. Pin to hold the two layers together. Stitch the front crotch seam and the back crotch seam. Hem the two lower leg edges by turning up twice and stitching (Figure 5).

2 Open up the shorts or pants and place the two crotch seams together. Pin the underleg seam from one hem to the other, and stitch.

3 Make a casing at the waist, measure the elastic around the waist of the doll, and insert in the casing.

Basic Pinafore

1 Make the template for the pinafore bodice as instructed. Both front and back pieces are cut from the same template.

2 Cut a rectangle for the skirt, 7½ inches long by 30 inches wide. Join the two short sides, right sides together, and stitch with a ¼ inch seam. Make a ½ inch hem along one long edge. You may like to machine-embroider a decorative pattern 1 inch up from the lower edge.

Run a line of gathering stitch along the other long side, for the waist.

3 Fold the remaining fabric in half, right sides together, and place the complete pinafore bodice template centrally on top, allowing sufficient space for seam allowances. Trace, pin, and then machine stitch along the curved edges, from one side, around the straps,

necklines, and underarms, to the other side; do not stitch the side seams yet. Do a second piece in the same way.

4 Cut both out, adding ¼ inch seam allowances all around. Snip curves and trim corners. Turn right side out and press carefully. Open up sides, matching backs to fronts on each side; pin, stitch, fold back, and press in place (Figure 6).

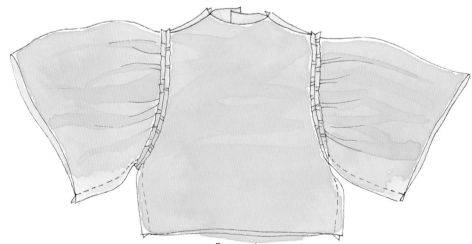

Figure 4

Figure 5

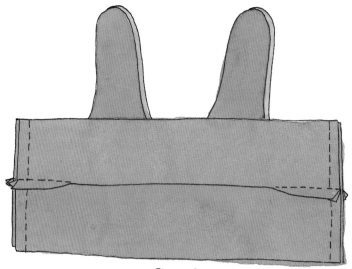

Figure 6

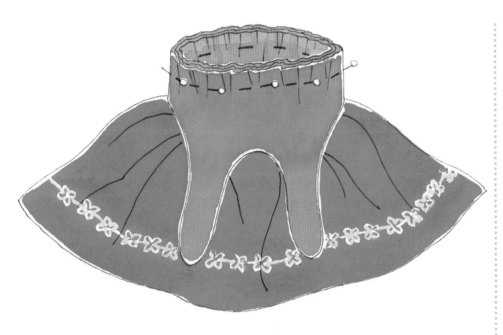

Figure 7

2 Pin and stitch the side and underarm seams. Hem both sides of the back opening, and then hem lower edge.

3 To finish neck, cut a strip of either ribbing or stretch fabric 1 inch wide and a bit shorter than the neck edge. Fold in half and place on the T-shirt neck, raw edges matching. Stretch it to fit and stitch with an overlock stitch. Fold up and press. Alternatively, simply turn a narrow hem on the T-shirt neck edge and hem in place by hand. Finish the back opening with two press studs (Figure 8).

Basic Reversible Vest

1 Make the template as instructed.

2 Place the two fabrics right sides together. Position the template centrally on top, to allow for seam allowances. Trace around the template, pin to hold the layers together, and stitch around, leaving an opening in the center of the lower edge as indicated (Figure 9).

5 Pull up the gathers on the skirt to fit the lower edge of the bodice. Treating the two bodice layers as one, right sides together, pin the skirt to the bodice and stitch in place. Press the seam toward the bodice (Figure 7).

6 Make two buttonholes on the ends of the front straps and stitch buttons to match on the back straps. Alternatively use press studs.

Basic T-shirt

1 Make the two pattern pieces as instructed. Fold the fabric in half, right sides together, place the front to the fold, and the back on double fabric and cut out. Right sides together, join the two backs to the front at the shoulders, pin, and stitch. Make narrow double hems on the sleeve edges.

3 Turn right side out and press. Turn in the opening edges and hand hem to close. Overlap the shoulders and machine stitch across. Make a buttonhole on the pointed front edge and attach a button to the other side. Alternatively sew on a press stud, or leave without a fastening.

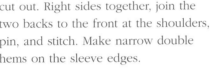

Figure 8

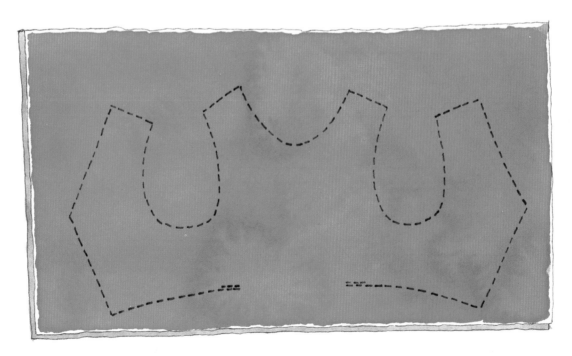

Figure 9

Basic Dress

The dress is made by simply making a slightly shorter blouse or T-shirt, and then attaching it to a skirt made in the same way as the pinafore. The only differences are that there is no need to hem the lower edge of the blouse, and that a 1½ inch opening should be left on the skirt seam at the waist end, so that it matches the overlap on the blouse back (Figure 10).

Basic Shoes

1 When using felt, you may find it easier to make a complete shoe pattern by joining two halves along the "fold" line. Prepare your chosen pattern (closed shoes or ankle-strap shoes) as instructed.

2 Place the shoe pattern on the felt, pin in place, and cut out. Repeat for the second shoe (Figures 11 and 12).

3 Fold each shoe in half and pin around the curved seams. Machine stitch ¼ inch from the edge. For the closed shoes, stitch the complete seam. For the ankle-strap shoes, stitch the shoe section only, leaving the straps unstitched.

4 Turn the shoes right side out and try them on the doll. For the ankle-strap shoes, attach a bead to one strap on each shoe, and make a tiny cut on the other strap for the buttonhole.

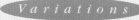

Variations

Many more dolls can be made by using other flesh-colored fabrics, combining different faces, hairstyles, and clothes from the basic selection. You may like to bind the edges of your garments with contrasting colors, embroider decorative motifs, add pockets, make vents in skirts, or add pants turn-ups—the permutations are endless.

Figure 10

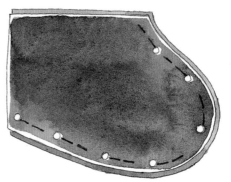

Figure 11

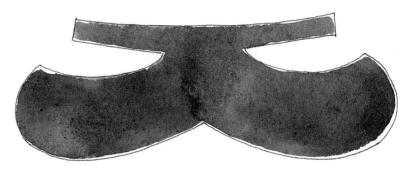

Figure 12

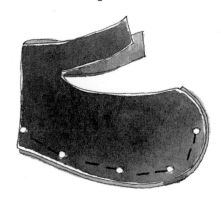

Folk Art Doll
Jessica

★

This small rag doll, with its naive style, is simple and quick to make. She's cuddly and quite portable—you might say almost a "pocket" doll. At only 12 inches tall, she's small enough to be put in a purse should the doll owner get tired of carrying her. The doll's brightly colored clothes are simply gathered tightly onto the body, although they can be made removable by inserting elastic instead of gathering. There are few seams and all the edges of the clothes are cut with pinking shears to avoid hemming.

Making the Doll

The patterns and templates for this doll are on page 151. The clothes are made from rectangles, so the dimensions for these are given in the relevant section.

1 Fold the flesh-colored fabric in half, right sides together. Trace around the body and stitch on the marked lines, leaving the lower edge open. Cut out, adding ¼ inch seam allowances. Carefully snip into the seam allowance under the arms and at the neck. Paint the cut edges with fray-stop solution or white craft glue. Leave to dry.

2 Turn right side out. Stuff the head and neck very firmly. Stuff the arms to within ½ inch of the underarm point. Stitch across from the shoulder to the underarm corner to make a flexible shoulder joint. Tack a small hem on the lower edge of the body, and finish stuffing it, giving it firm shoulders.

3 Fold the leg fabric in half (I chose blue fabric), right sides together, and draw around the leg template twice. Stitch on the marked lines, leaving the tops open. Cut out, adding the seam allowances as for the body. Snip the curved seams. Turn right side out. Stuff the legs to about 1 inch from the top.

4 With the feet pointing outward, place the tops of the legs inside the body. Pin both back and front edges to the legs, stitch twice across for strength. Remove the tacking (Figure 1).

The Face

1 To prepare a paper template for transferring the features, first make a tracing of the face. Then make small holes where the eyes, the nostrils, and the mouth corners are. Place the tracing carefully over the doll's face, matching the top and neck edges, and mark these points on the fabric with a pencil. Remove the pattern.

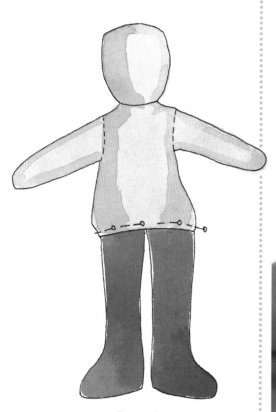

Figure 1

2 With the blue waterproof drawing pen, draw circles about ⅛ inch in diameter for the eyes and fill in with the same color. Draw a curved line for the mouth with the red pen. Using the brown pen, draw small curved lines for the eyebrows, ⅛ inch above the eyes. Make two tiny lines for the nostrils in the middle of the face, and if a freckled doll is wanted, mark some light brown dots over the nose and cheeks.

Making the Clothes

All the clothes pieces are cut out with pinking shears, and do not have hems. But, if you prefer to make removable clothes, elastic can be inserted into casings instead of gathering. For this, follow the instructions for the elasticated waist for the pantaloons of Hannah, the Pioneer Doll on page 60. Casings for elastic can also be made for the pantaloon legs, and for the neck and sleeves of the dress.

1 To make the pantaloons, cut two fabric rectangles from the green cotton, each 9 x 7 inches. Place them on top of

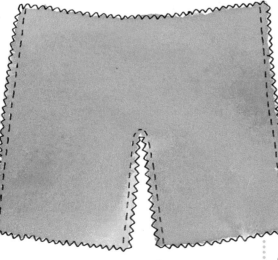

Figure 2

each other, right sides together, and using a pencil, mark a center line upward from the lower edge, 3½ inches long. This will be the underleg. To stitch the leg division, first stitch a seam ¼ inch from the pencil line, working up toward the center. Stitch across the top for ½ inch and then back down the other side, taking a ¼ inch seam. Cut along the pencil line (Figure 2).

Figure 3

2 Stitch the two side seams, and turn right side out.

3 Run a row of gathering stitches, by hand, ½ inch below the waist edge. Place the pantaloons on the doll, pull up the gathers tightly around the waist, knot, and finish.

4 On each leg, run a row of gathering stitches, by hand, ½ inch from the lower edge. Pull up the gathers and finish as for the waist (Figure 3).

5 Cut two 15 inch lengths of red ribbon, and tie with a bow over the gathered legs.

6 To make the dress, cut four rectangles from the red fabric: two for the dress, each 9 x 6 inches and two for the sleeves, each 4 x 5 inches. Place the two dress rectangles on top of each other, right sides together, and do the same with the sleeves matching them carefully.

7 To make raglan sleeves, you need to cut off the top corners of both the dress and the sleeves. On each top corner, mark points 2 inches in both directions. Draw a line between them to make triangles, and cut them off (Figure 4).

8 Pin and stitch the sleeves to the front and back dress sections, right sides together, along the diagonal raglan line (Figure 5). Fold the dress over and stitch the underarm seams from sleeve edge to dress edge. Turn through to the right side (Figure 6).

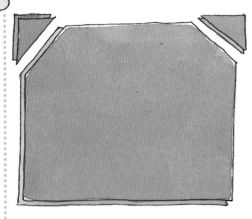

Figure 4

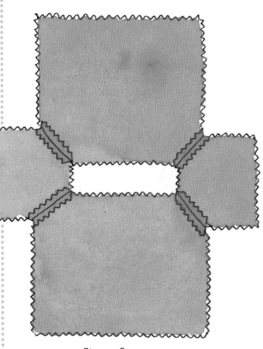

Figure 5

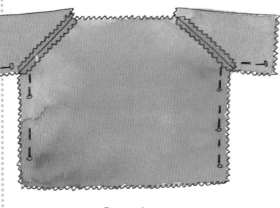

Figure 6

9 Run a row of gathering stitches, by hand, ½ inch from the neck edge. Place the dress on the doll, pull the gathers (not too tightly) around the neck, and knot to finish. Repeat for the sleeves, but here pull a little bit tighter (Figure 7).

Figure 7

10 Tie the blue ribbon around the neck, and secure it with a few stitches at the back and sides of the neck (otherwise it may slip off) and finish with a bow.

Making the Hair

It is always best to make the hair last of all, otherwise it gets in the way when the clothes are being attached to the doll.

1 Wind the yarn to a length of 10 inches and a width of 7 inches, as explained on page 26. Tie the loops at one end, fairly tightly, with a length of the same yarn; we will call this "the knot." Cut the loops at the other end, and spread the yarn out, double fan shape from the knot outward (Figure 8).

2 Place the knot centrally on top of the head, and stitch it firmly in position. Spread the rest of the hair to the front, sides, and back of the head, leaving no areas empty, and then backstitch it to the head along the hairline and the back neck (Figure 9).

3 Sweep the front hair toward the back and bring the hair and the sides upward to make a ponytail. Do not pull tightly over the forehead, on the contrary, leave it slightly loose for a better shape. Tie the ponytail first with a length of the same yarn (Figure 10) and then wrap the remaining 24 inches of red ribbon around it, and make a bow. Arrange the hair to look attractive, and trim any yarn ends that may be sticking out.

Figure 8

Figure 9

Figure 10

Traditional Doll
Beth

★ ★

*R*ag dolls appeal to everyone, young and old. They have traditionally been
made from whatever scraps of fabric there were at hand—but nowadays there are many
wonderful fabrics in the stores, small quantities of which can easily be transformed into a
beautiful, three-dimensional plaything.

Materials

You will need
For a doll 19 inches tall

For the body
- 12 x 38 in unbleached muslin
- 8 x 24 in striped fabric for the legs, with the stripes parallel to the short side
- 8 oz loose polyester stuffing
- 2 oz wool or acrylic yarn for the hair
- A fine-point permanent drawing pen or a waterproof fabric pen, in brown or black

- Acrylic or fabric paints in white, black, red, brown, and blue
- A fine, good quality painting brush (size 1 or 2)
- 1 yd x ⅝ in ribbon for hair

For the clothes
- 42 x 10 in white fine cotton or polycotton for the pantaloons and petticoat
- 43 x 1 in white broderie anglaise trim
- 18 in narrow white elastic
- 42 x 20 in cotton or polycotton print fabric, for the dress

- 3 small press studs, metal or plastic
- 7 in narrow white elastic
- 42 x 20 in plain color cotton or polycotton fabric for the pinafore
- 2 small press studs, metal or plastic
- 3 buttons to match color of pinafore, ½ inch diameter
- Two pieces 12 x 5 in felt for the shoes
- 12 x 5 in fusible bonding web
- 2 small buttons or beads in color to match

Making the Doll

The patterns and templates for this doll are on page 152.

Marking, Stitching, and Cutting

1 Begin with the legs; fold the striped fabric in half lengthwise, and place the leg template on it with the back to the fold. Trace around, and repeat for the second leg, checking that the stripes match on the front seam. Leaving both the top and toe areas open, stitch the front seam from top to toe and the underfoot seam on both legs.

2 Cut out the two legs, adding a ¼ inch seam allowance all round. Open up the toe area so the front and underfoot seams meet in the center, and the angled lines are on the outside edge of the foot. Stitch the toe seam following the shape in a slightly rounded way (Figure 1).

3 Fold the muslin in half, place the other templates on the straight grain and trace around the body, the head back and the face once, and round the arms twice. Stitch around the body and the arms, leaving openings as indicated on the templates. Stitch the center seam of the head back.

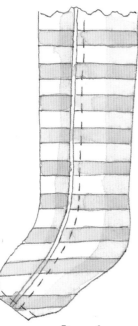

Figure 1

4 Cut out the arms and the body, adding ¼ inch seam allowances all round. Cut out the face and the head back on the marked cutting lines.

The Face

1 Using a soft pencil, trace the features on the wrong side of the muslin face by placing the fabric over the paper pattern and taping them both to a window, as explained on page 23.

2 Place the fabric face on a sheet of white paper, pencil side down, and trace the features on the right side with a fine, brown permanent drawing pen.

3 Paint the face as follows, beginning with the eyes. Paint the irises with a mixture of blue and white paint. Then paint the lips with a mixture of red and white to make a pink. For a more peachy color add a touch of brown. For the pupils, paint a largish black dot on each eye. When the eyes are dry, paint a tiny white dot at the top right of each iris (on the edge of the pupil), for the highlights. When all paint is quite dry, go over the pen lines again to make them darker if they look too pale, especially the top line of the eyes.

Alternative: Embroidering the face

If you prefer to embroider the face, work the eyes and mouth in satin stitch, using two strands of embroidery thread in the colors indicated. Then go over the pen lines using dark brown thread, working stem stitch for the lip-parting line, the eyebrows, and eyelash line, and straight stitches for the eyelashes (see pages 15 and 25).

Stitching the Head

1 On the head back, finger-press the seam open. Right sides together, join the face to the head back section matching the curved sides. Pin and stitch around, leaving the lower neck edge open.

2 Pin and stitch the dart on the neck front. Trim to a ⅛ inch seam allowance, and turn the head right side out. Trim the seam allowance around the thumb also to ⅛ inch.

Stuffing

1 Stuff the head very firmly, making sure any creases are stretched out with extra stuffing. Do not fill the neck area.

2 To stuff the arms, first stuff the thumb, and the hand (keeping it reasonably flat), then the forearm, to the elbow line. Stuff the second arm in the same way, making sure they are both even. Stitch a straight line across both arms at the elbows. Continue stuffing the upper arms, but stop about 1 inch before the top edge.

3 To stuff the legs, first fill the feet and ankles very firmly. Continue stuffing up to the knees. Open up each leg so that the front seam is in the middle of the leg. Stitch across the knees as for the elbows. Stuff the top part of the legs to within 1 inch of the top. Do not stuff the body yet.

Assembling the Doll

1 Tack together the raw edges at the top of the legs. With the feet pointing up, place them on the body front, right sides together, about 1 inch up from the lower edge. Stitch firmly in place (Figure 2).

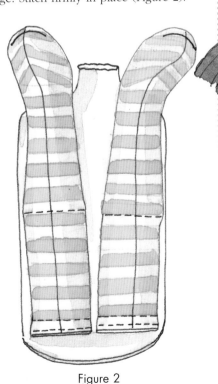

Figure 2

2 Stuff the body firmly, giving special attention to the neck tab and shoulders. Bring the lower back edge of the body toward the front, fold under a ¼ inch

turning, pin, tack, and hem stitch to the back of the legs. Add more stuffing to the doll's bottom if necessary.

3 At the top of each arm make ¼ inch turnings. Neaten with small running stitches on the very edge, pulling slightly as you go along, to gather the top edge of the arm. Stitch each arm to a shoulder, making sure that the thumbs face forward.

4 Make a ⅜ inch turning on the lower edge of the head, and tack to hold. Fit the head over the neck tab, and add stuffing if necessary. Pin the head to the neck edge all round. Stitch to the body with tiny, inconspicuous stitches. Remove the tacking (Figure 3).

5 Make the fingers by stitching three rows of running or stab stitch on each hand. Pull each stitch firmly as you go along to indent the finger separations.

Figure 3

Making the Hair

1 Wind the wool or acrylic yarn onto a piece of stiff card 22 inches long. Draw a pencil line on a piece of scrap paper, 4¾ inches long.

2 Remove the yarn from the card, and place it centrally on the paper over the drawn line. For the center-parting line, machine stitch the yarn to the paper along the drawn line and then tear the paper away.

3 Place the hair on the doll, with the parting line in the center of the head, extending from the front hairline (approximately ¾ inch below the head seam) to the back of the neck. For positioning, pin in place and backstitch securely to the head.

4 Smooth the yarn with your fingers, divide into bunches and use some wool to tie them in place. Trim the hair evenly. Cut the ribbon in half and tie bows around each bunch. Secure the hair to the head at the neck level with a few stitches taken through the under-strands of the wool only.

Making the Clothes

The patterns and templates for the clothes are on pages 153–54.

The Underwear

1 For the pantaloons, fold over 12 inches of the white fabric, pin the complete pantaloons pattern in place, and cut out both layers.

2 Turn up a ⅜ inch hem on each lower leg and press the fold. Cut two 8½ inch lengths of broderie anglaise, and pin one to each folded edge, with the raw edge of the trim against the raw edge of the folded hem. Pin and machine stitch ⅛ inch from the folded edge.

3 Place the two pieces right sides together, pin, and stitch each of the two center crotch seams. Open up and refold the pantaloons so the front and back center seams meet. Pin and stitch the underleg seams.

Figure 4

4 Make a casing at the waist edge. Measure the elastic on the doll's waist and thread it through the casing. Turn the pantaloons right side out and try them on the doll (Figure 4).

5 For the petticoat, cut a rectangle measuring 9½ x 22 inches from the remaining white fabric. Fold under ⅜ inch on one long edge and attach the remainder of the broderie anglaise to the edge as described for the pantaloons.

6 Right sides together, pin and stitch the two short edges of the petticoat. On the waist edge, make a casing and thread elastic through and finish as for the pantaloons (Figure 5).

Figure 5

The Dress

1 From the dress fabric, cut a rectangle 9½ x 32 inches for the skirt. Make a hem on one long side, and machine stitch twice: place the first row of stitching close to the folded edge, and the second row about ¼ inch away. Run two rows of gathering stitch along the other long side of the skirt, ⅛ inch apart.

2 Right sides together, fold the remaining dress fabric in half. Pin in place the patterns for the bodice front and back and the sleeves. Cut out. From the remaining fabric, cut one strip on the bias grain, 2 x 8 inches long, for the collar. Placing right sides together, join the bodice backs to the bodice front at the shoulders.

3 Run two rows of gathering stitch along the top edge of the sleeves. Pull up the gathers, distributing them evenly over the curved edge of the sleeve. Right sides together, place each gathered sleeve edge onto each armhole edge on the bodice. Adjust the gathers to fit the armhole, pin, and stitch.

4 Fold the bodice front toward the back along the shoulder line, right sides together. Match the underarm seams from the edge of the bodice to the edge of the sleeves. Pin and stitch together.

5 Make a casing on the wrist edge of each sleeve. Measure the elastic on the doll's arm and thread one piece through each casing. On the bodice center back edges, make ¼ inch turnings and press.

6 On the skirt section, pull up the gathers to match the size of the bodice waist. Right sides together, raw edges matching, pin and stitch the skirt to the bodice. Press the seam toward the bodice.

Helpful Tip

Our rag doll has a muslin body, striped legs (for stockings), underwear edged with broderie anglaise, a flower print dress, and a plain pinafore. She wears felt shoes and her hair is arranged in bunches held by ribbons. She sits well because she has stitched knees and elbows that allow her mobility and poseability. Her face is painted, using a very easy transfer method, but it can also be embroidered.

skirt. Run two rows of gathering stitch on the remaining long edge. You may like to add a row of decorative machine embroidery parallel to the long lower hem of the pinafore.

2 For the pinafore top, cut a long strip, 30 x 6 inches, from the remaining fabric. Fold it in half, right sides together. Place the template for the whole pinafore top on it, leaving space to add ¼ inch seam allowances all round. Pin in place and draw the outline. Starting at the waist edge of the center back, stitch on the marked lines all the way around, including the armholes, shoulders, and neck edges, to the other back waist edge, leaving the lower edge open. This makes a self-lined top.

3 Cut out the pinafore top, adding ¼ inch seam allowances. Snip the curved seams, trim off the corners, and turn right side out, carefully pushing out all corners and seams with an appropriate blunt tool. Press flat.

4 Pull up the skirt gathers, match them to the waist edge of the pinafore top, pin right sides together, and stitch as for the dress skirt. Press the seam toward the top.

5 Put two press studs at the back, one on the neck line and one on the waist. Decorate the front with three buttons. Stitch the shoulders together, with a machine embroidery stitch, back overlapping front (Figure 7).

Figure 6

7 Join the skirt at the center back by matching the short edges of the skirt, pinning and then stitching the lower 5 inches. On the dress opening, fold back the edges, press, and hem in place by hand or machine.

8 Pin the collar band to the neck edge, right sides together, allowing the ends to extend evenly at each end. Stitch, and press the band upward. Fold the short edges in to neaten. Fold the long edges twice to make a hem, allowing about ½ inch of the collar to show at the neck

edge. Handstitch the hem to the dress on the inside (Figure 6).

9 Stitch three press studs on the back opening—one at the neck edge, one at waist level, and one half way between the two.

The Pinafore

1 For the pinafore skirt, cut a rectangle 8½ x 36 inches from the plain fabric. Hem one long edge and the two short sides in the same way as for the dress

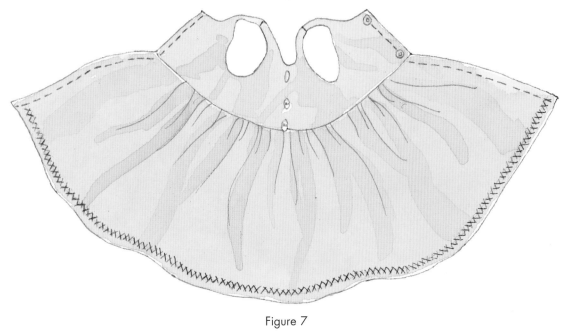

Figure 7

The Shoes

1 Begin by fusing the two layers of felt together. Place the fusible bonding web on one piece of felt, sticky side down. Following manufacturer's instructions, press with a medium heat.

2 When cool, peel off the paper backing and place the second piece of felt on top, cover with a wet cloth, and press again. The two pieces of felt should be now bonded together, and should be treated as a single layer.

3 Place the shoe and sole patterns on the felt and mark them twice each, cut out. Then, carefully cut out the area marked in the center of each shoe.

4 Right sides together, overlap the back edges of the shoes by ¼ inch, and stab stitch together. Turn the shoes wrong side out. Fit one sole on the lower edge of each shoe, pin in place, and hand stitch around, with backstitch, worked with an up-and-down movement.

5 Turn right side out, and stitch one small button to each shoe on the outside edge of the strap area, on opposite sides of each shoe. Put the shoes on the doll, making sure the buttons are on the outer sides of the feet (Figure 8).

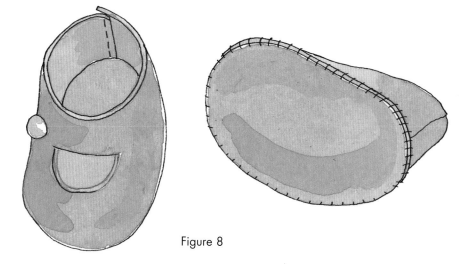

Figure 8

Variations

Beth can be made in other colors and variations. Her companion here is made in a similar way, but she has all-in-one legs with velvet boots, made by the same method as Susanna, the Spring Doll on page 63. Instead of wearing a dress under her pinafore, she wears a long-sleeve blouse and a pinafore which is closed at the back.

Pioneer Doll
Hannah

★ ★

This is a simple rag doll, dressed as a pioneer girl would have been, with lace-edged pantaloons, and a printed cotton dress and apron. Her features are very simply drawn and painted directly onto the muslin—as are her hair and boots. The muslin fabric has been dyed with tea to give a more antique look.

5 Turn the arms and legs right side out, and stuff firmly, leaving the last ½ inch unstuffed. Stitch the raw edges closed to hold the stuffing in (do not turn edges in). Make sure the legs have front-pointing feet.

5 Turn the arms and legs right side out, and stuff firmly, leaving the last ½ inch unstuffed. Stitch the raw edges closed to hold the stuffing in (do not turn edges in). Make sure the legs have front-pointing feet.

6 Place the legs on the right side of the front body, raw edges of the legs matching the lower edge of the body, and legs pointing up (Figure 1). Pin and tack in place, then stitch about ⅜ inch from the raw edges.

7 Place the arms on the right side of the body front, raw edges of the arms and body sides matching, with the arms pointing toward the inside of the body (Figure 2). Pin and tack in place, then stitch about ¼ inch inside the raw edges.

8 Move the legs out of the way of the body, but keep the arms inside. Right sides together, place the body back on top of the body front and pin, matching the top and the sides of the head, neck, and sides of body down to the lower edges (Figure 3). Stitch in place, making sure you catch the arms accurately.

Materials

You will need
For a doll 16 inches tall

For the body
- ❖ 34 x 11 in beige cotton fabric or unbleached muslin dyed with tea (see box below)
- ❖ Brown waterproof drawing pen
- ❖ Acrylic or fabric paints in red, white, black, light brown, dark brown, yellow ocher, and blue, and a fine brush
- ❖ Acrylic textile medium for thinning the paint

For the clothes
- ❖ 10 x 15 in cream cotton fabric for the pantaloons
- ❖ 32 x ¾ in cream cotton lace
- ❖ 7 in long narrow elastic
- ❖ 20 x 22 in cotton fabric in a small darkish print
- ❖ 3 press studs for the dress
- ❖ 10 x 22 in contrast print cotton fabric in a lighter color

Making the Doll

The patterns and templates for this doll are on page 155. Note that the arms and legs are templates while the body pieces are patterns. Remember to transfer marks and other useful information.

Dyeing fabric with tea

To dye white or unbleached muslin to a nicely worn (antiqued) flesh color, cold tea can be used instead of commercial dyes. Make a strong solution of tea with about three pints of boiling water, and let it cool to blood temperature. Use a large bowl if possible, which will allow the fabric to remain flat and not creased. Put the fabric in the tea for about 20 minutes, stirring from time to time with a wooden spoon. Rinse well and dry. Do not worry if the dye is not totally even, this gives a charm of its own to the doll.

1 Place the body front paper pattern on single muslin and cut out. Fold the remaining muslin in half, pin the body back pattern in place, and cut out. Trace around the leg and arm templates twice.

2 Stitch around the arms and legs on the marked lines, leaving openings where indicated. Cut out adding ¼ inch seam allowance.

3 Place the body front fabric wrong side up, over the body front paper pattern, matching them carefully, and with a soft pencil, trace the doll's features and hairline.

4 Pin the two body back pieces together from the top of the head to the mark just below the neck and stitch.

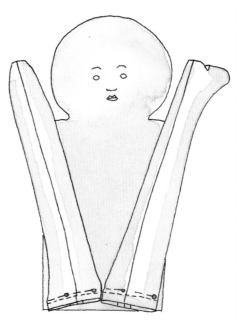

Figure 1

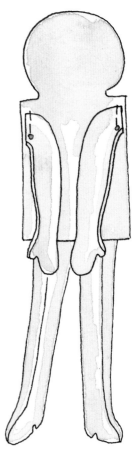

Figure 2

9 Right sides together, pin the rest of the body back center seam, from the neck to the lower edge, and stitch (Figure 4). Snip the neck curves, and turn the doll right side out. The arms should be in the right places now.

10 Stuff the body very firmly, especially the head, neck, and shoulders. Bring the lower edge of the body back toward the front, turn a narrow hem and stitch to the front, matching the leg seams (Figure 5).

11 Paint the boots with dark brown. When very dry, paint lines in yellow ocher for the boot laces (Figure 6, page 60).

The Face

1 Following the previously traced outlines, now draw the doll's features on the right side of the face using the brown pen.

2 For the eyes, paint the irises light blue or light brown and paint the area outside the irises white. When dry, paint the black pupils and the white highlights.

3 Paint the mouth a darkish pink, by mixing red with a little white. Go over the brown lines again if necessary.

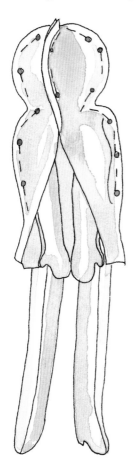

Figure 3

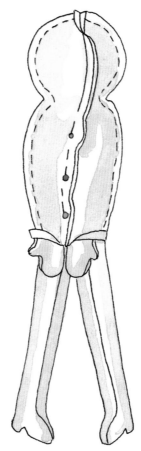

Figure 4

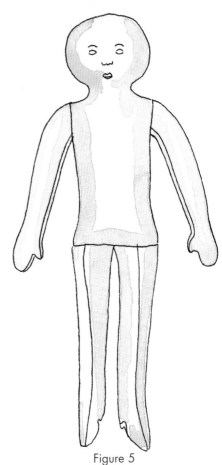

Figure 5

4 For the cheeks, pick up pink paint with a flat brush, and then wipe most of it off on a wad of paper towels. Brush the cheeks lightly to give them a slight pinkish tone (try this first on a spare piece of fabric). Alternatively apply make-up blush to the cheeks.

5 Paint the hair light brown, keeping within the hairline at the front, and painting down to the neck at the back. Should you need to thin the paint, use the appropriate textile medium (Figure 6).

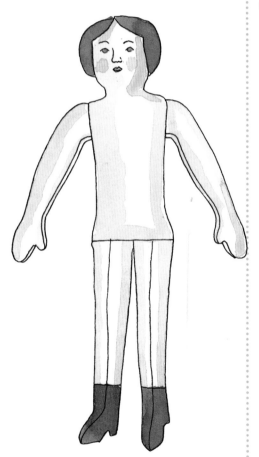

Figure 6

Making the Pantaloons

1 For the pantaloons, cut two rectangles of cream fabric, each 9¼ inches long by 7 inches wide. Place them on top of each other, and mark the center of the lower edge. Draw a 5 inch line from that center point toward the opposite side. This will divide the two leg sections. Cut along the line.

2 Placing right sides together, pin and stitch the underleg seams ¼ inch inside the cut edges, stitching first along one side, then down the other (Figure 7). Open up each leg section, turn up ¼ inch hems on each lower leg and then pin and stitch a length of lace on the edge.

3 Right sides together, pin and stitch the sides of the pantaloons.

4 Make a casing on the waist edge by turning first ⅜ inch and then ¾ inch. Stitch along the folded edge, and then again along the top edge, leaving an opening to insert the elastic (Figure 8).

Making the Dress

1 From print fabric, cut a rectangle 22 inches by 9 inches for the skirt. Fold the rest of the fabric in half, right sides together, pin the paper patterns in place, and cut out the front bodice, the back bodice, and the sleeves, the front facing and the back facing.

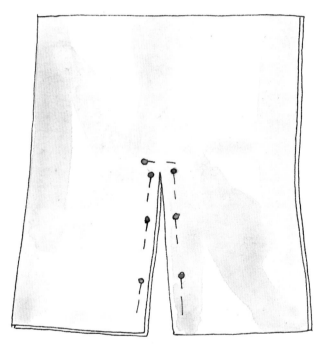

Figure 7

Figure 8

Figure 9

2 Right sides together, match the front and back bodice pieces at the shoulders, pin, and stitch. Match the shoulders of the front and back facings, pin, and stitch. Press the seams open on both pieces.

3 Right sides together, pin the neck facing to the bodice neck, and stitch along the neck edge (Figure 9). Clip into the curves, turn the facing to the wrong side, press, and top stitch along the edge.

4 Run two rows of gathering stitch along the curved top edge of the sleeves. Pull up the gathers to fit the armhole of the bodice. Right sides together, pin in place (Figure 10) and stitch.

5 Turn ¼ inch hems on the wrist edge of each sleeve and stitch. Fold the bodice, right sides together, and then pin and stitch each side from the wrist through the underarm to the waist edge.

6 On the skirt section, make a double ¼ inch hem along one long edge and stitch. Make a tuck by folding the skirt fabric lengthwise, wrong sides together, 1 inch from the hem edge, and stitching ¼ inch from the folded edge. Press the tuck toward the hem.

7 Run two rows of gathering stitch along the waist edge. Pull up the gathers to fit the bodice waist, and with the two pieces right sides together, pin and stitch.

8 Pin the short sides of the skirt right sides together and stitch to 1 inch below the waist. Turn in the raw back edges to make a hem, and stitch in place. Finish

the dress with three press studs, one on the neck edge, one on the waist, and one in-between (Figure 11).

Making the Apron

1 Cut a strip of fabric for the combined waistband and ties, 22 x 2¼ inches. Fold it in half, wrong sides together, and press. On each edge, fold in ½ inch, press again.

2 For the apron, cut a piece of fabric 7 x 7½ inches. Make small hems on three sides, leaving one 7½ inch side for the waist. Run a row of gathering stitch on this edge. Pull up the gathers to measure 3½ inches. Matching the center of the apron with the center of the waistband, fit the gathered edge in-between the folded waistband. Pin and stitch along the waist and then continue around the ties to finish (Figure 12). Put on the doll and tie a bow at the back.

Figure 11

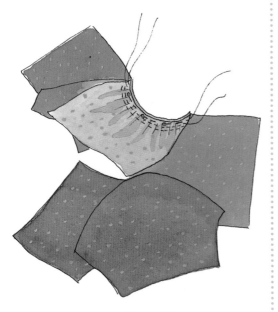

Figure 10

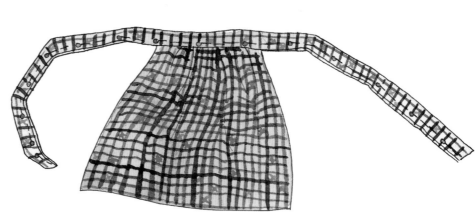

Figure 12

Spring Doll
Suzanna

This doll represents the freshness of spring, with its bright green shoots and colorful flowers. She has a nicely shaped body and a round girlish face, and her underclothes and boots are part of her body. Her long curly hair flows down to frame her face, and her wide-brimmed hat complements a pretty outfit.

Making the Doll

The patterns and templates for this doll are on pages 156–57.

The Legs

1 The leg and the boot are cut in one piece by joining the fabrics first. Cut a strip of leg fabric, 14 x 7 inches, and a strip of boot fabric, 14 x 4 inches. Right sides together, join the two fabrics on one 14 inch side. Press the seam toward the boot fabric. Machine embroider a row of decorative top-stitching on the boot edge, with a contrasting colored thread (optional) (Figure 1).

2 Right sides together, fold the two sides of the fabric toward the center matching the boot seams. Place the leg template on the double fabric, matching both boot lines, pin, and draw around, twice. Stitch on the marked line, leaving the top open. Cut out, adding ¼ inch seam allowances (Figure 2).

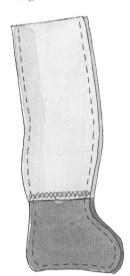

Figure 2

3 Make the feet while the legs are still wrong side out. First snip the corners of the seam allowance at the toe and heel. Then open the sole seam and finger press it. Press the corners out, forming a small triangular shape at the toe and heel. Pin across, about ¼ inch from each point, and stitch across (Figure 3).

4 Turn the legs right side out, and stuff very firmly, stopping about 1 inch below the top. Match the seams at the center of the leg so that the toes point forward and tack the tops closed.

The Body

1 Fold the remaining body fabric in half right sides together. Mark the back and front body templates on the fabric. Machine stitch the center seams only at this stage, leaving the opening at the center back as indicated. Cut out, adding seam allowances on the center seams.

2 Transfer the dart marking to the underside of the body back. Open up the two pieces and press the seams open. Make the two darts as indicated.

3 Right sides together, join the front and back body sections, stitching the two sides from the neck edge to the lower edge, leaving the neck and the lower edge open (Figure 4).

4 Turn up ¼ inch on the lower edge of the body, and tack. Do not stuff the body yet.

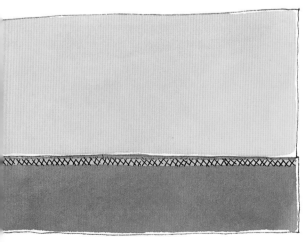

Figure 1

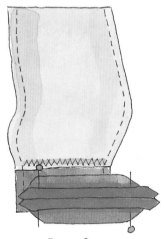

Figure 3

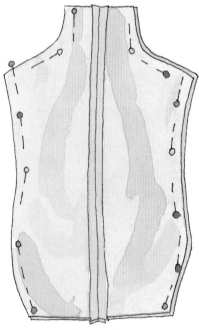

Figure 4

The Arms and Head

1 Fold your chosen fabric in half, pin the head pattern in place, mark it including the darts on the head, and then cut it out.

2 Draw around the arm template twice and stitch around the traced lines, leaving an opening for turning through. Cut out, adding ¼ inch seam allowances. Turn right side out (Figure 5).

3 Stuff the hands first, and stitch three lines for the four fingers. Make sure you fill the thumb well. Stuff the rest of the arm firmly, and close the openings.

4 On the head, mark the darts on the underside. Place the face trace pattern under one of the layers, and trace the features on the wrong side, using a soft pencil and placing the paper and fabric against a window.

5 Make the two darts on each head piece (Figure 6). Right sides together and matching the darts, stitch around the head, leaving the lower edge open as indicated.

6 Stuff the head very firmly, but do not close the opening.

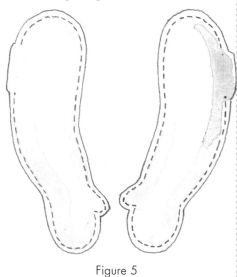

Figure 5

Figure 6

The Face

1 Trace the features on the right side of the head with a fine, brown permanent pen, following the pencil lines traced earlier which should be visible.

2 Paint the eyes green or blue. Paint the mouth with a pink/peach color made by mixing red, white, and yellow. Paint the black pupils and the white highlights on the eyes when the iris colors are dry. Go over the lines for the eyelids and eyebrows, if needed (see page 24).

Assembling the Doll

1 Insert the tops of the legs into the body, and pin the body back and front over the legs. Tack and stitch securely in place, catching all four layers. Remove the tacking (Figure 7).

2 Stuff the body very firmly through the back opening, adding a little more stuffing to the neck to make it firm. Leave the small pointed corners on the shoulders only loosely stuffed, but stuff the rest of the shoulders firmly. Close the back body opening.

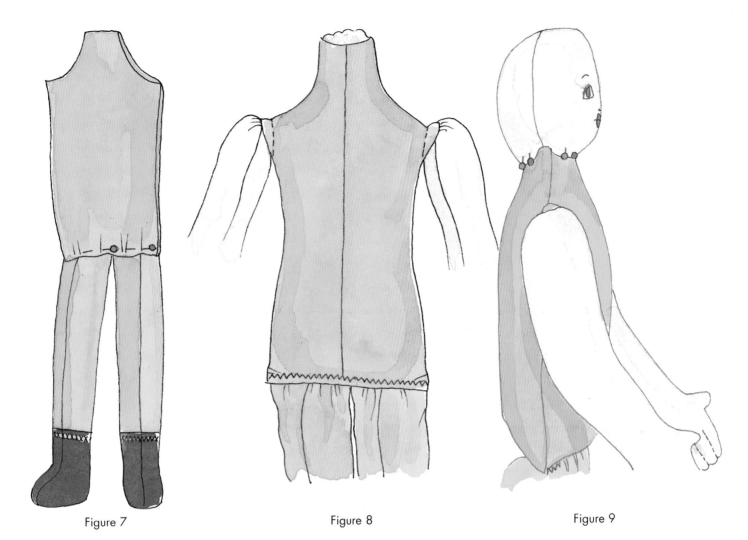

Figure 7

Figure 8

Figure 9

3 To join the arms to the body, pull the shoulder corners flat and place the top of an arm under one, making sure the thumbs are pointing forward. Stitch the top of each arm securely to the shoulder point (Figure 8).

4 Make a "hole" in the head stuffing so that the neck can be inserted. Pull the back and front of the head well over the neck, hold firmly in place with pins (Figure 9) and add more stuffing if necessary. Stitch in place with carefully concealed stitches.

Making the Hair

Wind the yarn onto a piece of card 18 inches long by 4 inches wide. Remove the card, and stitch across the center of the yarn by hand or machine. Attach to the head with backstitch along the parting line. Trim hair length evenly (see pages 26–27).

Making the Clothes

The Dress

1 Make patterns for the dress: bodice front and back, and the sleeves, and also a template for the armhole as instructed.

2 For the skirt cut out the fabric to the following measurements. For the skirt front, cut one rectangle 10 x 18 inches, and for the skirt back cut two rectangles 10 x 9 inches each.

3 Place the armhole template on one corner of the skirt front; mark and cut out the armhole. Repeat for the other side, turning the template over. Do the same for the backs, cutting one armhole only on each section, turning the template over, as before. Run two rows of gathering stitches across the top end of each skirt piece, stopping at the armholes.

4 Fold the remaining fabric in half right sides together, cut out two sleeves, two bodice fronts, and four bodice backs (for the self-lined bodice). Prepare the

bodice and the bodice lining by joining the front to the backs at the shoulders on each one.

5 Place the two bodices right sides together, pin, and stitch along the neckline and the center back seams only (Figure 10). Turn right side out, and press. This makes a neat neckline, without having to fold fiddly edges.

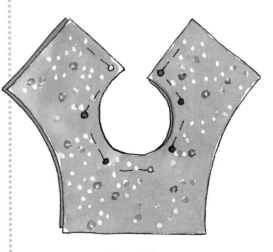

Figure 10

6 Pull the gathers of the skirt front to fit the size of the bodice front. Treat the two layers of the bodice as one. Right sides together, pin and stitch. You will see the complete armhole appearing when the two pieces are joined. Repeat for the two back pieces, matching the armholes to the sides, and the straight edges to the center back (Figure 11).

7 Run two rows of gathering stitch along the curved edge of the sleeves. Pull up the gathers to match the armhole. Pin the sleeves into the armholes, right sides together, and stitch in place.

8 Fold the backs over the front, right sides together. Pin the underarm seams from the sleeve edge to the skirt edge, and stitch. Snip underarm curve.

9 Join the back skirt seam, right sides together, stitching from lower edge halfway to the waist. Press the opening edges to the wrong side. Turn the dress right side out.

10 On the sleeves, make casings 1 inch up from the lower edge by folding fabric up, first ¼ inch and then 1¼ inches. Stitch on the fold and make the casing just below, leaving an opening for the elastic. Measure the elastic on the doll's arm, and thread through the casing. This will produce a ruffle effect on the edge of the sleeve.

11 Hem the lower edge of the skirt, and sew two press studs on the back opening of the dress.

The Hat

Make the hat templates as instructed.

1 Cut out one hat brim in felt, and four crown pieces. Make ¼ inch snips on the inner edge of the brim as shown in the pattern.

2 Pin and stitch together two crown pieces along the middle seams. Repeat for the second pair. Then place the two crown halves right sides together and stitch along the curved sides. Turn right side out.

3 Place the crown over the brim, matching the lower edges of the crown with the snipped edge of the brim. Stitch in place with small running stitches. Place on the doll, folding the front brim upward at a stylish angle (Figure 12).

4 Tie a ribbon bow around her neck to finish.

Figure 11

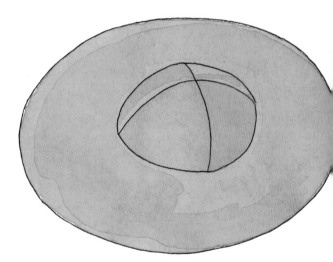

Figure 12

Toddler Doll
Joe

★ ★ ★

*T*his is a soft playful doll, cuddly and rounded with button-jointed limbs.
The doll has an embroidered face, a "button" nose, attached ears, and curly-yarn hair,
easy-fit clothes, and a baseball-style cap.

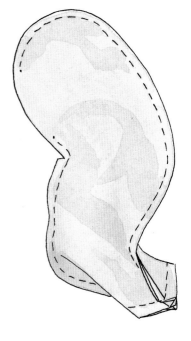

Figure 1

Figure 2

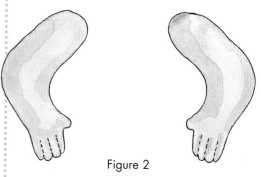

Materials

You will need
For a doll approximately 16 inches tall

For the body
- ❖ 14 x 44 in flesh-colored robe velour (the soft brushed side used as right side) for the body. If this material is not available, use muslin or other woven cotton fabric, cut on the bias grain to give maximum stretch
- ❖ 6 oz loose polyester stuffing
- ❖ 4 buttons for joints, approximately ⅝ in diameter
- ❖ 80 in strong carpet thread for joints, in white or matching flesh color
- ❖ 7 in long toy-maker's needle for assembling joints
- ❖ 1 oz yarn for hair, plain or fancy

For the face
- ❖ 1 yd each blue, light brown, pinky beige, black, and white embroidery thread

For the hair
- ❖ 1 oz double knitting yarn, plain or fancy

For the clothes
- ❖ 14 x 7 in ribbed stretch fabric for the T-shirt
- ❖ 10 x 16 in woven cotton fabric for the shorts, striped, plain, or print
- ❖ 12 in narrow elastic for the shorts
- ❖ 15 x 15 in thick woven cotton fabric such as cotton gabardine for the cap, in navy or other dark color
- ❖ 7 x 6 in thick woven cotton fabric for the cap's sun visor in a lighter color
- ❖ 7 x 6 in cotton or stretch fabric for the visor lining in a bright color
- ❖ 6 x 5 in thick non-woven interlining or buckram for the visor
- ❖ One button for the cap, about ½ in diameter

Making the Doll

The patterns and templates for this doll are on page 158. Test the robe velour fabric for the direction which gives maximum stretch, this should run from side to side on the body pieces. Remember to place the patterns on the fabric with the double arrow pointing in the direction of the stretch. Alternatively, place the patterns on the bias grain if you are using a woven fabric such as muslin.

Marking, Stitching, and Cutting

1 On the wrong side of a single layer of your chosen body fabric, position the patterns for the front head, the body gusset, and the nose. Pin in place and cut out. Trace the eyes and mouth on the reverse side of the face section, with the trace pattern underneath the fabric and taped to a window.

2 Fold the remaining fabric in half, right sides together, and trace around the templates twice; the arm, leg, and ear. Pin the patterns in place for the body side and the head side sections. Mark the openings, darts, and joint points. Cut out

the patterns only. Transfer the marks for the joints to the right side of the fabric with a pencil or a stitch in different colored thread.

3 For the arms, legs, and ears, machine stitch the traced outlines, leaving openings where indicated. Cut out these pieces, adding a ¼ inch seam allowance.

Making the Arms and Legs

1 Still wrong side out, toe seams meeting in the center, stitch across the lower feet in a slightly rounded way, to make the toes (Figure 1).

2 Snip the curves and the thumb/finger area, and turn the arms and legs right side out. Stuff firmly. Close the openings.

3 Stitch the fingers and toes (Figure 2) as explained on pages 118 and 139.

Making the Body

1 Right sides together, pin one side of the body gusset to the tummy side of one body side piece. Stitch in place.

2 Pin the other side of the gusset to the second tummy piece. Machine stitch, and then continue stitching along the center

back seam, leaving the opening as indicated (Figure 3).

3 Stitch the two neck darts. Turn right side out.

4 Stuff firmly. Run a row of gathering stitches around the neck. Pull up the gathers to partially close the opening, knot, and finish. Push extra stuffing well into the neck and shoulders, adding more if necessary. Then close the back opening.

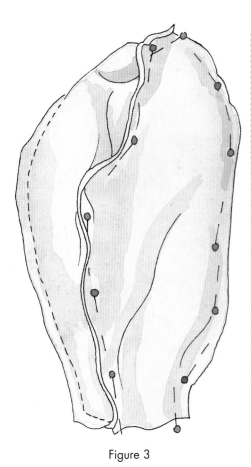

Figure 3

Making the Head

1 Right sides together, pin one head side to the center head piece, matching front, top, and back edges carefully, and stitch (Figure 4).

2 Pin and stitch the second side in the same way (Figure 5). Then pin and stitch the front face dart and the two side darts (Figure 6).

3 Turn right side out. Stuff the head firmly. Turn under the lower edge ¼ inch and tack in place.

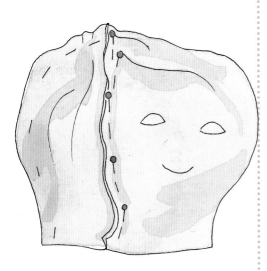

Figure 4

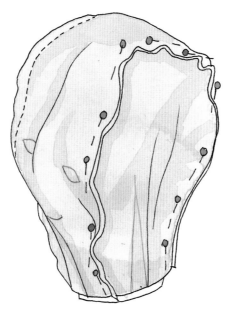

Figure 5

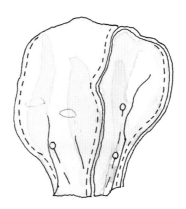

Figure 6

4 Make the nose by running a gathering stitch around the edge of the nose circle. Put a wisp of stuffing inside it, pull up the gathers, and close securely. Place the nose on the face and attach it using ladder stitch, see page 26.

5 Turn the ears right side out, but do not stuff. Top stitch ⅛ inch from the edges to indicate ear folds, and attach to the head as shown on page 24 (Figure 7).

Figure 7

The Face

Robe velour does not take paint or drawing pens very well, so it is best to embroider it. If you are using muslin or woven cotton then the face can be painted instead.

Figure 8

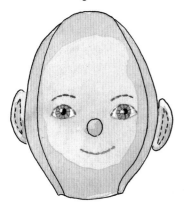

Figure 9

1 For the eyes, embroider the irises with blue embroidery thread and blanket stitch worked in a circle (Figure 8).

2 In the center, embroider black circles with satin stitch for the pupils, and a small white dot for the highlight.

3 Using brown embroidery thread, and stem stitch, embroider the lines for the eyelids and eyebrows.

4 Embroider the mouth in stem stitch with pinky beige thread (Figure 9).

Assembling the Doll

1 Place the head on the body, push the neck up into the head, and pin in place. Stitch firmly around using ladder stitch. Remove the tacking if visible (Figure 10).

2 Check that the joint points on the body and limbs are even. Thread 20 inches of strong carpet thread on the 7 inch long needle; use it double, but do not knot the ends. Insert the needle at one joint point, take it through one leg, then through the lower body, then through the other leg, and pull the thread through. Cut the thread next to the needle eye, and leave the threads hanging (Figure 11).

3 Pass the threads through the two holes in each button, then make a knot, and pull on each side alternately until the joint feels firm enough. Tie a second knot, and twist the ends under the button, knot several times, and cut off.

Figure 10

Figure 11

4 Repeat for the arms (for more details of jointing see page 21).

Making the Hair

1 Fold a sheet of paper lengthwise to obtain a strip 2¼ inches wide, and repeat to make two more strips. Wind the yarn around each one, and stitch lengthwise along the center. A total length of about 36 inches will be

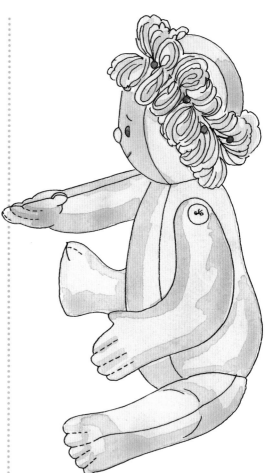

Figure 12

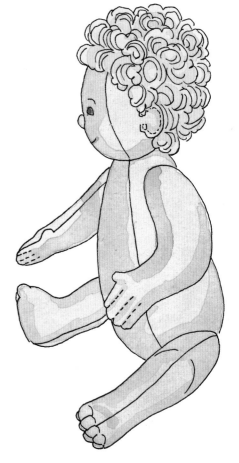

Figure 13

needed, see page 28 for making short yarn hairstyles.

2 Tear off the paper, and pin the lengths of looped yarn to the doll's head along the stitched line, in a spiral shape, starting at the hairline. Backstitch by hand along the stitch lines, starting on the outside row and finishing at the center top (Figures 12 and 13).

Making the Clothes

The patterns and templates for the clothes are on page 159.

The T-shirt

1 With the arrow on your pattern positioned for horizontal stretch, cut one front and one back from the ribbed stretch fabric. This type of fabric should not require hemming; instead, neaten with a small machine zig zag stitch on the neck, armhole, and lower edges.

Figure 14

2 Right sides together, join the shoulders and the sides with narrow seams. This completes the T-shirt (Figure 14). Alternatively, use any other type of non-stretch fabric, but cut the shapes ¼ inch larger all round and neaten with small hems.

The Shorts

1 Make two copies of the shorts paper pattern; cut one using the front waistline, and the second one using the back waistline. Join the two paper patterns together along the "Place on Fold" line. Now use this complete pattern to cut the shorts with.

2 Fold the fabric in half, right sides together. Place the paper pattern on top, and cut out. Still right sides together, pin and stitch the center front seam and the center back seam.

3 Turn up a ¼ inch hem along each lower leg, and machine stitch in place. Still right sides together, refold the shorts so center seams meet, and stitch across the crotch seam (Figure 15).

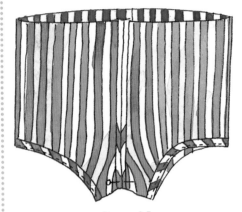

Figure 15

Figure 16

4 Make a casing on the waist edge by folding the fabric twice, first ¼ inch and then ½ inch. Pin and stitch the casing close to the hem fold and again close to the outer edge, leaving an opening. Insert the elastic (Figure 16).

The Cap

1 From the hat fabric, cut a strip 15 inches long and 1¼ inches wide. Lengthwise, fold the edges so that they meet in the center and make a narrower strip. Machine stitch close to one folded edge only; set aside.

2 Fold the rest of the fabric in half, and using the cap side pattern, cut out three times—to give the required six pieces.

3 Right sides together, pin the pieces in pairs, along one long curved edge, and machine stitch.

4 Right sides together, pin and stitch the pairs to each other to make a complete cap. Turn under the lower edge ¼ inch and tack in place.

5 Cut a circle of contrasting stretch fabric about 1 inch in diameter. Run a gathering stitch around the edge. Place the button inside, pull up the gathers, and knot. Place the covered button at the center top of the cap, and stitch in place with ladder stitch.

6 For the sun visor, cut out the reinforcing material using the visor template.

7 Using the visor pattern, cut out one section from thick cotton fabric. Right sides together, place the cotton fabric on top of the stretch fabric, and stitch around the curved outside line, ¼ inch from the cut edge. Trim the stretch fabric to the same size as the cotton fabric.

8 Turn right side out. Insert the reinforcing material, and tack the raw edges together. For decoration, top stitch several rows on the visor following the curved outline.

9 Right sides together, pin the visor to the front of the cap. Take the strip made earlier, and starting at the back, pin the non-stitched edge around the inside of the cap, covering the turned raw edges of the cap and the visor. Carefully stitch in place. Remove any tacking (Figure 17).

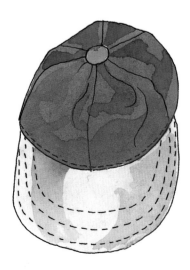

Figure 17

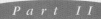

Fantasy Dolls

Let your imagination fly, and angels, fairies, witches, clowns, and all sorts of dolls with their own unique character will add magic to your life.

Decorative String Doll
Delilah

*T*his is a deceptively simple but versatile doll, which is meant to be hung on
the wall as a decoration. Her arms and legs are made of cord (piping cord is a very good type
to use) and she has a flat muslin face. The doll can be made extremely attractive by carefully
blending colors and the choice of fabric for the dress and hair. Fantasy yarn is used here
for the hair, to complement a glittery painted face.

Materials

You will need
For a doll approximately 16 inches tall

For the body
- 42 x ¼ in cotton piping cord for the arms and legs
- 5 x 8 in muslin for face
- Handful loose polyester stuffing
- For the face: drawing pens in brown, black, and red; acrylic paints in blue or violet, black, and white; and pale

blue, pale pink, and clear transparent glitter paints
- 1 oz fantasy yarn for hair

For the clothes
- 18 x 8 in fabric for dress
- 4 x 5 in felt for shoes
- 18 in narrow ribbon
- 6 in narrow ribbon or decorative trimming to hang doll from

Making the Head

1 The patterns and templates for this doll are on page 160. On double muslin, trace around the face template. Insert the template between the two layers and trace the features clearly with a soft pencil. Remove the template. Stitch the two layers around the traced outline, leaving the neck open.

2 Turn right side out, stuff well but keep the head fairly flat. Stitch the raw edges of the neck together.

The Face

Draw the face on the right side with a fine brown pen. Paint the irises in blue or violet; paint the mouth red with either a pen or acrylic paint. Paint black dots for the pupils. Paint clear transparent glitter paint over the eyes. Lightly brush pale blue transparent glitter paint over the eyelids for eyeshadow. Smear a little pale pink transparent glitter paint over the cheeks. Put a tiny white dot on each eye for the highlights. Go over the eyelashes if the lines are not clear.

Making the Clothes

The Dress

1 Fold the dress fabric in half, right sides together. Pin the pattern in place and cut out. Stitch the two sides, leaving openings for the arms as indicated. Turn right side out.

2 Make a narrow hem on the lower edge and machine stitch. Turn in the neck edge ¼ inch and press.

The Shoes

Fold the felt in half, and cut out the shoe pattern twice. Stitch around three sides, leaving the top open. The shoes are attached with the seam allowances showing.

Making the Body

Making the String Arms and Legs

1 Bind the ends of the piping cord with sticky tape to stop them unraveling.

2 Fold the cord in half and in the center make two knots (in mirror image) for the hands. Push them upward while tightening them, until they are in the middle of the cord (Figures 1 and 2).

Figure 1

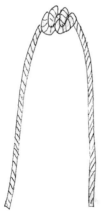

Figure 2

3 The legs are formed with the remainder of the cord. Fold and knot the cord as shown (Figure 3). The doll can now be assembled.

Figure 3

Assembling the Doll

1 Place the knotted hands on the dress. Insert the ends of the cords into the armholes, pull them (the legs) down from inside the dress, and arrange them to a pleasing length, balancing out with the arms and hands (Figure 4).

2 Insert the head into the dress through the neck hole, and stitch in place using ladder stitch.

3 Arrange the legs so they follow the natural twist of the cord and insert the bound ends into the shoes with the sticky tape intact. Stitch the shoes to the cord legs at the back only.

Figure 4

Making the Hair

1 Wind the fantasy yarn to a length of 18 inches and a width of 3½ inches. Loosely wrap a spare length of yarn around the center, making sure the width remains 3½ inches and knot.

2 Place the hair on the doll, with the wrapped middle as a center parting, starting at the hairline (about ½ inch below the top of the head). Pin in place along the parting, and backstitch to the head.

Finishing Details

1 Tie narrow ribbon around the head or neck finishing in a bow.

2 Make a loop with a short length of narrow ribbon and stitch to the back of the neck so that the doll can be hung on the wall. If the doll is for an older child or a teenager, it can be further decorated with beads, buttons, feathers, flowers, and so on.

Witch
Hepzibah

★ ★

*Halloween is the time for witches—when they come in all colors and shapes.
They may be old or young, wear all kinds of costumes, have lots of charm, and wear a smile.
Our witch will sit quite happily on a bookshelf or bedhead. She has a completely poseable body,
as her knees and elbows are jointed with buttons, as are her shoulders and hips.
Every section of her body is a different color.*

You will need
For a doll 21 inches tall

For the body
- 8 x 8 in cotton fabric for the lower legs/boots
- 5 x 14 in contrast 1 cotton fabric for the upper legs/stockings (stripes are attractive)
- 10 x 10 in contrast 2 cotton fabric for the body
- 9 x 6 in contrast 3 cotton fabric for the lower arm/gloves
- 10 x 5 in contrast 4 cotton fabric for the upper arms/sleeves
- 10 x 6 in unbleached muslin for the head
- Buttons for joints: 8 x ½ in diameter for elbows and knees and 4 x ¾ in diameter for shoulders and hips
- 3 yd strong thread (linen carpet thread) for jointing
- 8 oz loose polyester stuffing
- 2 oz wool or acrylic yarn for hair

- For the features: a fine black permanent pen, acrylic or glitter paints in blue and red, acrylic or fabric paints in black and white (alternatively, fabric pens in the same colors) and a size 1 or 2 fine paintbrush
- Glittery embroidery thread, or a fine-nozzle tube of puffy glitter paint for the boot laces
- 7 in long needle for jointing
- Fine long needle for sculpting the nose (optional) and white quilting thread

For the clothes and accessories
- 36 x 36 in cotton fabric for front-opening dress
- 2 pieces of cotton fabric (colors chosen from the other fabrics used), each 9 x 14 in, for the hat
- 1½ in strip Velcro™, or 3 press studs for fastening robe
- A short stick from the yard, or dowel, and some raffia or straw for the broom

Making the Doll

The patterns and templates for this doll are on pages 161–63.

The Head

1 Pin the head back pattern on one end of the muslin and cut out. Fold the dart toward the wrong side, pin, and stitch.

2 Fold the remaining muslin in half and trace the front face template on it. Stitch the profile only, on the marked line. Cut out, adding a ⅛ inch seam. Cut out the side of the head on the pencil line.

3 Slip the face pattern between the two layers of fabric, tape to a window, and trace the features with a soft pencil, first on one (wrong) side, and then on the other (wrong) side. Remove the pattern.

4 Snip into the curved seams, and finger-press open. Right sides together, match head front and back, pin, and stitch with a ⅛ inch seam allowance, leaving the neck open (Figure 1). Turn right side out.

The Body and Limbs

1 Fold the body fabric in half right sides together, place the body template on top, and trace around. Pin and stitch on the marked line, leaving a side opening as indicated. Turn right side out.

2 For the upper and lower sections of the arms and legs, fold each piece of fabric in half right sides together. Trace around each template twice (for right and left limbs), and then proceed as for the body, finishing with the limbs turned right side out.

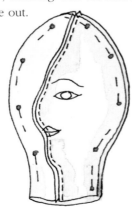

Figure 1

Stuffing

1 Stuff all parts very firmly including the body, limbs, and head sections. Close the body and limb openings with invisible ladder stitch.

2 Stuff the head really firmly, smoothing out any creases with more filling if needed. Leave the neck empty and do not close. Turn the neck edge in ¼ inch, and tack in place.

The Face

1 Working on the right side and following the pencil lines, draw the outlines of the eyes, eyebrows, and mouth, with a fine black permanent pen.

2 Paint the irises of the eyes with blue acrylic or glitter paint. Alternatively you can paint them with plain acrylic or fabric paint, and add a layer of transparent glitter paint on top.

3 Paint the mouth with red glitter paint. Alternatively, repeat as for the eyes.

4 When the eyes are dry, paint a fairly large black dot in the middle for the pupils. Lastly paint a tiny white dot on the edge of each pupil, for the highlight.

5 When everything is dry, go over the black lines again with either pen or black paint, thickening the eyebrows and eyelids especially.

6 Gently paint a layer of pale blue glitter above the eyes for eyeshadow, and pale pink on the cheeks.

Soft-Sculpting the Nose

1 Using a fine, long needle and single quilting or polyester thread, insert it at the back of the head and bring out to one side of the bridge of the nose, level with the eye.

2 Pass the needle under the nose, from one side to the other, taking tiny stitches on each side, going over them twice and pulling as you go along, to shape the nose.

3 When you get to where the nose widens, make a loop on the outside with the thread, from this point to the nostril on the same side; hold the thread out with a pin, and pull to get a round fleshy

side to the nose; take the thread back to the entry point above the nostril. Go over it again to hold it in place. Repeat for the other nostril.

4 Go back to the bridge of the nose and stitch backward and forward twice to secure (Figure 2).

5 Take the needle out through the back of the head, knot, and cut the thread off.

Assembling the Doll

1 To attach the head, slip the body neck inside the head neck cavity. Add more stuffing to the head to make it

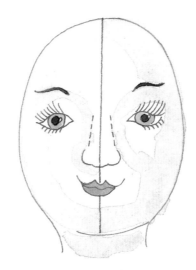

Figure 2

firmer if needed. Pin the head to the body, stretching the edges so it is firmly attached. Stitch in place with ladder stitch. Remove the tacking thread in the neck.

2 Mark the jointing points on the limbs and body as indicated on the patterns. Following the instructions for button jointing on page 21, attach the upper arms and upper legs to the doll's shoulders and hips respectively, using ¾ inch buttons in matching or contrasting colors. Finish by knotting the threads tightly so that the joints feel fairly stiff. Make three knots on each

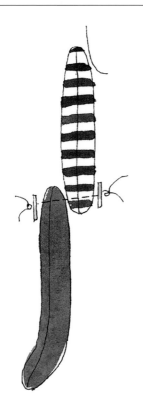

Figure 3

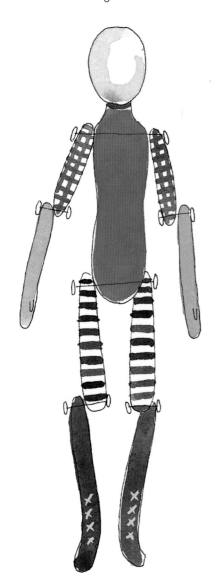

Figure 4

side. Take the tails under the buttons, twist them around several times, and make further knots underneath them until the limbs feel secure. Then cut the tails off, and leave short ends hidden under the button.

3 Join the lower leg/boot to the upper leg/stocking at the knee (Figure 3) and the upper arm/sleeve to the lower arm/glove at the elbow, using ½ inch buttons in matching or contrasting colors. You can also use different colored buttons on each side if you wish. Place the boot on the outside of each stocking, and the glove on the outside of the sleeve (Figure 4).

The Hair

1 Wind the black yarn onto a piece of thick card 18 inches long by 4 inches wide. Place the yarn on scrap paper where you have marked a 4 inch long line in the center, at right angles to its length. Pin the center of the length of hair on the center line. Stitch across the yarn to secure.

2 Tear away the paper. Place the hair on the doll, with the stitching line as a center parting, checking the correct placement, from the hairline at the front to the neckline at the back. Pin in place. Using double thread, backstitch to the doll's head.

Making the Clothes

The Dress

To be able to show off all the different fabrics that make up her body and her stockings and boots, our witch wears a front opening dress. It also has a large stand-up collar and pointed sleeves.

1 Fold the fabric in half, right sides together, pin the patterns in place, and cut out as instructed.

2 Right sides together, pin and stitch the back center seam of the dress with a ¼ inch seam allowance. Snip the seam allowance where the collar and dress meet, and press open.

3 Right sides together, place the two dress fronts on the back, match the collar, shoulders, sleeves, and side seams, and pin together. Stitch the collar/shoulder seam.

Figure 5

4 For the facing, pin the back collar facing to the front facings right sides together, and stitch. Turn under the inner edges of the facing to make a small hem, and stitch in place.

5 Right sides together, pin the complete facing to the dress around the edges of the collar and the center front edges and stitch. Turn the facing inside the dress and press in place.

6 Fold the front over the back right sides together, pin, and stitch the underarm and side seams. Make a double hem on the dress, stitching across the facings to hold them in place.

7 Make narrow hems on the sleeves, folding in the pointed ends carefully (Figure 5).

8 Fit the dress on the doll. Turn out the collar, cross over the fronts and mark where the fastenings should go. Sew three press studs or Velcro™ to the center section of the dress, leaving the neck and the lower part of the skirt open, so that you can see the colors of her body.

The Hat

1 Note that one fabric is used for the outside of the hat and the other for the lining/brim. Fold each fabric in half, right sides together, place the pattern on one double fabric, mark, and cut out. Repeat for the second fabric. Stitch around the curved back, top, and front of the hat, to make one hat and one lining.

Figure 6

2 Turn the hat lining right side out, and place it inside the hat, right sides together. Match the brim edges, pin, and stitch around, leaving a small opening. Turn right side out. Stitch the opening closed. Place on the witch, with the more concave seam toward the face, and turn up the brim at the front only (Figure 6).

The Broom

Tie a bunch of raffia or straw to one end of the stick to make a broom (Figure 7).

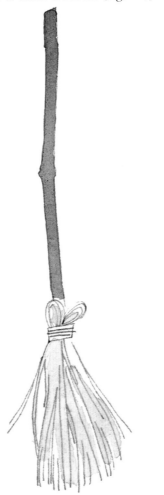

Figure 7

Finishing Details

1 Make laces for the boots by painting them with puffy paint from a tube, or alternatively by cross-stitching them with contrast embroidery thread onto the legs/boots (Figure 8).

2 Attach a folded piece of fabric from her costume, showing a star or other appropriate motif, around her neck to hide the head/body join. If you are making the witch for a grown-up, you may wish to further embellish her costume with beads, ribbons, or bows.

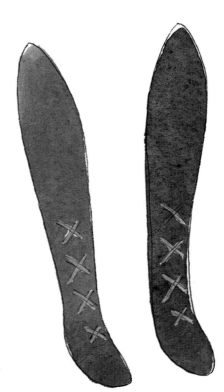

Figure 8

Angel
Araminta

★ ★

Angels have a special sort of magic. They symbolize a protective love, a love that is non-demanding and always there. Our angel doll is made mainly from crisp cottons. She has a fixed pose and a face drawn with colored pencils so she is very simple to make. She also has long golden hair, removable wings, and a cord attached so that you can hang her up—on a wall, over the bedhead, on the window or door—the choice is yours.

82

You will need
For a doll 20 inches tall

For the body
- 18 x 22 in cotton fabric for the body
- 8 oz loose polyester stuffing
- 2 oz silky yarn for the hair
- 30 yd gold knitting or embroidery thread, for the hair
- 12 x 4 in piece of thick card
- Fabric glue
- Fine black permanent pen, for the features
- Colored pencils, acrylic or fabric paints (dark brown, pink, light and dark eye color, and shadow color)

- White paint and a small paintbrush

For the clothes
- ¾ yd x 40 in/45 in wide lightweight, loosely-woven cotton fabric for the dress
- 18 x 22 in gold-printed cotton fabric for the overdress
- 14 x 24 in lightweight loose open-weave fabric or voile for the pantaloons
- 2 yds x 1½ in lace for dress
- 24 in x 1 in lace for pantaloons
- 9 in of ⅛ in narrow ribbon for pantaloons

- 4½ yds x ⅛ in gold ribbon for overdress, ties, bows, and hanging loop
- 2½ yds x 1½ in gold-printed ribbon for overdress edges
- 12 x 12 in gold-printed cotton fabric for the (removable) wings
- 2 in Velcro™ strip
- 6 x 12 in iron-on polyester wadding
- 6 x 12 in non-iron, non-woven interfacing (medium stiff)
- 12 in thick silky cord for "halo"
- Fray stop solution (the clear, liquid sort is best for this doll)

Making the Doll

The patterns and templates for this doll are on pages 164–65.

The Body

1 Fold the body fabric lengthwise in half and trace around the body templates as instructed, leaving about ½ inch between each piece.

2 Sew around the body, limbs, and head on the traced lines, leaving openings for turning where indicated.

3 Apply fray stop solution around the stitched lines and openings and leave to dry (this strengthens the seam and allows you to trim it closely and still stuff the doll firmly).

4 Using pinking shears, if you have them, trim around the stitched lines leaving a wider turning at the openings. Otherwise trim closely and clip the curves.

5 Match the top and bottom foot seams together and stitch across the toe ¼ inch from the edge.

6 Slip the face trace pattern inside the two layers of the head, put it against a window and trace the features using the dark brown pencil (which should be well sharpened).

7 Turn all pieces right side out and mark the facial features again on the right side.

8 Stuff all parts very firmly and close the openings with invisible ladder stitch.

Assembling the Doll

1 Pin the arms to the back of the shoulder as shown so that they are spread open wide. Sew firmly around the tops of the arms (Figure 1).

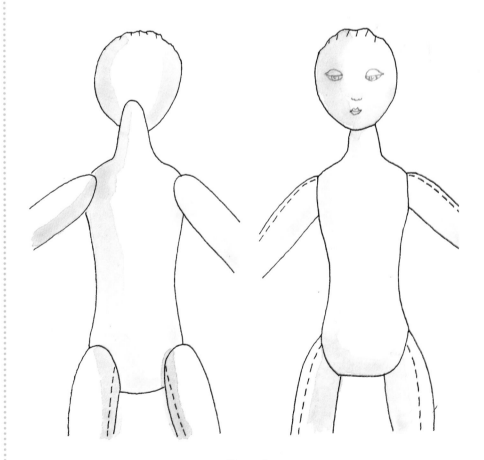

Figure 1

2 Pin the top of the legs slightly to the back of the hips so that the toes are pointing outward and the heels are together. Sew firmly around the tops of the legs.

3 Pin the head to the neck tilting it slightly to one side. The chin should overlap the top of the neck by around 1¼ inches. Sew firmly around the top of the neck using ladder stitch.

4 If you want to hang the doll on a wall then cut a 12 inch length of ⅛ inch wide ribbon. Fold the ribbon in half then turn over ¼ inch at the cut edges. Sew to the center back waist of the doll so the loop is just behind the neck.

The Face

I've used colored pencils for the facial features as they're cheap and readily available, but since they are not permanent you may prefer to paint or embroider the details.

1 Accentuate the eyelash line using the well-sharpened dark brown pencil.

2 Fill in the iris using the light eye-color pencil, shading it darker at the top of the iris and fading it to almost nothing at the twenty before eight position. Draw around the iris under the darker shade.

3 Color the mouth pink and accentuate the lips and nose with the dark brown pencil if necessary.

4 Color the cheeks, temples, and chin lightly with the pink. Test the color on a scrap of fabric and rub a clean damp finger over it to see if the pencil blends: if it does then you can blend in the cheeks.

5 Apply the eyeshadow color to each side of the upper lid leaving a small gap in the center. Run it very lightly underneath the eye. Blend as for the cheeks if desired.

6 Make large dots with the permanent black pen for the pupils and add a touch of white paint at the ten after twelve position for the highlights.

The Hair

It is best to make the hair now but attach it after the Angel is dressed.

1 Divide the gold thread into three. Wind a quantity of the silky yarn into a second ball.

2 Wind together one strand of gold thread and two of yarn around the 12 inch length of card until the gold thread runs out. The hank should be about 2½ inches across (Figure 2).

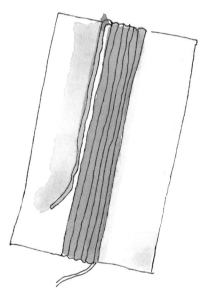

Figure 2

3 Remove from the card, open up the hank (welt) and machine stitch across the width of the hank, see page 27. Cut the end of the hank opposite the stitching (Figures 3 and 4).

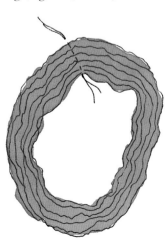

Figure 3

Figure 4

4 Repeat steps 2–3 twice giving you three hanks of hair. Select the neatest for the front edge. Set aside until the Angel is fully dressed.

Making the Clothes

The Pantaloons

1 Fold the fabric in half, right sides together, taking the short sides to the center. Pin the pattern to the two fold lines and cut out giving you two pieces.

2 Right sides together, stitch 1 inch wide lace to the bottom of each leg; open up, and press the seam toward the fabric.

3 Pin and stitch the front crotch seam. Repeat for the back crotch seam.

4 Turn the top of the pantaloons under ½ inch and press.

5 If you wish to machine gather the waist and ankles then run two rows of gathering stitches ¼ inch and ⅜ inch from the turned edge of the fabric. Otherwise hand gather after the pantaloons are turned right side out.

6 Placing right sides together, pin and stitch the underleg seam from one ankle to the other. Clip the curved seam, turn, and press.

7 Put the pantaloons on the doll and pull up the gathering threads at the waist and tie off. Repeat with the threads at the ankles.

8 Make two small bows from the ⅛ inch wide ribbon and stitch to the center front at the ankles.

The Dress

1 Cut the skirt from the dress fabric, 15½ inches long by the width of the fabric. Cut this in half to give two pieces 15½ x 20 inches, then cut one of the two pieces in half again. The wider piece will form the front and the two narrower pieces the back skirts. Press under ¼ inch at one side of each back skirt section making sure you have a left and a right side.

2 Cut two sleeves 6½ inches long by 13 inches wide. Right sides together, attach 1½ inches wide lace to the lower edge of each sleeve and skirt section. Press the seams toward the fabric.

3 The dress bodice is self-lined. Fold the remaining fabric wrong sides together. Pin the pattern pieces in place and cut two dress backs and two dress fronts. Mark the outside of each bodice back with a pin; the folded edges become the neatened back opening (make sure you have a right and a left), the inside forms the lining. Mark the bodice front with a pin too.

4 Open out the dress backs. Right sides together, pin the dress backs to the dress front at the shoulders. Next pin the dress front lining to the dress back linings at the shoulder. If you lay out the pieces they should be in the form of a cross. Stitch ¼ inch seams. Press open (Figure 5).

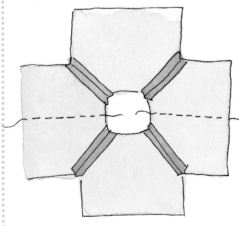

Figure 5

5 Right sides together, fold the dress back folds so that the bodice and lining are together. Pin around the neckline making sure the shoulder seams match. Stitch ¼ inch from the edge (Figure 6). Trim, clip, and turn the bodice right side

out. Treat this as one piece from now on (Figure 7).

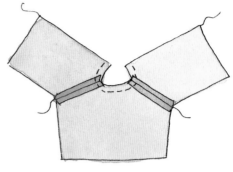

Figure 6

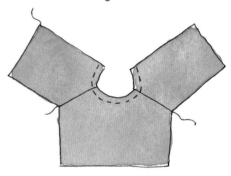

Figure 7

6 On the skirt waist edge, run three rows of gathering threads about ⅛ inch apart starting ⅛ inch below the raw edge. The stitches should start ⅜ inch from the side seam and continue over the folded edges at the center back. Gather the front skirt in the same way. Pull up tightly and press lightly with a steam iron. Loosen the gathers, if necessary, and pin to the appropriate bodice section at the waist with the right sides together. Stitch ¼ inch from the edge and neaten. Pull out any gathering threads that show.

7 Press the waist seams toward the bodice. Open the bodice and skirt sections out flat with the right side facing (Figure 8).

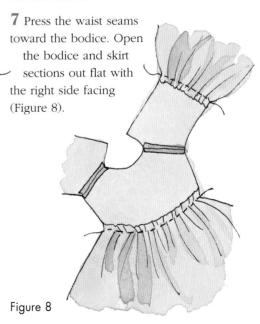

Figure 8

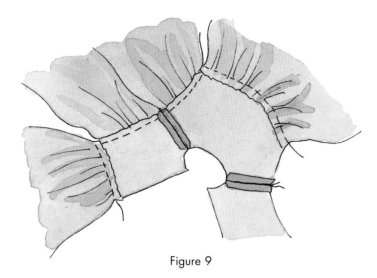

Figure 9

8 Mark the center of the sleeves with a pin and gather the top as for the skirt front, leaving ⅜ inch ungathered at the seams. Pull up to fit the bodice armhole.

9 Pin the sleeve in place, right sides together, matching the center of the sleeve to the shoulder seam and the edges of the sleeve with the waist seam. Stitch ¼ inch from the edge. Press seam toward the sleeve (Figure 9).

10 Fold the dress right sides together and stitch the side seams from the bottom of the skirt, turning at the waist and continuing to the wrist (Figure 10). Clip the seam allowance at the waist. At the center back, unfold the previously pressed edges, pin the back seam right sides together and sew along the creased line to 2 inches below the waist. Turn right side out and press seam open.

Figure 10

11 Hand gather the center of the sleeves for 2 inches at right angles to the lace. Pull up tightly and fasten off (Figure 11).

Figure 11

12 Make two small bows from ⅛ inch wide ribbon and stitch over the gathers.

13 Put the dress on the doll and sew up the back seam.

The Overdress

1 The overdress is constructed in a very similar way to the dress. Cut the skirt front 12 inches long by 9 inches wide and two back skirts 12 x 4½ inches.

2 Fold the remaining fabric in half, pin the pattern in place, and cut out the overdress top twice giving four pieces.

Fold two of the pieces wrong sides together for the back and self-lining and press the folds.

3 Follow steps 3–7 as for the dress.

4 Sew the back seam to within 2 inches of the waist.

5 Cut two lengths of 1½ inch wide ribbon to fit the sides of the overdress, from the lower back edge, over the shoulders, to the lower front edge. Pin, right sides together and stitch ¼ inch from the edge. Neaten the edge.

6 Cut two lengths of ribbon 1 inch longer than the width of the skirt (including the ribbon). Fold in each cut edge ¼ inch and again ¼ inch, pin to the bottom of the skirt, right sides together, and stitch. Hand or machine sew the edges.

7 Hand gather the ribbon at the waist seam on each side and pull up tightly.

8 Cut the remaining ⅛ inch wide ribbon into six and cut two of these pieces in half again. Sew the short ends under the gathered ribbon at the waist seam to form ties. Make small bows in the center of each length of remaining ribbon leaving long ends and sew to the overdress over the gathered ribbon.

9 Put the overdress on the doll and sew up the back using invisible ladder stitch. To complete, tie the short ribbons together under the arms.

The Wings

1 Pin the paper pattern onto the appropriate fabrics and cut out the wings as instructed.

2 Pin the wing interfacing to the back wing sections.

3 Trim ¼ inch from the edges of the iron-on wadding and iron onto the wrong side of the front sections.

4 Pin the wings together in pairs with the right sides of the fabric together, and stitch around the outside edge of the wadding leaving a gap at the center back.

5 Pin back the wing front fabric at the opening to keep it out of the way. Pin the wing back openings, right sides together, and stitch on the curved line. Finger-press seam open.

6 Unpin the wing front fabric, fold one edge over the other and hand sew closed.

7 Sew 2 inches of the hook side of Velcro™ to the center of the wing. Sew the loop side to the back of the overdress ready to attach the wings (Figure 12).

You can make an Angel to suit any season. The one shown in the project is a Christmas Angel, but you could make a Spring Angel by using a different fabric for the wings and halo (Figure 13).

Applying the Hair

1 Apply glue across the back of the head just above the neck, taking it just around the side of the face (Figure 14, line 1). Fold one hank of hair along the stitching line (Figure 15) and stick to the head with the hair falling down the back.

2 Apply more glue to the back of the head up to the top seam line (Figure 14, line 2), fold the next hank of yarn as before (Figure 15), and stick the stitched line to the top of the head with the hair again falling down the back.

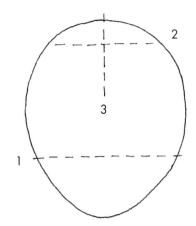

Figure 14

Figure 12

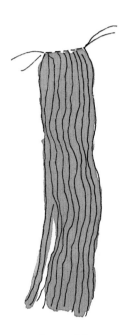

Figure 15

3 Open up the remaining hank. Apply glue to the top of the face (Figure 14, line 3) and along the stitching line of the third hank of hair. Stick this parting line starting at the face about ½ inch from the top of the head over to the back, overlapping the second layer. Arrange the front of the hair so that it falls down the side of the face.

4 Trim the hair when the glue is dry.

The Halo

Wrap the silky cord around the angel's head above the eyes and tie in a knot. To avoid the cord unraveling, cover the cord tails with fray stop solution about ½ inch from the knot and leave to dry. Cut the cord through the sealed area.

Figure 13

Bead-Jointed Doll
Vanessa

★ ★

This is a more adult doll, dressed for a special occasion, with gracefully styled red curly hair and extremely elegant clothes. Her elbows and knees are jointed with macrame beads which have large holes, so that the limb fabric can pass through them. If the doll is for a teenager or adult, she could have further decorative touches of beads and ribbons.

You will need

For a doll 18 inches tall

For the body

- 5 x 8 in flesh-colored cotton fabric, or unbleached muslin, for the face
- 10 x 8 in print or checked cotton fabric for the body
- 17 x 11 in cotton fabric with horizontal stripes for the legs
- 10 x 8 in plain cotton fabric for the arms
- 4 buttons, about ½ in diameter, for the arm and leg joints

- 1 yd strong carpet thread
- 4 oz loose polyester stuffing
- ¼ oz fine curly wool or mohair for the hair
- 4 macrame beads, ⅝ in across and with ¼ in holes for elbow and knee joints
- 5 in long needle
- Acrylic or fabric paints in white, black, brown, red, and an eye color such as blue, green, or violet, and a fine brush
- Glitter paint for the eyeshadows, in blue or green

- Dark brown or black fine-point permanent ink fabric pen
- All-purpose or fabric glue to attach the hair

For the clothes

- 10 x 12 in cotton print fabric for the skirt
- 3 press studs or Velcro™
- Two contrasting plain colors for the jacket (yellow and red), each 10 x 9 in
- Decorative trimmings such as cotton lace, thin silk or rayon ribbon, and small beads

Making the Doll

The patterns and templates for this doll are on page 166.

The Face

1 From the flesh-colored fabric, cut two rectangles, each 4 x 5 inches. Put one fabric rectangle aside to make the back of the head later.

2 Place the face pattern under the fabric, tape them onto a window pane, and trace the features and the head on the wrong side of the fabric, using a pencil.

3 Place the fabric, features side down, on white paper, so that the pencil lines show clearly on the right side. With the black or dark brown permanent ink pen, carefully retrace the features on the right side of the fabric. Now paint the face (see page 24).

Painting the Face

1 Beginning with the eyes, paint the irises brown or any other suitable eye color. When dry, paint the pupils black, and then add white dots for highlights. Paint the mouth with "lipstick" red. Add glitter paint above the eyes for eyeshadow. Emphasize the brown or black lines of the eyebrows and eyelids by going over them either with the pen, or black paint and a fine brush. Draw or paint the eyelashes over the glitter paint.

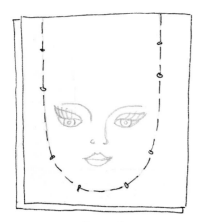

Figure 1

Figure 2

2 When the paint is dry, place the face onto the fabric reserved for the back head, right sides together. Pin along the curved line, and stitch ¼ inch inside the marked line, leaving the top open (Figure 1). Cut on the marked line and turn right side out. Stuff very firmly, until the face is very smooth. Run a row of gathering stitch around the top, pull up the gathers, and close the opening (Figure 2).

The Body and Limbs

1 Trace the body template onto double fabric, right sides together. Machine stitch around leaving the opening on the side as indicated. Cut out, adding ¼ inch seam allowances. Turn right side out.

2 Using horizontal striped fabric for the legs, folded right sides together, trace around the leg template twice. Machine stitch around, leaving openings at the toes and the side.

3 Cut out the legs, adding ¼ inch seam allowances. Open up the foot area and fold flat, bringing together the seams in

the center. Mark a curved line for the toes, stitch, and trim the seam. Turn right side out.

4 Make the arms in plain fabric as for the legs, leaving one opening as shown. Snip the curved seams, particularly between the hand and thumb. Turn right side out.

The Bead Elbows and Knees

1 Stuff the arms and legs firmly up to the knees and elbows only. Make sure the thumb and hand are stuffed well before continuing up the arm. Stuff the feet and ankles quite firmly.

2 When you reach the elbows and knees, slip the macrame beads (Figure 3) in position by pushing the unstuffed fabric through the holes, until the beads reach the stuffing. (Alternatively, if suitable beads are not available, gather the fabric at the elbows and knees, pull the gathers, and tie securely.)

3 Stuff the rest of the arms and legs firmly, and close the openings.

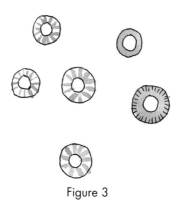

Figure 3

Assembling the Doll

1 Stuff the doll's body firmly and close the opening. Mark the hip and shoulder joints on the outside of the body and limbs.

2 Attach the button-jointed limbs to the body (Figure 4) following the instructions on page 21.

3 Place the head on the neck tab so that there is a good chin in front, and handstitch firmly in place (Figure 5).

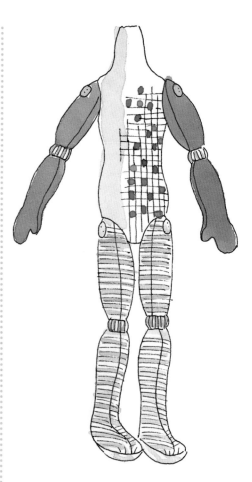

Figure 4

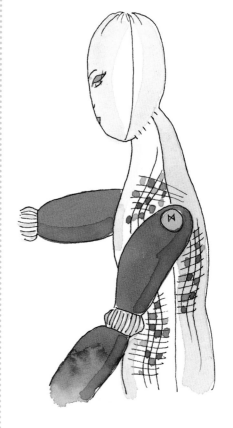

Figure 5

Making the Hair

1 Make the hair from curly mohair or curly wool. Cut sufficient 10 inch lengths to cover the head completely so that the fabric underneath does not show.

2 Once you are satisfied with the arrangement, spread glue on the head and fix the hair in place. Leave to dry thoroughly. Trim the ends if needed (Figure 6).

Figure 6

Making the Clothes

The Skirt

1 Cut a 10 x 12 inch rectangle of print fabric for the wrap-around skirt and, make ⅜ inch hems on all four sides.

Figure 7

Along one of the 12 inch sides, make five pleats at regular intervals to reduce the waist width from 12 inches to 7½ inches (Figure 7). Top stitch the waist edge twice to hold the pleats in place.

2 Try the skirt on the doll and mark the crossover with pins. Stitch pieces of Velcro™ or press studs to secure the waist edge (Figure 8).

The Jacket

1 Cut two 5 x 9 inch rectangles from each of the two jacket fabrics, and place two contrasting colors together, to make two pairs.

Figure 8

2 Along one 9 inch side, yellow side up, stitch a ¼ inch seam from the edge, for 4 inches only. Repeat for the other piece, also yellow side up. Press the seams open.

3 Now place the pieces, right sides together, seams matching, so that the colors alternate. Place the jacket template on top with the relevant edge along the stitched seam. Mark around it, turn it over the other side, and mark again. Hold with pins, and stitch around, leaving an opening at the back as indicated.

4 Cut out, adding a ¼ inch seam allowance all round (Figure 9). Turn right side out through the back opening. Push the seams out with a blunt tool, press flat, and close the opening with invisible stitching.

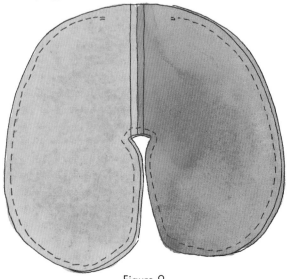

Figure 9

5 Fold the lapels out, with a 1 inch maximum width. Stitch in place with a decorative machine embroidery flower or other stitch, in contrasting colors. Try on the doll. Cross over the fronts so that they overlap about ½ inch. Attach a press stud or a piece of Velcro™ to hold it together (Figure 10).

6 With the jacket on the doll, mark the underarm seam so that it looks comfortable on the doll. Secure with three flowers or other embroidery stitches, also in contrasting colors.

Finishing Details

1 You may like to decorate the neck with a piece of cotton lace. Further decorations, such as seed bead jewelry, can be added if the doll is for an adult.

2 For the slipper laces, cut two pieces of soft silk or rayon ribbon, 24 inches long. Stitch them on the doll's feet as shown, with four beads at the holding points on each foot. Tie the remaining lace above the ankles (Figure 11).

Figure 10

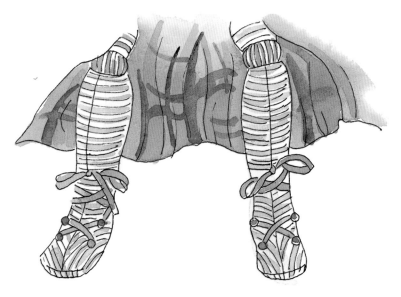

Figure 11

Mermaid
Melody

★ ★ ★

*O*ur beautiful mermaid, with her sea-green waist-length hair and glittery green
fish tail stitched with silver, will attract all who are interested in fantasy and fairy tales. She has
trapunto features, a smart silver sun-top, and wears enticing green nail varnish.

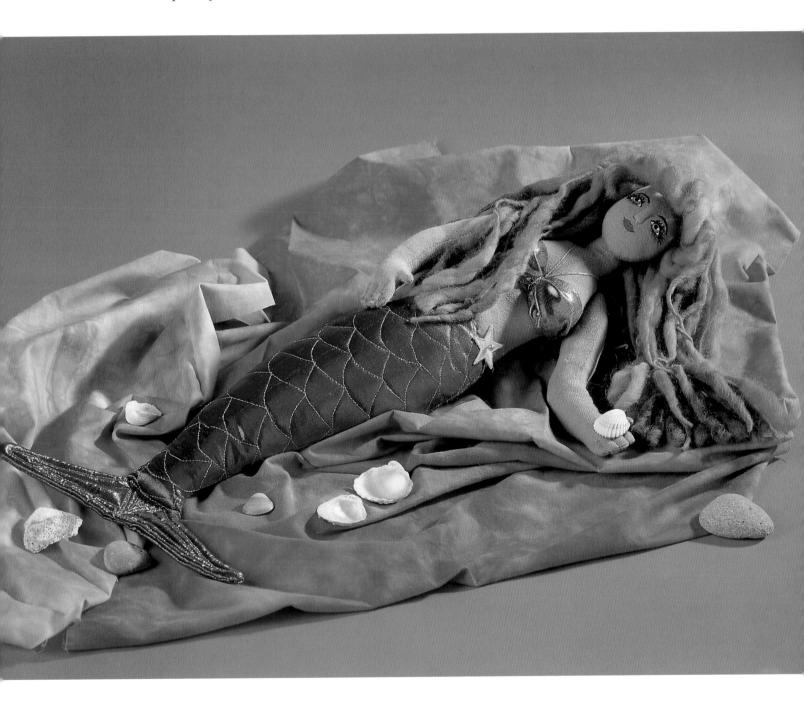

93

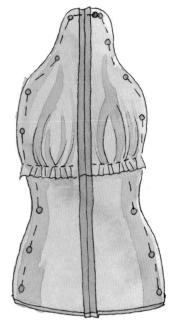

Figure 3

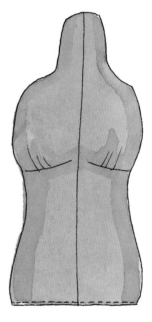

Figure 4

Making the Doll

The patterns and templates for this doll are on page 167.

The Body

1 Cut a piece of body fabric 10 x 3 inches and put aside for making the head. Fold the remaining fabric right sides together, position the templates for the body back, the upper body front, the lower body front, and two arms and draw around as instructed.

2 Pin and stitch the center seams only of all the body pieces. Stitch around the arms, leaving openings where indicated.

3 Cut out, adding ¼ inch seam allowances to the stitched seams. Press the center seams open (Figure 1).

4 Make the bust by running two short rows of gathering stitch along the lower edge of the upper body front where indicated. Pull up the gathers to fit lower body front edge. Right sides together, pin and stitch to make a complete front body (Figure 2).

5 Right sides together, pin and stitch around the body front and back with a ¼ inch seam, leaving the lower edge open (Figure 3).

6 Turn right side out, and stuff firmly, especially the neck and shoulders. Shape

the bust by molding the stuffing into the slightly stretchy fabric. Oversew the raw lower edges together; do not turn in, as this end will fit inside the tail (Figure 4).

7 Needle-sculpt the bust slightly, by taking small stitches from the center of the bust to the back (where they will be covered later by her sun-top and hair).

8 Turn the arms right side out, stuff, and close the opening. Stitch the fingers. As a finishing detail, paint her nails with green glitter paint (Figure 5).

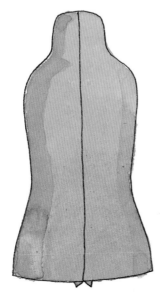

Figure 1

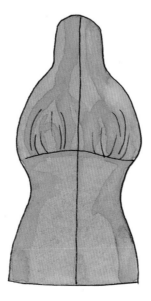

Figure 2

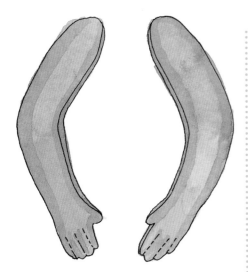

Figure 5

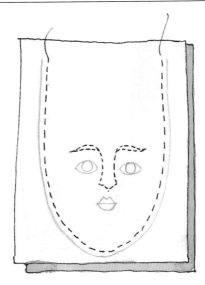

Figure 6

Figure 9

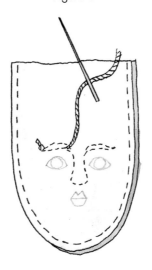

Figure 7

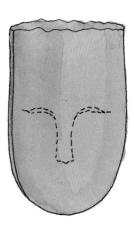

Figure 10

The Head

1 Cut two pieces of body fabric and one of muslin, each 3 x 4 inches. Place the face pattern under the muslin, and trace the head and the face features with a soft pencil. Do not cut out.

2 Place one piece of stretch fabric under the muslin, wrong sides together, drawn features uppermost.

3 Pin and machine stitch around the head, ⅛ inch in from the curved outline, leaving the top open.

4 Part of the face is made by the quilting technique known as trapunto. Stitch through the two layers of fabric along the eyebrows and nose outlines as shown (Figure 6).

5 Cut out along the marked line. Insert wisps of stuffing into the nose, from the top, checking on the stretch fabric side to give it a good shape. For the eyebrows, insert a needle threaded with soft, thick embroidery thread. From the muslin side trim the ends (Figure 7).

6 Place the stitched face on the second piece of stretch fabric, right sides together, muslin side up. Pin and stitch through all thicknesses, ¼ inch in from the cut curved edge; leave the top open (Figure 8). Cut the head back fabric along the edge of the front, leaving a bit more fabric on the top (Figure 9).

7 Turn the face right side out. Stuff the head thoroughly, so the fabric is stretched and does not pucker at the seams (Figure 10). Run a row of gathering stitch along the top, pull together, and close.

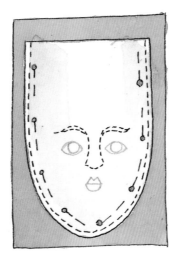

Figure 8

The Face

1 Using the nose and eyebrows as guidelines, draw the eyes and mouth with a sharp pencil. Then go over them with black and red waterproof drawing pens; draw the eyebrows (see page 24).

Helpful Tip

If you are not familiar with the technique of trapunto, or feel that it is a little too difficult, you could make an alternative face, following the steps for making the face of the Bead-Jointed Doll on page 89.

---

2 Paint the whole of the eye white. When dry, redraw the iris and paint it green. When dry, paint the black pupils and the white highlights. Add glitter paint as eyeshadow.

3 Paint the mouth with a good "lipstick" shade of red.

4 When dry, redraw all the black lines with the pen and then paint the eyebrows and eyelashes black.

Making the Clothes

The Sun-top

Cut a strip of silver fabric 10 x 2 inches. Wrap a length of silver thread around the center, gather it tightly, and knot firmly. Leave long thread ends. Place on the doll, turn the edges in if necessary. Stitch the sun-top to the doll at the center, sides, and back as needed. Tie the silver thread around her neck and trim the ends (Figure 11).

Assembling the Doll

1 Pin the head to the neck tab, making sure the neck is not too long. Position the head at a slight angle for more interest. Stitch firmly in place with ladder stitch.

2 Attach the arms to the body (Figure 12) with a button joint, see page 21.

Making the Tail

1 Cut two pieces of green glitter fabric and two pieces of wadding, approximately 10 x 16 inches. Place wadding under each piece of green fabric, and pin together. Mark the tail shape with pins or chalk, extending the outline by 1 inch all round. Repeat on the second piece making sure it is a mirror image—one for the back and one for the front.

2 Using silver machine embroidery thread on the top of the machine, and plain white thread in the bobbin, quilt

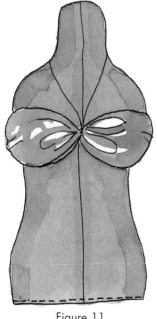

Figure 11

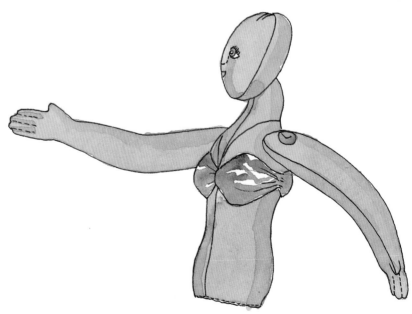

Figure 12

the scale pattern indicated on the tail template. There is no need to draw and measure here, just stitch freely over the wider tail width (Figure 13).

3 Place the back and front tails, right sides together. Position the template on top and mark the precise tail outline with pins. Stitch around the shape, leaving the top open. Carefully turn the tail right side out. Now stitch the lines on the tail fins, through all thicknesses, with the front side of the tail uppermost, to show the silver thread lines (Figure 14).

4 Stuff the lower section of the tail, just up to where the body will fit in. Turn in the top edge and tack. Place the body inside the tail, positioning it level with the navel. Pin the tail to the body and ladder stitch in place.

Making the Hair

1 Using space-dyed novelty yarn if available, or a mixture of green, blue, and yellow ocher yarn, wind a 14 inch length, and sufficient to make a good thick fringe. Tie the yarn about 2½ inches from one looped end. Place on the doll's head, shape a curly fringe, and stitch the tied section onto the head (Figure 15).

2 Wind a second section of yarn, this time 24 inches long, and sufficient to cover the top of the head with a thick head of hair. Stitch a center parting on a piece of paper, see page 27. Tear off the paper (Figure 16).

3 Place this second section across the mermaid's head and backstitch in place. Trim the lower ends to an even length. The fringe can be cut if desired, or left with loops.

Figure 13

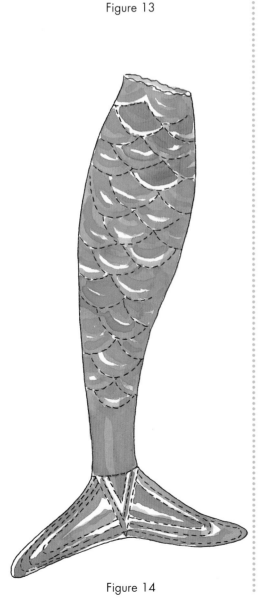

Figure 14

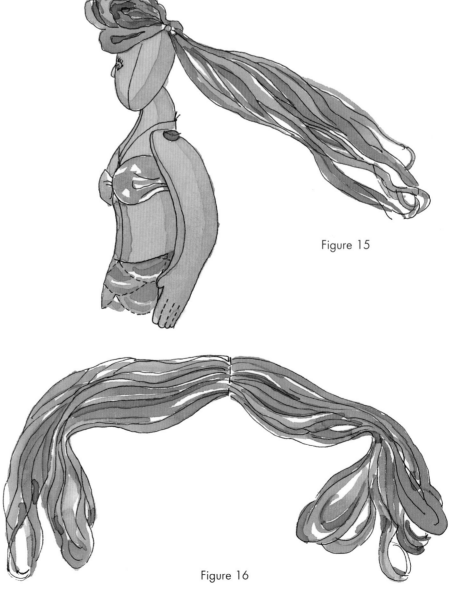

Figure 15

Figure 16

Rose Fairy
Rosalind

★ ★ ★

This delightful fairy doll is dressed, as you would imagine, in a skirt made from rose "petals" and shoes from "leaves." She has beautiful translucent wings made from metallic organza, and silky soft hair decorated with tiny flowers. In good flower-fairy style, her silk shift and pantaloons are delicately trimmed with "spider-web" lace. The doll's limbs are fully jointed so she can be artistically posed, and makes an excellent collectors' piece— she's not, however, recommended for young children.

Making the Doll

The patterns and templates for this doll are on pages 168–70.

The Body

1 Fold the body fabric in half lengthwise and trace around the body templates as instructed, leaving about ½ inch between each piece. Stitch around the body, limbs, and head on the traced lines leaving openings where marked for turning.

2 Apply fray stop solution to the stitched lines and openings and leave to dry (this strengthens the seam).

3 Using pinking shears, if you have them, cut closely around the stitched lines leaving wider turnings at the openings. Otherwise cut out with ⅛ inch seam allowances and snip the curves.

4 Slip the face trace pattern inside the two layers of the head, tape to a window, and trace the features using a sharp pencil or fade-away marker pen.

5 Turn the body pieces right side out. Stuff all parts very firmly and sew the openings closed using invisible ladder stitch.

Assembling and Jointing the Doll

The jointing of this doll is very simple: the two parts of each limb are overlapped, a thread is taken through both sections and held in place with buttons at either side.

1 Join the upper and lower arms using linen thread and a long needle. Thread one ⅜ inch button onto the end of the thread leaving a long end. Sew right through the upper arm from the outside, as marked, and then through the lower arm. Thread on another ⅜ inch button and sew back through the arms leaving a long thread underneath the outside button. Squash the arm sections together firmly and tie off the thread tightly. Repeat for the other arm but reverse the order of threading so that you have both the right and left arms (Figure 1).

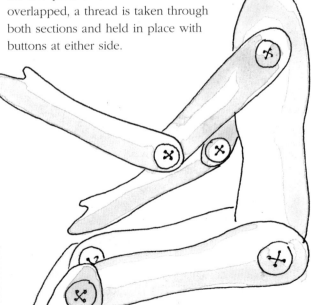

Figure 1

2 Joint the lower and upper legs in the same way using ½ inch buttons (Figure 1).

3 Arrange the doll so that the upper arms are on the outside of the lower arm and the upper legs are on the inside when placed against the body. This makes the doll pose more naturally. Using the same technique, attach the arms to the shoulders using ½ inch buttons, taking the thread all the way through one arm, then from one side of the body to the other, through the other arm and back again before tying off as tightly as possible. Do the same with the legs using ⅝ inch buttons.

4 Pin the back of the head to the front of the neck with the chin about ¾-inch below the top of the neck. Sew firmly twice around the neck form using invisible ladder stitch (Figure 2).

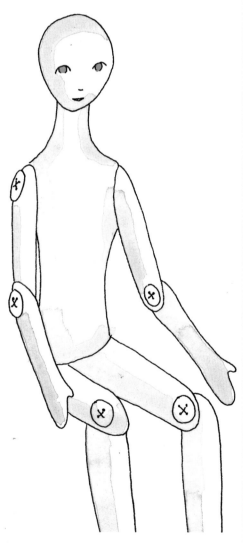

Figure 2

The Face

1 Mark the features on the face using the guidelines traced earlier.

2 Paint the whites of the eyes using the opaque white fabric paint and outline the nose and lips with pink (deepen the pink with a spot of black if necessary).

3 Pour a reasonable quantity of the pearl white (or white) fabric paint into a mixing dish, add a touch of gold paint, and mix thoroughly. Don't use too much gold to start with as you don't want the doll to look gold-plated. It is easier to add more gold if it's too pale than to tone it down if it's too bright.

4 Using the large brush, paint over the face of the doll (missing the eyes but don't worry about the nose and lips as the pink should show through enough for you to repaint), under the chin, and the back of the neck.

5 Paint the irises using a mixture of gold and green. With the other, dry, brush, wipe off a little of the color at the twenty before eight position. Add some more green to the eye paint and draw a fine line around the outside of the iris.

6 Outline the eye with the eyeshadow color from the inside corner of the upper lid to halfway along the lower lid. Before it dries, soften the shadow with the other brush rinsed in clear water. Repeat more than once if you wish to build up the color and shading.

7 Outline the top lid with a fine line of black paint and make a large dot nearer to the top of the eye for the pupil. When the pupils are dry, make a small dot with white paint at the ten after twelve position for the highlight.

8 The lips require three shades of pink which can be mixed from your existing colors. (Experiment with adding gold or white to the pink for the lightest shade and black for the darkest.) Outline the lips and nostrils in the darkest pink, then paint the lower lip using the lighter shade and the upper lip using the middle shade. Leave to dry in a warm place.

Painting the Body

1 Using the same paint mix as used for the base color for the face, paint the body from the neck to mid-chest, the arms from hands to the elbow joints, and the legs from the ankles up to the knee joints. The rest of the body won't show.

2 Mix some gold and green paint and paint the low boots as shown (Figure 3).

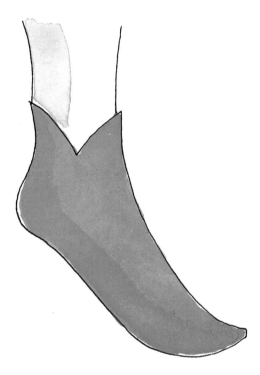

Figure 3

The Hair

It's best to leave this stage until after the fairy is dressed but I've included it here for completeness.

1 Divide the viscose or mohair lengthwise into three equal sections. Spread each section to a width of 1½–2 inches. Machine sew down the center of each section using a short stitch. If you find that it gets caught in your machine then sew it between two layers of tissue paper and tear the paper away afterward.

2 Select the best length of hair for the front and put aside. Spread the head with glue from ¼ inch below the seam line at the front over the back of the head to the neck.

5 The hair is going to look quite thick and messy at this stage. Once the glue is dry, comb the hair from the bottom very carefully with a wide-toothed comb. You may find that you lose half the bulk, and that the hair looks much more realistic. Lightly trim.

The Wings

1 Place the wing fabric centrally in the embroidery hoop and place it flat side down over the wing templates. You should be able to fit a right and left wing in the hoop if you place the outside of each wing to the center. Trace the outline and markings for each wing using the gold pen.

2 Cut the wire in two. If you're using a machine embroidery hoop then leave the fabric in the hoop, otherwise take the fabric out of the hoop and tack tissue paper to the back. Put a strong needle in the machine and set the machine speed to its slowest setting. Set the machine to a fairly wide zig-zag stitch in order to clear the wire easily.

3 The wire is stitched to the inside edges of the wing only. Apply fray stop solution to the wing tips, and push each end of the wire through the fabric from the front, and leave loose (Figure 4).

3 Fold the other two hair sections in half along the stitched lines. Stick one of the sections across the back of the head level with the top of the neck and the other above it, just below the top seam line.

4 Open up the remaining hair section and spread glue along the stitching line. Glue the hair along the center parting from the front of the head and over the previously applied hair.

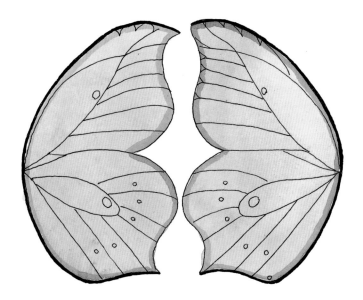

Figure 4

4 Zig-zag stitch carefully over the wire between the points. Cut the wire on the wrong side about ¼ inch from each hole and bend the wire over securely. Carefully remove the tissue paper if used.

5 Stretch the fabric back in the hoop right side on top. You can use gold silk-painting gutta to outline the veins and when dry apply silk paint to give the wings more shading. Alternatively, use the gold fabric paint to outline the veins.

6 Apply fray stop solution around the outside edges of the wing. Outline the wing with pink and paint the markings at the edge.

7 Decorate the wing with small crystals to finish.

8 Leave the wings in the hoop to protect them until the doll is dressed.

Making the Clothes

The Pantaloons

1 Fold the fabric right sides together, pin the paper pattern in place, and cut out. Right sides together, sew lace to the bottom edges.

2 Pin and stitch the center front seam. Turn ⅜ inch to the wrong side at the waist and press. Open up the pressed turning at the back seam, pin the seam together, stitch, and press again.

3 Pin and stitch the underleg seam, from one lace edge, through the crotch seam, to the other side. Turn and press.

4 Run a gathering stitch ¼ inch from the top edge starting and ending at the center back. Leave the needle in the back without finishing off. Using two other needles, repeat for each of the legs just above the lace, starting and ending at the center front.

5 Put the pantaloons on the doll and pull the threads up to fit. Finish off the ends and sew a little ribbon bow at the bottom of each leg.

The Blouse or Shift

The only difference between the blouse and the shift is that the blouse has a double hem while the shift is edged with lace and is therefore longer. It is your choice.

1 Fold the fabric right sides together, pin the two paper patterns in place and cut out the shift sections.

2 Right sides together, sew lace to the bottom of the raglan sleeves. Fold over the top edges of the sleeves and bodice and press. Pin the sleeves to the front, right sides together, and sew the diagonal front shoulder seams. Repeat for the back shoulder seams.

3 Pin and stitch one side of the front to the back and continue stitching around the armhole to the elbow.

4 Either sew lace to the bottom of the shift or turn a double ¼ inch hem to the wrong side, press, and stitch.

5 Stitch the other front and back together as before.

6 Gather the elbows and necklines in the same way as for the pantaloons. Put the shift on the doll. Arrange the neckline so that it is fairly wide and sew on a small ribbon bow to the front. Pull the elbows up tightly and again finish off with a small bow.

The Underskirts

There are two underskirts each made in the same way. If you wish to increase the number of underskirts then make each one smaller than the others and put them on first. The doll has a very slim waist so she can take the bulk required.

1 From the pale pink silk, cut a strip 1½ inches wide from one short end. Cut 5¼ inches off the strip for the waistband.

2 Turn a hem on one long edge of the skirt, first ¼ inch and then ⅜ inch, press, and stitch. Press in ¼ inch at each end.

3 Fold the waistband lengthwise, wrong sides together, and press. Turn under ¼ inch at each end and press.

4 On the skirt run three rows of machine gathering near the top edge. Pull up to fit the waistband, pin, and stitch ¼ inch from the edge. Pull out any gathering stitches which show.

5 Open up the folds at the back seam and stitch from the hem to within 2 inches of the waistband. Put to one side.

6 Make the outer underskirt in exactly the same way, but starting with a length of fabric 7 x 45 inches and making the waistband 5½ inches long.

The Petal Skirt

The petals are made separately, then gathered together, and applied to a band.

1 Fold the fabric in half right sides together. Draw around the petal template five times leaving a ½ inch gap between each petal. You should be able to fit three petals along one edge and two, between them, on the other.

2 Stitch around the outside, curved edge. Apply fray stop solution all around the outside edge, leave to dry, and cut out the petals leaving a small margin. Clip in curves. Turn the petals right side out and press.

3 Cut a piece of fabric from the scraps, 1¾ x 5½ inches. Prepare as for the underskirt waistband.

4 Line the petals along a table, overlapping them by 1½–2 inches at the top, and pin the overlap. Run three rows of machine gathering near the cut edge and pull up to fit the waistband arranging the petals evenly. Pin the petal skirt to the waistband, right sides together, and stitch ¼ inch from the edge. Pull out any gathering stitches which show. Press.

5 To curl the petals naturalistically, place a pencil across one petal near the bottom, at about 45 degrees. Roll the petal over the pencil so that it completely overlaps it. Pin and secure the overlap with one or two stitches from the underside so that it doesn't show. Repeat for the other side of the petal and for the remaining petals. Do not press (Figure 5).

6 Put the petal skirt to one side.

The Cummerbund with Sepals

1 Fold the fabric, right sides together, and draw around the template for the cummerbund once on the double fabric. Then draw around the template for the sepals five times. Leave up to ½ inch between the drawn pieces for the seam allowance.

Figure 5

2 Stitch around each piece on the traced line leaving the cummerbund open at one short end and the sepals open at the top. Apply fray stop solution to the seam lines and leave to dry.

3 Cut out the cummerbund and sepals close to the stitched line using pinking shears, or trim and clip curves. Turn right side out. Press.

4 Arrange the sepals to fall between the petals with the fifth sepal at one end of the band. Pin the sepals to the outside of the petal waistband, overlapping the waistband about ¼ inch and hand stitch. Put the cummerbund to one side.

Assembling the Clothes and Wings

The doll should already be dressed in her shift and pantaloons.

1 Put the smallest underskirt on over the shift. Overlap the ends of the waistband pulling it tightly, and hand sew closed.

2 Repeat for the second underskirt and the petal skirt.

3 Remove the wings from the hoop and carefully cut them out using sharp scissors to give an even edge of color.

4 The wings have to be attached securely to the back of the doll, just below the shoulder blade. Use dressmaker's pins to attach the wings temporarily while you determine the best position. The doll should be able to sit without crumpling the wings. Thread a very long needle with a doubled thread to match the wings or the blouse. Secure the thread to the back of the blouse, then wrap it over the wire at the center of the wing and take the needle diagonally through the doll's body to the center front at the waist. Don't worry about the stitches showing on top of the petal waistband. Take the needle back through the body, sew over the wire again and repeat a few times so that the wing is secure. Do the same with the other wing.

5 Wrap the cummerbund over the waistbands with the finished end on top and pull tight. Hand sew closed.

Finishing Details

Decorate the doll's hair with a few small fabric flowers and sew a crystal bead to one of the petals to represent a dewdrop.

Clown

Jojo

★ ★ ★

*W*hat toy would be more pleasing for a child than this charming clown
dressed in shiny satin clothes with tinkling bells attached—he makes a jolly, colorful companion.
His face is painted with fabric paints mixed with glitter for a truly stunning effect.

You will need
For a doll about 19 inches tall

For the body
- ❖ 7 x 8 in white, slightly stretchy knit fabric (or muslin cut on the bias grain) for the head
- ❖ 11 x 8 in purple satin for the body
- ❖ 16 x 16 in blue satin for the legs
- ❖ 9 x 16 in yellow satin for the arms
- ❖ 5½ oz loose polyester stuffing
- ❖ Acrylic or fabric paints for painting the face in magenta or bright pink, purple, blue/green, yellow, and metallic gold; and glitter paints in red and white
- ❖ Two ½ in diameter buttons for jointing the doll; 20 in thick carpet thread and a 7 in long needle
- ❖ ½ oz yellow yarn, for the hair

For the clothes
- ❖ 20 x 12 in yellow satin for the pants
- ❖ 20 x 5 in blue satin for the pants edge lining
- ❖ 15 in narrow elastic for the pants and neck bow
- ❖ 12 x 12 in each purple and pink satin for the top
- ❖ A small piece of Velcro™ or a press stud for closing the top
- ❖ 9 x 3 in each purple and pink satin for the cuffs
- ❖ 8 x 8 in each purple and pink satin for the hat
- ❖ 9 x 6 in blue satin for the neck bow
- ❖ Scraps of pink and purple satin for the shoe bows
- ❖ Ten cap bells, ⅜ in diameter

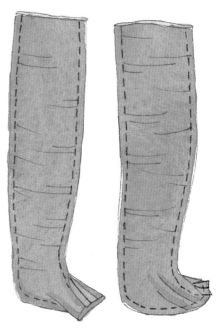

Figure 3

Making the Doll

The patterns and templates for this doll are on pages 171–2.

The Body

1 Handle the satin very carefully, leave ½ inch seam allowance because it frays easily. Fold the purple satin in half, right sides together, trace around the body template, pin, and stitch around, leaving the neck open. Cut out, adding a ½ inch seam allowance. Turn right side out and stuff firmly but carefully, leaving space in the stuffing for the neck. Do not close the opening (Figure 1).

2 Fold the yellow satin in half, right sides together, trace around the arm template twice, pin, and stitch around, leaving the opening as indicated. Cut out, adding ½ inch seam allowances. Turn right side out, stuff carefully, and close the opening. Stitch the fingers (Figure 2).

3 Fold the blue satin in half, right sides together, trace around the leg template twice, pin, and stitch around, leaving

openings at the top and toes. Cut out, adding ½ inch seam allowances. Match the toe seams, pin, and stitch with a curved seam to make the toes (Figure 3). Trim, turn right side out, stuff firmly but carefully to about 1 inch from the top. Turn top edges in and close with ladder stitch, gathering slightly.

4 Fold the head fabric in half, right sides together, trace around the head template, pin, and stitch around leaving the top open. Cut out, adding a ¼ inch seam allowance (Figure 4). Stuff firmly, especially the neck, molding the stuffing as you go to give the head a good shape. Gather the top edge and pull to close.

Figure 1

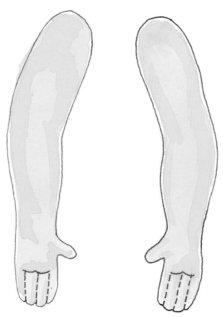

Figure 2

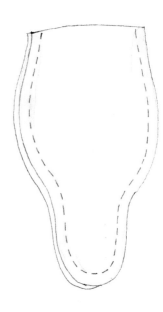

Figure 4

Painting the Face

1 Make a copy of the paper template of the clown's face with the features drawn on it. Cut out the paper outlines of the eyes, the round nose, the eyebrows, and the mouth.

2 Position the cut-out face template centrally on the stuffed head, and pin in place. With a soft pencil, or an air-vanishing pen, draw the outlines of the eyes, nose, eyebrows, and mouth. Remove the template.

3 Paint the eye shapes white. Then mix a little white glitter paint with each of the following colors and paint the nose yellow, the mouth magenta or bright pink, and the eyebrows purple. When the white is dry, paint the irises blue-green, the pupil black, and the highlights white. The features will then be beautifully glittery when they catch the light.

4 Paint red or pink glitter above the eyes for the eyelids. Paint decorative shapes on the cheeks in gold metallic paint. When everything is dry, outline the eyes, irises, and the eyelashes with a black pen. With a brown pen, draw around the nose and the line to join it to the eyebrows, and finish with the middle line for the lips.

Assembling the Doll

1 Fit the neck into the body, leaving about ½ inch showing below the head. Add stuffing if necessary to make a firm join. Pin and stitch with ladder stitch (Figure 5).

2 Pin the legs to the front of the body, 1 inch above the lower edge. Ladder stitch in place, around the front and the back of the legs (Figure 6).

Figure 7

Figure 5

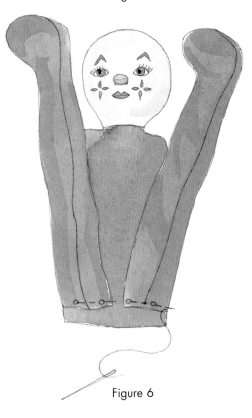

Figure 6

3 Joint the arms to the body with two matching buttons using strong thread and a long needle, see page 21. Make the joint tight so the arms do not flop (Figure 7).

The Hair

It is recommended to make and fit the clothes before attaching the hair.

1 Wind the yarn for a fringe on a piece of card, 7 inches long by 3 inches wide, see page 27. Remove from the card, and stitch a seam across the yarn, 2 inches from one looped end.

2 Wind the yarn for the main hair on card, 10 inches long by 2 inches wide. Remove and stitch a seam across the center (Figure 8).

3 Pin the fringe on the doll, with the seam across the top of the head, and backstitch in place. Place the main hair across the previous one, with the parting line placed in the center of the head, starting just on top of the fringe seam. Backstitch in place. Cut off the loops and trim the hair evenly (Figure 9).

Figure 8

Figure 9

Making the Clothes

Pants

1 Cut a rectangle of yellow satin 12 x 20 inches and fold the two 12-inch edges so that they meet in the center, right sides together. Pin the pattern on top placing the side to one fold, and cut out—do not cut out the points, instead cut a straight edge enclosing the points. Repeat again on the other fold, reversing the pattern.

2 Cut two strips of blue satin for the lining, each 10 x 5 inches. Right sides together, pin them along the lower edges of the pants. Now cut away the shaded area on the paper pattern, replace it on top, and mark the points. Stitch the points, trim the fabric leaving a ½ inch seam allowance, snip into the points to within ⅛ inch of the stitching, and snip into the corners. Turn right side out. Push out the points very carefully with a blunt tool, press (Figures 10, 11, and 12).

3 Place the two pieces right sides together, join the center front seam, and the center back seam. Press open, snip curves. Refold so that seams meet, pin, and stitch the underleg seam (Figure 13). Turn in the waist edge twice to make a casing, stitch, and insert elastic to fit.

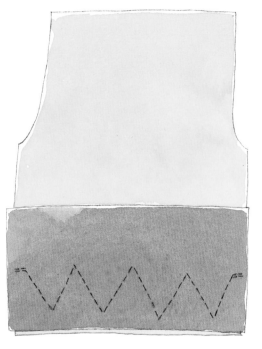

Figure 10

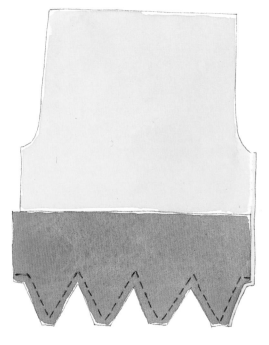

Figure 11

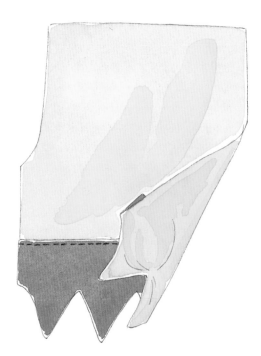

Figure 12

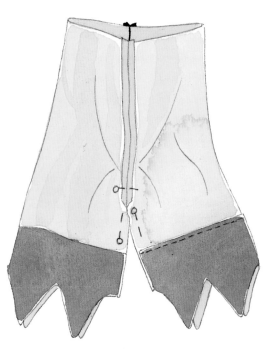

Figure 13

Top

1 Pin the pink and purple rectangles of satin right sides together. Place the template on top and draw around. Stitch around the neck, the two back seams (leaving the openings as shown), and around the points (Figure 14). Trim the fabric, snip into the points, and turn right side out as explained for the pants. Close the openings (Figure 15).

Figure 14

2 Try on the doll, mark where the fastener should go on the back (one at the top is usually sufficient), and where to top stitch a short seam or machine-embroider a flower to join the underarms. Attach the fastener and stitch the seam.

3 To make the cuffs, cut each strip widthwise in half to make two cuffs. Match the two different colors for each cuff, right sides together. Draw around the template, pin, stitch, leaving the straight edge open. Trim, finish the points as before, and turn through. Turn raw edges in, machine stitch (Figure 16). Stitch the cuffs around the wrists, points up, and with a different color showing on each cuff.

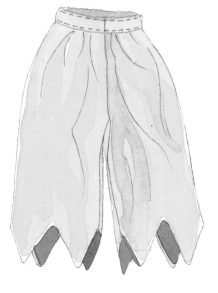

Figure 15

Figure 16

Neck Bow

1 To make the neck bow, fold a piece of blue satin, 8 x 6 inches lengthwise in half right sides together, and stitch along the long edge, leaving an opening in the center. Press the seam open, refold with the seam in the middle, and stitch. Turn right side out, press.

Figure 17

2 Cut a strip of blue satin, 1½ x 3 inches; wrong sides together fold the long edges to the middle and press. Run a gathering stitch down the center of the bow, pull up the gathers, cover with the folded strip, and stitch at the back. Cut a piece of elastic long enough to fit snuggly around the neck, and attach the ends to the back of the bow (Figure 17). Place round the clown's neck.

Shoe Bows

To make the shoe bows, cut two rectangles of pink and purple satin, each 1¼ x 2 inches, using pinking shears. Gather the center of each rectangle to form a bow, and stitch them to the upper part of the feet.

Hat and Bells

1 To make the hat, place the two squares, purple and pink, right sides together, and the hat template on top. Draw around the shape, pin, and stitch around the two long sides, leaving the lower edge open. Cut out, adding ½ inch seam allowance. Turn in the lower edge twice, and stitch a hem; do a second row of stitching (Figure 18). Place on the doll, with one seam to the front, so that the two colors show.

2 To finish the costume, attach the cap bells to the point of the hat, the center of the shoe bows, and to the points of the top.

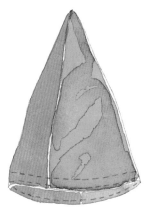

Figure 18

Santa

★ ★ ★

*Santa Claus or Father Christmas is such a popular character
we could not leave him out of our collection of dolls. Here he is, traditionally dressed in a
beautifully soft red velvet suit edged with white fur. He has a long, white beard,
wears jet black boots, and in this case, a pair of gold spectacles.*

You will need
For a doll 21 inches tall

For the body
- ❖ 24 x 24 in unbleached muslin for the body
- ❖ 5 x 10 in white or cream stretch fabric with Lycra™, for the head
- ❖ 9 oz loose polyester stuffing
- ❖ 4 white chenille stems for shaping the fingers
- ❖ Fray stop solution or white glue
- ❖ Strong thin thread (such as hand-quilting thread), and a fine long needle for needle-sculpting the face
- ❖ A brown waterproof pen

- ❖ Acrylic or fabric paints in white, black, brown, red, green, and yellow ocher; and a fine brush for painting the face

For the clothes
- ❖ 30 x 24 in red velvet for the suit
- ❖ 9 in narrow elastic
- ❖ 3 press-studs or Velcro™
- ❖ 6 x 42 in white fake fur
- ❖ 12 x 12 in black felt for the boots
- ❖ 2 small black buttons, ³⁄₈ in diameter
- ❖ 2 oz white fancy, curly wool for the beard
- ❖ All-purpose glue
- ❖ Pair of gold spectacles (optional)

Making the Doll

The patterns and templates for this doll are on pages 173–75.

The Body

1 Fold the muslin in half, position the templates and patterns for two arms, two legs, body back, body front, and body gusset, and draw around.

2 Stitch around the arms and legs, leaving open where indicated. Stitch the center back seam on the body back. Cut out the body back, the body front, the body gusset (on single fabric), and the arms and legs, adding a ¼ inch seam allowance to the stitched seams.

3 Right sides together, match the body front gusset to the two center edges of the body front; pin and stitch. The crotch section of the gusset is longer than the side bodies, and should remain loose for the time being.

4 Right sides together, join the body front to the body back, pin, and stitch around, leaving the neck and the lower edges open (Figure 1). Turn right side out, and stuff the body firmly.

5 Snip the curved seams on the arms and legs. Snip carefully between the fingers. To avoid the seams bursting, apply a very small amount of fray stop solution to the edges. Leave to dry. Turn right side out, being specially careful with the fingers. Stitch along the middle finger separation.

6 Cut the chenille stems into ten 4 inch lengths. Fold over one end of each piece by 1 inch, and catch the merest wisp of stuffing in it (Figure 2). Insert each chenille stem into one finger, folded end toward the point of the finger. Push the other ends toward the center of the palm, and fill the hand with stuffing so that the stems cannot be felt. Stuff the rest of the arm firmly, and close the opening (Figure 3).

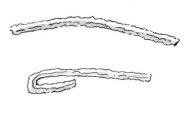

Figure 2

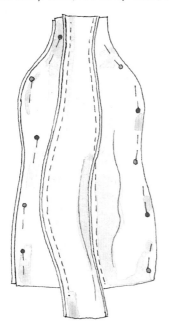

Figure 1

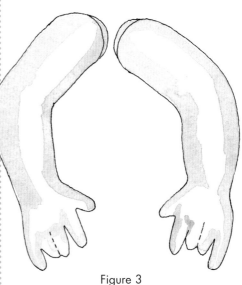

Figure 3

7 Match the foot seams in the center, pin, and stitch across in a rounded shape to form the toes. Trim the corners (Figure 4). Turn the legs right side out, stuff very firmly to the top.

The Head

1 Fold the stretch fabric in half, right sides together, place the template in the center and draw around. Pin and stitch, leaving the back open as indicated. Cut out, adding a ¼ inch seam allowance. Turn right side out and stuff well. Close the opening.

2 To needle-sculpt the face, thread a fine needle with strong thread. Insert it at the back, and bring it out at the nose point just above the nostril. Stitch the nose, nostrils, and mouth (Figures 5, 6, 7, 8, and 9) and as shown on page 26.

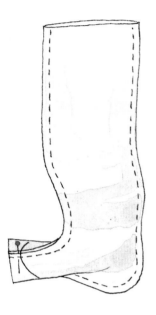

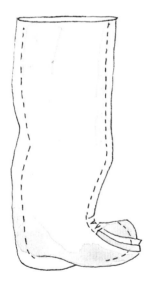

Figure 4

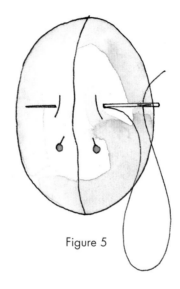

Figure 5

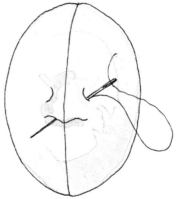

Figure 6

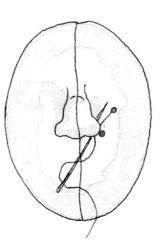

Figure 7

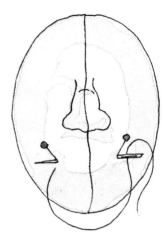

Figure 8

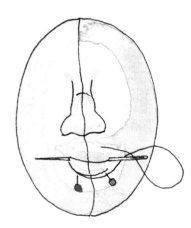

Figure 9

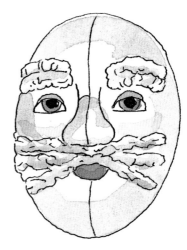

Figure 11

middle by wrapping yarn around, and glue in place above the mouth (Figure 11).

3 For the beard, wind the wool around card 12 x 6 inches. Remove the wool, stitch across the center, fold along the stitched line, and pin to the face. Backstitch in place, see page 27.

4 For the hair, wind the wool around card 8 x 6 inches. As before, remove and stitch along the center, fold along the stitched line, and pin around the middle part of the head (the top of Santa's head is bald). Backstitch in place (Figure 12). Trim the hair and beard to a pleasing shape.

The Face

1 Draw the eyes and mouth with pencil first and then with brown waterproof pen. Paint the eyes green, the eyelids yellow ocher, and the mouth pinkish peach. Add the black pupils and the white highlights. The eyebrows are made later from white wool.

2 Finish the needle-sculpting by taking a stitch from the corner of the mouth to the inner corner of the eye, and then from the mouth to the outer corner of the eye; repeat for the other side. Pull slightly to form cheeks. Paint the cheeks and nose a reddish pink with a very dry brush (blot it on paper first) or make-up blusher (Figure 10).

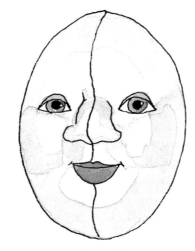

Figure 10

The Hair and Beard

1 For the eyebrows, cut two lengths of white wool 1½ inches long for each eyebrow, and glue in place.

2 For the moustache, cut three pieces of wool, 3 inches long. Join them in the

Figure 12

Assembling the Doll

It is recommended that the body is assembled and the clothes made before the head, with its hair and beard, is attached to the body.

1 Our Santa doll is designed to stand up on his two strong legs, so the fully-stuffed legs are inserted into the lower edge of the body (where stuffing should be removed if necessary). The crotch of the gusset is placed between the legs and secured at the back to prevent stuffing coming out. First tack a small hem to the body and gusset edges, then pin the legs in place and hemstitch to body—twice for safety. Remove tacking if visible (Figure 13).

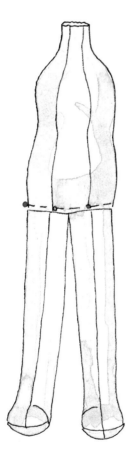

Figure 13

2 Using ladder stitch attach the tops of the arms to the shoulders, stitching around the top, and under the arm, for strength (Figure 14).

3 Make sure the neck is stuffed really firmly, and oversew the raw edges. The head is attached to the body after the clothes have been fitted, otherwise the beard gets in the way.

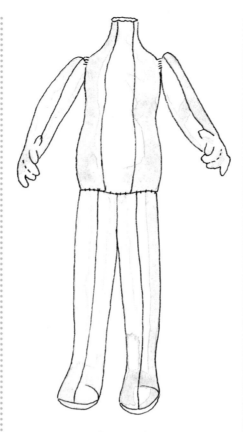

Figure 14

Making the Clothes

Boots

For the boots, fold the black felt in half, pin the boot and sole patterns in place, and cut out. Stitch the front of the boot from points A to B. Insert the soles, right sides together, matching front and back points, pin, and stitch. Turn right side out. Stitch one button to each boot, as indicated on the pattern. Cut a tiny buttonhole on the other side (Figure 15).

Suit

Before cutting out the velvet suit, mark the back of the fabric with several arrows, in pencil, to indicate the direction of the nap. This should fall in the same direction on all pattern pieces.

Pants

1 To make the pants, cut two pieces of velvet big enough to accommodate the pattern. Right sides together, naps matching, pin the pattern in place and cut out.

2 Stitch the center back and front seams, snip into the curves (Figure 16). As velvet frays, all unseamed edges should be neatened first with zig-zag machine stitch. Neaten the two lower legs and the waist edge. Match the underleg seam, pin, and stitch. Make a casing for the waist with a single ½ inch turning. Stitch, leaving an opening. Insert elastic to fit.

Figure 16

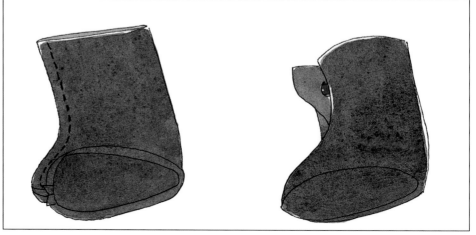

Figure 15

114

Jacket

1 For the jacket, fold the velvet in half, making sure naps match, pin, mark, and cut the back on the fold, and the front. Right sides together, stitch the shoulders. Neaten the cuff, neck, and front edges. Right sides together, match and stitch the underarm seams. Neaten the lower edge (Figure 17).

2 Make fur fabric trim by cutting 1 inch wide strips. The lengths required are as follows (but check your own set of clothes): lower edge of pants, 8½ inches each; sleeve cuffs, 8 inches each; lower jacket edge, 17 inches; overlapped front jacket strip, 5 inches; jacket neck, 9 inches. Cut one 13½ inch strip for the hat.

3 Pin and backstitch the strips to all the required edges. Stitch three fasteners on the jacket front (press studs or Velcro™) (Figure 18).

Hat

For the hat, fold the remaining piece of velvet in half, right sides together. Position the pattern and cut out. Pin and stitch the curved seam and turn right side out. Zig-zag stitch to neaten the lower edge, turn under a ½ inch hem, and attach the fur fabric trim. For the pompom, cut a square of fur fabric, roll it into a tube, right side out. Secure one end with several stitches, slip the hollow end over the point of the hat and stitch around so that it is quite firm (Figure 19).

Finishing

1 Attach the head by placing it in a good position on the neck, pin, and stitch in place—several times around for security (Figure 20).

2 Dress the doll, put on the hat and the gold spectacles to complete Santa.

Figure 20

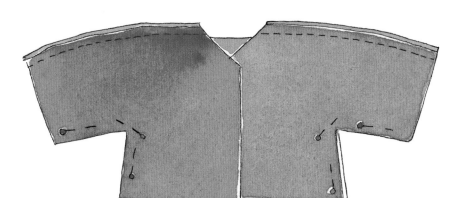

Figure 17

Figure 18

Figure 19

Safety

If this doll is for a young child, it is recommended that the chenille stems are not used for the fingers, and gold spectacles are not added.

Fantasy Flapper
Clarissa Bow

★ ★ ★ ★

*Inspired by the long-legged chorus girls of the 1920s, the Fantasy Flapper doll,
or boudoir doll as they were called, is a real collector's piece. Her joints are stylishly hinged
and decorated with large covered buttons. With her dreamy eyes, long eyelashes, and sleek, bobbed hair,
she's quite grown up. She wears a flapper's jazzy colored dancing dress trimmed with gold,
and black dancing shoes with heels.*

Materials

You will need
For a doll 26 inches tall

For the body
❖ 12 x 24 in cotton fabric for the body, arms, and head (allow extra if you use an embroidery hoop for the face)
❖ 12 x 15 in cotton fabric for the legs (abstract print or stripes)
❖ 9 x 7 in cotton fabric (plain) for the shoes
❖ 9 x 7 in fusible bonding web for the shoes
❖ 8 oz loose polyester stuffing
❖ ¼ in pompom for nose
❖ 5 in embroidery hoop for the features

❖ Shiny embroidery thread in the following colors: red, dark red, blue, green, black, white (or 2 very small white beads); black stranded embroidery thread
❖ Fabric crayons for make-up and cheeks, dark blue, red
❖ Long needle and strong linen thread for jointing
❖ Four ⅝ in self-cover buttons for elbows, six ¾ in for knees and shoulders, two ⅞ in for hips
❖ Clear fray stop solution
❖ 1 oz chenille yarn for the hair
❖ 6 x 4 in piece of card
❖ Fabric glue

For the clothes
❖ 15 x 45 in cotton fabric (patterned) for the dress
❖ 10 x 45 in cotton fabric (plain) for bow and bands on dress and French knickers
❖ 6½ x 45 in cotton organdie or silk organza for underskirt
❖ 45 x 2½ in wide and 45 x 1 in wide metallic ribbon or silk organza for ruffles and underskirt edge
❖ 24 x 1½ in and 24 x 1 in metallic ribbon for hair and shoe bows
❖ 9 x ⅛ in narrow metallic ribbon for trimming underwear
❖ 18 x ⅛ in elastic for underwear
❖ 18 in x 1 in lace for underwear

Making the Doll

The patterns and templates for this doll are on pages 176–77.

Cutting Out the Body

1 Fold the body fabric in half, pin the paper patterns in place and cut out the body, upper arms, lower arms, and arm hinge as many times as instructed. Save the fabric scraps.

2 Fold the leg fabric in half, pin the paper patterns in place, and cut out the upper legs, lower legs, and leg hinge making sure the front of the lower leg is on the straight grain of the fabric. Save the fabric scraps.

The Face

1 On a piece of remaining fabric (large enough to fit the hoop) trace the head pattern in the center by placing the trace pattern underneath and taping the two fabrics to a window. Trace the features using a fine fade-away marking pen or a hard pencil on the right side.

2 Embroider the mouth in red using satin stitch then outline the lips with the darker red using backstitch (Figure 1).

3 (Refer to picture on page 118, for subsequent steps for the face). Embroider

the irises using two strands of thread (one of each eye color) in buttonhole stitch.

4 Work the pupils in black satin stitch.

5 Test your fabric crayon or eyeshadow on a scrap of fabric. If it smudges badly when ironed then leave this step until after the eyelashes. Outline the eyes softly in dark blue fabric crayon or eyeshadow, stopping in the center underneath the eye.

6 Outline the nose in backstitch using dark red thread.

7 Embroider the eyelashes using Turkey stitch (loop stitch) using two strands of black thread. Gently press the loops upward using your iron. Trim the eyelashes graduating them from around ⅛ inch at the inside eye to ¼ inch at the outside. Don't leave the eyelashes too long or the doll will appear startled.

8 Embroider a white French knot or sew a small white bead to the iris at the ten after two position on each eye.

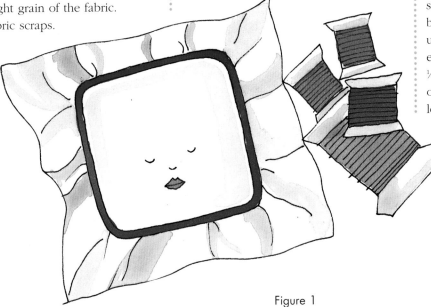

Figure 1

5 If you require fingers, press the hands, mark three lines, and stitch down each line (Figure 2). Apply fray stop solution to the stitching lines and when dry, cut the ends of the threads.

Figure 2

Stitching the Head and Body

1 For the head back, pin the face (embroidery side down) to the remaining fabric and cut out on the marked line. Right sides together, stitch ¼ inch from the edge leaving the top open as indicated. Repeat for the body.

2 Run fray stop solution around the seam lines and leave to dry.

3 Snip curves and turn right side out.

Stitching the Arms

1 Fold the arm hinges along the dotted line, making sure the wrong sides are together, and press to mark the center. Open the hinge out flat.

2 Right sides together, pin the hand. Pin one side of the hinge to the top of the lower arm (right sides together) and stitch around from one side of the fold to the other. Pin the opposite side of the hinge to the other arm piece and stitch as before.

3 Pin around the rest of the arm from one side of the hinge to the other and stitch ¼ inch from the edge remembering to leave an opening at the back. Repeat for the other arm. Turn right side out.

4 Pin the upper arms and stitch ¼ inch from the edge, leaving an opening where marked. Apply fray stop solution, snip curves, and turn right side out. Press the arm hinges.

Stitching the Legs

1 Iron the fusible bonding web to the back of the shoe fabric. Using the template given, draw around the shoes (1 pair in reverse) and cut out on the marked line.

2 Iron the shoes onto the feet. If the shoe fabric frays then run fray stop solution around the strap and the top of the shoe.

3 Stitch the lower legs in the same way as the lower arms, inserting the leg hinge, but leave the foot open at the toe. Press the foot seams open with your fingers and apply fray stop solution. Match the top and bottom foot seams together and stitch across the toe. Apply fray stop solution, snip curves, and turn right side out. Press the leg hinges.

4 Stitch the upper legs as the upper arms and turn right side out.

Stuffing and Jointing

1 Stuff the head, body, upper arms, and upper legs very firmly. Push the polyester pompom between the head fabric and the stuffing to accentuate the nose. Close the openings with invisible ladder stitch. Stuff the lower legs and lower arms as far as the opening. Do not close at this stage.

2 Cover four ⅝ inch buttons and two ¾ inch buttons using scraps of the body fabric. Cover four ¾ inch buttons and two ⅞ inch buttons using scraps of the leg fabric.

3 Apply fray stop solution to the centers of the arm and leg hinges where marked. When dry make small holes with your scissors. Push the shanks of the self-cover buttons through the holes from the outside: ⅝ inch buttons for the elbows and ¾ inch buttons for the knees (Figure 3).

5 Following the procedure for button jointing, see page 21, join the arms at the shoulders using the remaining ¾ inch buttons and ⅞ inch buttons on the legs at the hips.

The Hair

1 Wind the chenille yarn on the 6 inch side of the card to a width of 3½ inches (Figure 5). Slide the yarn off the card and opening up the hank, machine stitch across the yarn (Figure 6). Cut the hank through at the opposite end from the stitching (Figure 7). Apply fabric glue to the back and sides of the doll's head from ear level down to the neck. Fold the hank of yarn along the stitching line (Figure 8) and glue it to the back and sides of the head.

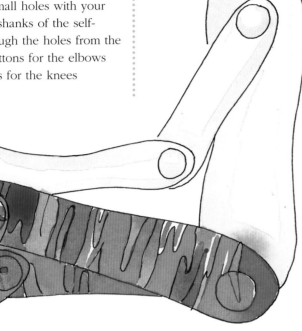

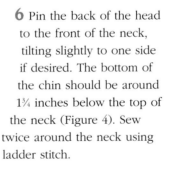

Figure 3

4 Using linen thread and a long needle, thread through one ⅝ inch button leaving a long end, sew through the upper arm, thread through the opposite button, back through the arm, and tie off very tightly under the button (squeeze the upper arm as you tie). Repeat for the other arm and legs. Finish stuffing the lower arms and legs and ladder stitch closed.

6 Pin the back of the head to the front of the neck, tilting slightly to one side if desired. The bottom of the chin should be around 1¾ inches below the top of the neck (Figure 4). Sew twice around the neck using ladder stitch.

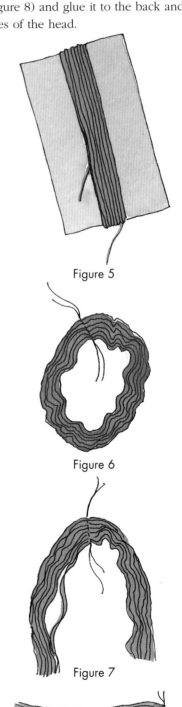

Figure 5

Figure 6

Figure 7

Figure 8

Figure 4

2 Wind more yarn, this time to a width of 2 inches around the 4 inch end of the card. Open up the hank and stitch as before but cut the hank about 2 inches from the stitching (Figure 9). Apply glue to the face from ¼ inch below the head seam and to the bare back of the head. Apply the hair so that the stitching line falls along the seam line at the top of the head and the bangs reach the bottom of the eyes.

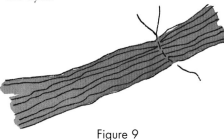

Figure 9

3 Wind a third set of yarn around the 6 inch length of the card to a width of 2 inches. Stitch as before and cut at the opposite end from the stitching. Apply glue to the existing hair at the center top of the head from ¼ inch below the head seam to the top of the first hair applied. Open up the hank of hair and stick along the stitching line. Once dry, trim the hair to chin level and the bangs to just above the eyes.

Making the Clothes

The Dress

1 From the dress fabric, cut a rectangle 6 x 45 inches for the skirt. For the bodice, cut another rectangle 24 x 9 inches. From the plain cotton, cut the skirt hem band 2½ x 45 inches, and the bodice band 1½ x 24 inches.

2 The dress bodice is self-lined and has an integral band to reduce bulk. Right sides together, pin the bodice band to the bottom of the main bodice fabric (Figure 10). Stitch ¼ inch from the edge. Press the seam open. Aligning the bottom of the pattern pieces along the bottom of the bodice band (Figure 11), cut out two bodice fronts. Fold the remaining fabric wrong sides together placing each end in the middle, and cut out two bodice backs on the folds, again aligning the bottom of the bodice pattern with the bottom of the band.

Figure 10

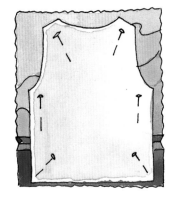

Figure 11

3 Open out the bodice backs. Mark with a pin each back section, making sure you have a right and left half—the other halves of each section form the lining. Pin the bodice front to the bodice back at the shoulders and the bodice front lining to the bodice back lining. If you spread out the bodice it should look like a cross (Figure 12). Stitch the seams and press open.

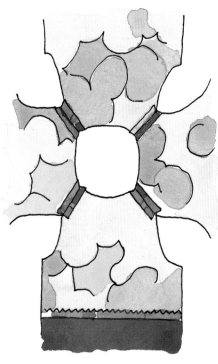

Figure 12

4 Now fold the bodice backs right sides together at the fold lines. Pin the bodice to the bodice lining around the neck and armholes, matching the shoulder seams (Figure 13). Stitch ¼ inch from the edge. Trim, clip, turn, and press. You should now have a bodice neatly finished around the neck and armholes but open at the sides (Figure 14).

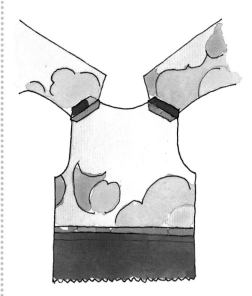

Figure 13

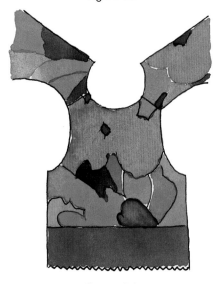

Figure 14

5 For the neck ruffle, cut a 24 inch length of 2½ inch wide ribbon. Remove the wire from one edge of the ribbon if necessary. Apply fray stop solution to each end of the ribbon.

6 Sew two rows of gathering thread along the unwired edge and pull up to fit the neckline. Pin the ruffle flat to the neckline and stitch using zig-zag stitch between the two rows of gathering. Remove the gathering threads.

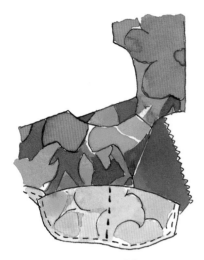

Figure 15

7 Fold the ruffle back onto itself and pin out of the way. Spread open the bodice and lining at the underarms. Pin the bodice front to the bodice back on one side, continue through the underarm seam to pin the linings. Stitch continuously from the bottom of the bodice to the bottom of the lining (Figure 15). Press the seam open, trim, fold the bodice lining down, and press the underarm area (this gives a neat finish to the underarm). Repeat for the other side, to complete the bodice (Figure 16).

Figure 16

8 For the skirt, fold the skirt band in half lengthwise and press. Pin the raw edges to the bottom of the skirt and stitch ¼ inch from the edge. Press the seam upward. Fold ¼ inch to wrong side of each end of skirt and press. Sew two or three lines of gathering at top of skirt. Pull up to fit bodice, pin, and stitch.

9 For the underskirt, attach the 1 inch wide metallic ribbon to the edge of the organdie, as for the skirt band. Gather the underskirt to fit the dress bodice, pin the right side of the underskirt on top of the wrong side of the skirt, stitch, and neaten the edge.

10 Unfold the sides of the skirt and underskirt (which you previously pressed under). Pin the sides of the skirt together and the sides of the underskirt together (separately) and stitch along the creased line from the bottom to 2 inches below the waist seam. The underskirt should show just below the skirt.

11 Put the dress on the doll and hand sew the back seam together.

12 For the dress bow, cut one piece of plain fabric 5½ x 12 inches and another 2½ x 4 inches. Form each piece into a tube lengthwise, stitch, turn, and press. Overlap the short ends of the larger tube in the center and hand-gather through all three layers to pull up the bow. Wrap the smaller tube around the center of the bow, overlap at the back, and stitch. Sew to the back of the dress at the waist.

The French Knickers

1 From plain fabric, cut out the knickers pattern twice on the fold.

2 Right sides together, stitch the lace to the bottom of each leg.

3 Stitch the center front seam and neaten.

4 Press under ½ inch at the waist edge. Zig-zag stitch over the elastic ¼ inch from the fold and pull up to 5½ inches. Pin the elastic at the back seam.

5 Stitch the center back seam, catching the elastic in the seam as you sew. Stitch the crotch.

6 Make two small ribbon bows and sew to the legs just above the lace.

The Wrist Ruffles

1 Cut two 12 inch lengths of 2½ inch wide ribbon. Stitch the short ends together.

2 Run a gathering thread along the middle of the ruffle, place on the doll's wrists, pull up, and tie off.

Finishing Details

1 Make two bows from 1 inch wide metallic ribbon and stitch onto the straps of the shoes. Decide where you want to cut the tails and apply fray stop solution and leave to dry before cutting.

2 Make a big bow from 1½ inch wide ribbon, apply fray stop solution as for the shoe bows. Stitch just below the head seam at the front of the head.

3 Apply blusher or fabric crayon to the doll's face on cheeks, chin, and temples. Touch up eyeshadow if necessary.

Part III

Special Dolls

Realistic, sometimes dramatic looks can be achieved by giving a doll a face with shaped features, through the use of a flexible mask covered with stretch fabric.

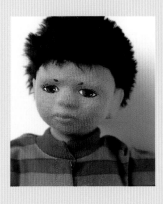

Baby Doll
Kamal

★ ★

*Y*ou can make this cuddly, baby boy doll in as many different flesh tones
as you like—perhaps Asian, Oriental, black, or white. He has a beautifully molded latex head
and face, and you'll find the techniques for making them on page 36. His neck is jointed,
so his head can be moved in all directions, and his short cropped hair is made from fur fabric.
He wears a one-piece playsuit, just like a real baby, and children adore him.

Materials

You will need
For a doll 15 inches tall

For the body
- A plaster head mold, with a head length of about 3 in
- 1 pint liquid latex
- 12 x 20 in flesh-colored cotton stockinette or stretch fabric for the body and head (if the right color is difficult to find, use a white T-shirt dyed with tea, see page 58, or fabric dye)
- Iron on non-woven interfacing (optional—depending on the stretch of the fabric)—same amount as for stockinette

- 5 oz high bulk polyester stuffing
- 10 x 5 in fur fabric for the wig
- Acrylic or fabric paints in white, brown, black, and peach
- Clear acrylic varnish (optional)
- Waterproof craft glue
- 1½ in plastic joint for the neck

For the clothes
- 30 x 20 in stretch fabric or jogging suit material for the playsuit (or cut up an existing sweat shirt)
- 2 x 30 in ribbing for the edges
- 3 press studs or a 4 in long piece of Velcro™

Making the Doll

The patterns and templates for this doll are on page 178.

The Head

1 For making a whole head with latex, follow the instructions on page 36.

2 For this particular doll you will need a plaster mold such as those used for casting a porcelain flange-neck doll head. To establish the head length, which should be 3 inches, open the mold and measure from the top of the head to the chin. This should measure 3 inches.

3 Once you have made the latex head, remove it from the mold when dry, and trim off the neck ½ inch below the chin, with strong, sharp scissors.

4 Using the paper pattern, cut out the head cover from your chosen flesh-colored stockinette and mark the center line top and bottom with chalk, or cut a little notch. Glue the fabric cover to the head as explained on page 36.

5 When the head is covered, the glue dry, and the stitching finished, fit the neck joint. Fit the disc with the central pin into the neck base. Gather the edge of the overhanging fabric with strong thread, and pull it tightly around the disc. Fasten off securely and then cover

liberally with glue, rubbing it into the gathers; leave to dry.

The Face

1 Following the shape of the features, draw the outline on the doll's face with a soft pencil. Using acrylic or fabric paints, paint the whole white of the eyes.

2 While the eyes are drying, you can paint the lips. For a baby or child, mix a peach or brownish pink for the lips (not bright red).

3 When the white is dry, paint a brown iris on each eye, making sure that the circle of the eye is cut off by the upper and lower eyelids, otherwise the doll will have a staring expression.

4 Paint the pupil with black, and using a fine brush, outline the eye and paint short eyebrows.

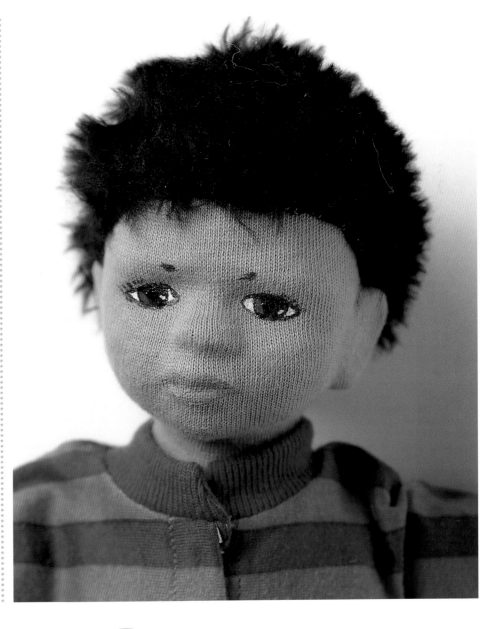

5 Finally paint a little white spot in each eye to the right of the iris; this gives them a life-like sparkle.

6 When all the paint is thoroughly dry, paint a clear acrylic gloss varnish on the eyes to give them extra shine (optional).

Making the Body

1 Fold the stockinette right sides together and pin the pattern pieces for the body, arms, and legs in place, making sure the crosswise arrows align with the maximum stretch of the fabric. If the stockinette is very stretchy, reinforce it by ironing on lightweight non-woven interfacing to the wrong side. Cut out the pieces.

2 On the body front sew the dart as marked. Gather the back slightly along the lower edge.

3 Stitch around the arms and legs, leaving openings as marked on the patterns. Snip into the angles of the seams and turn them right side out.

Assembling, Jointing, and Stuffing

1 Place the seams together at the top of the legs (Figure 1) and stitch across. Pin the legs to the body front as shown (Figure 2) and stitch along the seam line.

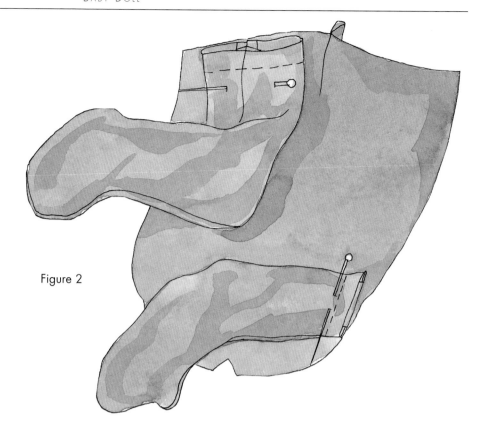

Figure 2

2 Place seam on seam at the top of the arms, make one or two tucks (Figure 3), and stitch across. Lay the arms on the body front with the thumbs pointing toward the top of the body and stitch along the seam line to secure.

Figure 3

3 Lay the body back on top of the body front, sandwiching the legs and arms in the middle, and pin all round taking care not to catch the arms and legs. Stitch across the bottom sandwiching the legs, and continue stitching up the side, across the shoulders and half way down the other side. Stitch the seam once again. Then stitch the lower side leaving a gap at the side, big enough for the neck disc to pass through (Figure 4).

Figure 1

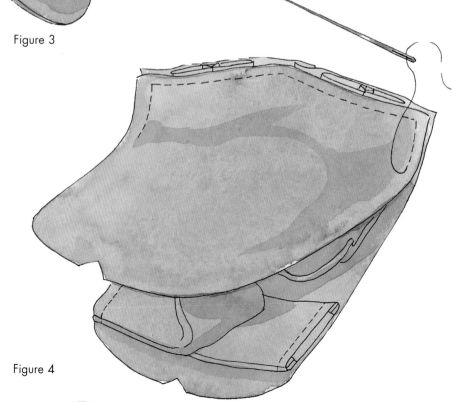

Figure 4

4 Snip the center of the shoulder seam, and rub glue around the cut to prevent the seam from coming undone. Check that the hole is big enough for the pin of the disc to pass through. Turn the body right side out, by pulling the legs and arms through the side opening.

5 Insert the disc pin through the hole in the shoulder seam, and push the other half of the disc over the pin from inside the body; then press on the safety washer. An old-fashioned wooden cotton reel is useful for pushing the washer home as far as it will go.

6 Stuff each part very firmly, starting with the arms and legs, and then the body. It is important to stuff firmly around the neck and shoulders. Close the openings in the legs, arms, and body using ladder stitch.

The Wig

1 Place the paper pattern on the wrong side of the fur fabric and cut out the wig. Pin the center back seam, check that it fits your doll's head, adjust if needed, and stitch (Figure 5).

Figure 5

2 Rub glue around the inside of the wig, and press it onto the head firmly. As an extra precaution, sew the wig to the head around the edges with matching thread (Figure 6).

Figure 6

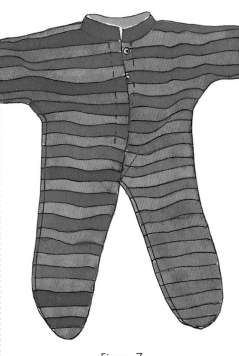

Figure 7

Making the Clothes

One-piece Playsuit

1 This garment can be made from stretch toweling or jogging suit material. If it is not available you could use a sweat shirt, which will provide both the fabric for the body of the suit and the ribbing for the cuffs and neck.

2 Prepare a front and back pattern, each one cut using the correct neckline. Fold the fabric in half, right sides together, position the paper patterns and cut out the back once, and the front section once, including the front facing as marked.

3 Pin and stitch the back seam, and the lower front seam as far as the marked opening. Fold back the front facings, allowing some overlap, and stitch on Velcro™, one half to each side, or 3 press studs.

4 Right sides together, stitch the front to the back at the shoulders.

5 Cut two lengths of ribbing, 2¾ x 1¼ inches for the cuffs, and fold in half lengthwise. Pin and stitch them to the sleeves, with a zig-zag stitch to hold the raw edges, and stretching the ribbing as you sew.

6 For the neck, cut a piece of ribbing 5½ x 1½ inches, fold the ribbing lengthwise in half, and sew across the ends. Turn right side out, pin it to the neck opening, and stitch in place, again using a zig-zag stitch.

7 Right sides together, sew the side seams from one cuff, down the side, around the legs, and back up to the other cuff. Turn right side out—and put it on your baby doll (Figure 7).

Child Dolls
Lara and Her Friends

★ ★ ★

*Lara is a beautiful child doll made with a latex mask face and
dressed in today's casual clothes—dungarees with pockets and a striped T-shirt.
She's jointed at the shoulders and hips so she can sit well. Her wonderful mop of black curly
hair is a wig made from "real hair" which can also be made from wool mohair.
She wears laced-up leather walking shoes and carries a backpack.*

Materials

You will need
For a doll 18 inches tall

For the body
- A latex front face mask about 3½ inches from head to chin
- 12 x 36 in flesh-colored cotton stockinette for the body, plus 8 x 9 in for the face cover
- 12 x 36 in woven cotton lining material: batiste, iron-on cotton, or any other thin cotton fabric, for lining the body fabric if it is too stretchy (optional)
- 8 x 9 in soft open-weave fabric for the first layer of the head cover (optional)
- 4 plastic joints, size 3 in
- 5 x 10 in thick non-woven interfacing or other stiff fabric for the neck support
- 7 oz loose polyester filling
- White craft glue and an old paintbrush
- Acrylic or fabric paints in white, black, red, brown, blue, yellow, for painting the face
- Clear acrylic varnish

- Hair wefts of "real hair" made from man-made fibers, hair unpicked from a full-size wig, or, alternatively, use wool mohair, for making the doll's hair
- 8 x 8 in felt for the wig skull cap, in a color similar to that of the hair weft
- A ball about 3½ in diameter, or a medium size orange covered in plastic wrap, to shape the skull cap

For the clothes
- 10 x 36 in cotton jersey for the T-shirt
- A small piece of Velcro™ or two press studs
- 32 x 20 in thin denim, chambray, or cotton gaberdine, for the dungarees
- 4 Poppa Snaps
- 14 x 6 in soft gloving leather or felt, for the shoes
- Piece of cardboard
- All-purpose glue
- Tool to make small holes in leather
- 30 in thick thread or fine cord for the laces
- For the socks, either buy a pair of doll socks, or cut down a pair of baby's socks or tights

Making the Doll

The patterns and templates for this doll are on pages 179–81.

The Face

1 Make a latex face mask as explained on page 33, using either an existing doll's head or modeling your own. The face should measure approximately 3½ inches from the top of the head to the chin (Figure 1).

2 Cut out the face-cover, once in the open-weave fabric (on the bias grain) and once in stockinette (with the maximum stretch on the width). Glue the open-weave fabric and then the stockinette to the head as explained on page 35. If soft, open-weave fabric is not available, and the stockinette used is thin, glue on two layers of stockinette instead (Figure 2).

3 Leave to dry thoroughly for two or three hours before painting.

Painting the Face

1 Draw the shape of eyes and mouth, and paint the eyes with white paint.

2 Draw the iris, making sure its edges touch the top and bottom of the eye shape. Paint the iris in a solid eye color—choose from brown, blue, gray, or green, and leave to dry.

3 Add a little white to the paint in the mixing dish, to lighten the eye color. Use this to put a lighter stroke in the lower left-hand quarter of the eye.

4 For the pupil, paint a black dot in the center of the iris. The bigger the iris and pupil, the friendlier the doll will look.

5 Paint a brown line on the top edge of the eye, to represent the eyelashes. Paint a second, parallel eyelid line, in a pink brownish color, ¹⁄₁₆ inch above the eye, for the eyelids.

6 Suggest the eyebrows with a suitable brown; if possible, paint small inclined strokes, simulating hairs.

7 Add a white dot for the highlight on the top right hand quarter of each eye.

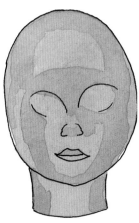

Figure 1

Figure 2

8 Mix a lip color, a fleshy, not red tone. Adding some brown to a mixture of red and white is a good way to get a pleasing color. Carefully paint the lips and leave to dry.

9 Add more brown (in the mixing dish) to half of the lip color, and use it to draw the middle line of the mouth. This should not be straight but should follow the shape of the upper lip.

10 Add white (in the dish) to the other half of the lip color, and lighten the center portion of the bottom lip.

11 If wanted, paint two dots for the nostrils in pink or light brown, or leave unpainted.

12 Paint a tiny pink dot in the inner corner of the eyes (optional).

13 When thoroughly dry, clear acrylic varnish can be painted over the eyes to give them a shine.

The Body

1 Place the stockinette and lining fabric wrong sides together, and hold with pins. The rib lines of the stockinette should be parallel to the short side and the maximum stretch should be on the width. (If using iron-on cotton, iron it now to the back of the stockinette.)

2 Treating the two pieces of fabric as one, fold them in half with the lining on the outside.

3 Position the templates on the folded stockinette remembering to leave sufficient space between them for seam

allowances, and draw around them, making one body front, one body back, two legs, and two arms. Notice that the body front and back templates include an "inner head" which will act as support to the face mask when it is attached to the doll later on (Figure 3).

4 Remove the templates and transfer the markings for the openings, position of joints, and so on. Insert some pins to hold the layers together.

5 Machine stitch around the traced lines on the arms and legs leaving openings where indicated. Stitch the center front and the center back seams of the body, leaving an opening in the back for stuffing and jointing.

6 Cut out the pieces, adding a ¼ inch seam allowance around them. Trim the seam to ⅛ inch around the hands. Tack around the stitching lines of the footsoles before cutting out.

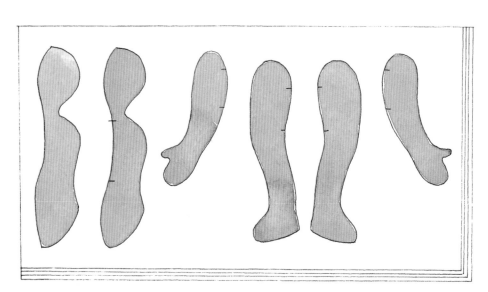

Figure 3

7 Open up the front and back body pieces, and finger press the seams open. Right sides together, pin them and stitch all around the combined head and body. Clip into the curves, especially between the fingers and thumbs and in the neck area of the body.

8 To make the feet, insert the footsoles in place, right sides together, matching toe and heel to front and back seams of the foot. Pin, tack, and stitch by machine or backstitch by hand.

9 Turn all the pieces right side out.

Jointing and Assembling

1 Prepare the neck support by tightly rolling up the piece of thick non-woven interfacing, and securing it with several stitches. Leave aside for the time being.

2 Using an awl or other blunt point, pierce the holes as marked on the inner sides of the arms and legs. Be sure to make one left and one right arm and leg.

3 Place the disc with the pin part of the plastic joint inside each arm and leg, pushing the pin out through the hole, so it sticks out of the limb.

4 Stuff the arms and legs, leaving the hands fairly flat. Close the openings with ladder stitch. Stitch three lines on the hands with small hand or machine stitches to indicate the fingers. Indicate toes with four loop stitches if wanted.

5 Place the body, arms, and legs on the table, arranged so that the limbs are clearly right and left. Pierce four holes in the body where indicated, for the joints, but check that they are evenly positioned, and adjust if necessary (Figure 4).

6 Push the pins from the completed arms and legs through the appropriate holes. Place a disc with a hole inside the body, over the pin, and finally slip the washer over it, pressing firmly to produce a tight joint. Use a wooden cotton reel to help press the joint tightly (see page 22).

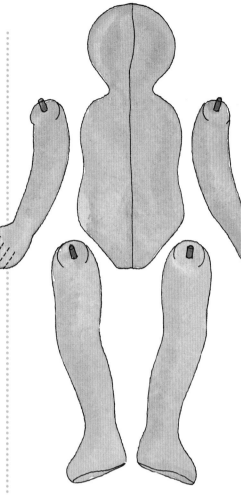

Figure 4

7 Now stuff the body, starting with the head. Place the roll of stiff fabric inside the neck area, and make sure it is firmly secured with stuffing around it, in the head, neck, and shoulder area. This will prevent the doll having a wobbly head (Figure 5).

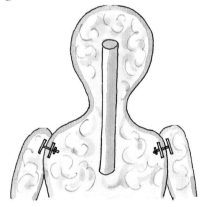

Figure 5

8 To complete the doll's body, finish the back body seam with ladder stitch.

Attaching the Face to the Head

Attach the face mask to the head following the instructions on page 35.

The Hair

1 Make a skull cap using the square of felt, as explained on page 29. When dry, place it on the head, trim to fit the hairline.

2 Following the appropriate instructions on page 29, prepare the wefts of hair, then pin and stitch them to the skull cap (Figure 6).

Figure 6

3 Attach the wig to the head securing it firmly with backstitch.

4 If you prefer to use wool mohair instead, apply it in a simpler way, following the instructions for making a yarn hairstyle (see page 26). Alternatively, stitch lengths of mohair to make them into wefts and stitch them to the skull cap as for "real hair" wefts.

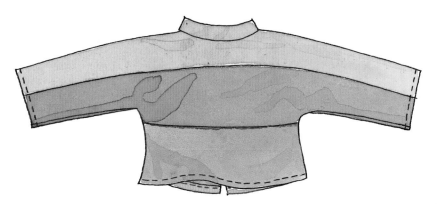

Figure 7

Making the Clothes

The T-shirt

1 Pin the two paper patterns on the jersey fabric and cut out the front and two back sections. Right sides together, stitch the shoulder seams. Turn sleeve edges and make a hem (Figure 7). Right sides together, stitch underarm seams from sleeve edge to lower edge.

2 Hem the bottom edge, and the back opening. Cut a strip of stretch fabric, 7 x 1½ inches, pin to the neck edge, right sides together, and stitch. Turn toward the back, leaving about ½ inch showing above the neck edge. Hand hem behind the neck, and also the ends (Figure 7).

3 Attach small pieces of Velcro™ or two press studs to fasten the T-shirt.

The Dungarees

These dungarees have double top stitching, as real denim clothes do. This may not be mentioned every time, so check the illustration for guidance.

1 Fold the fabric in half, right sides together, pin the patterns in place on the fold where indicated, and cut out.

2 Prepare the front and two back pockets: turn under the top edge, stitch twice along the edge. Fold and press all the other edges, set aside.

3 Right sides together, stitch the center seam of the pants back. Pin the two back pockets, about 1 inch either side of the seam, and about 1½ inches below the waist edge. Stitch around three sides leaving the top edges open.

4 Stitch the center seam of the back lining, press open, and pin to the pants back, right sides together. Stitch all edges, around the waist and straps (Figure 8). Turn out and press. Top stitch along all the edges.

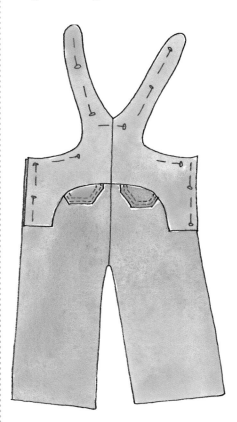

Figure 8

5 Right sides together, stitch center seam of pants front from A to B only. Fold the left extension piece, make a tiny hem on the lower edge, place over the other side, to imitate a fly opening, and stitch down.

6 Take the bib section, pin the front pocket to it centrally and stitch down as for the back pockets. Fold a hem on the lower edge of the bib and place over the front pants waist; stitch down.

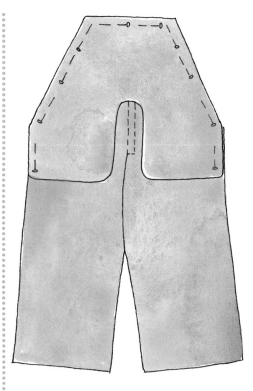

Figure 9

7 Right sides together, pin the front lining to the complete pants front, matching top and angled sides (Figure 9). Stitch around and turn right side out. Press and top stitch along all the edges.

Figure 10

8 Take the four rectangles for the big pocket lining; match them in pairs, and stitch along two sides only. Turn right side out, press, and top stitch on the stitched sides only. Put them behind the pants front, with the top-stitched corner showing behind the slanted edge of the big pockets. Pin in place, and stitch to make the actual pocket: start about 1 inch in from the corner of the pocket, down 2½ inches and rounding back to the side. Stitch again along the waistline to hold the fabric in place at the back (Figure 10).

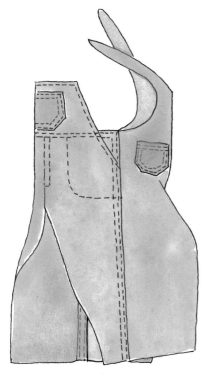

Figure 11

9 Join one side of the pants: place the front over the back, overlapping about ½ inch, and top stitch, starting only at the edge of the slanted pocket, and finishing at the lower pants edge; do not stitch the pocket lining, as Poppas will be fitted there. Do the same for the second side (Figure 11).

10 Hem the lower edges of the pants, and top stitch. Right sides together, join front to back and stitch the underleg seam.

11 Stitch two Poppas on the sides, and two to join the straps to the front (Figure 12).

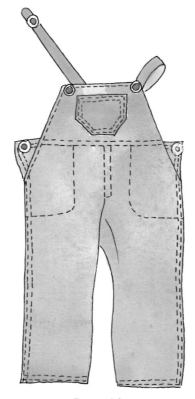

Figure 12

The Shoes

You can make Lara's shoes as detailed below or alternatively purchase a pair of doll shoes.

1 For each shoe, cut one front piece, two side pieces, and one sole from leather or felt, and one sole from card. Make three tiny holes with a leather punch or pointed scissors on the side pieces, as indicated.

2 Place the two sides over the front piece, overlapping as shown on the pattern; machine stitch them in place. Overlap one side over the other at the back, and glue in place. Snip ⅛ inch triangular cuts on the edges of the sole.

3 Cover the doll's feet with plastic wrap to protect them. Slip on a shoe and place a cardboard sole inside it. Apply glue to the snipped edges and fold them over the edges of the cardboard sole. When dry, glue the leather sole on top. Repeat for the other shoe. Leave to dry thoroughly.

4 Remove from doll, remove the plastic wrap, lace up each shoe with thick thread or fine cord (Figure 13), and place on doll on top of the socks.

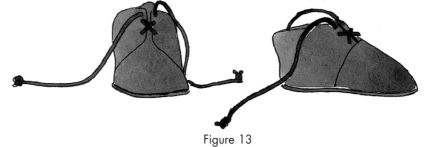

Figure 13

Variations

Lara's friends are made in exactly the same way, using different flesh-color fabrics for their bodies, different hairstyles, and dressed in different contemporary clothes.

African Boy
Chima

★ ★ ★

This is a playful boy doll, with a handsome face made with a latex head. He loves playing ball and will make a great companion for any child. Black fur fabric is used for a close-cropped hairstyle. His shoulders and neck are jointed so he can be moved into many lively poses—and he's easy to dress in a simple, bright colored shirt and knee-length shorts.

Materials

You will need
For a doll 19 inches tall

For the body
❖ A plaster head mold with a head length of about 4 inches
❖ 1 pint liquid latex
❖ 12 x 20 in light brown cotton stockinette or stretch fabric for the body and head
❖ Iron-on non-woven interfacing (optional—depending on the stretch of the fabric)—same amount as for stockinette
❖ 7 oz high bulk polyester stuffing
❖ 9 x 8 in fur fabric for the wig
❖ Acrylic or fabric paints in white, brown, black, and peach for the face

❖ Clear acrylic varnish (optional)
❖ Waterproof craft glue
❖ One 1½ in plastic joint for the neck, and two 1¼ in plastic joints for the arms

For the clothes
❖ 30 x 10 in plain cotton fabric for the pants
❖ 20 x 10 in patterned cotton fabric for the shirt
❖ 8 in narrow elastic
❖ Training or lace-up shoes: training shoes can be purchased from porcelain doll suppliers. Otherwise make a pair of lace-up shoes with the pattern given for Lara (see page 133)

Making the Doll

The patterns and templates for this doll are on pages 182–84.

The Head

1 For making a whole latex head follow the instructions given on page 36. For this particular doll you will need a plaster mold such as those used for casting a porcelain flange-neck doll head. To establish whether the head length is what is needed, about 4 inches, open the mold and measure from the top of the head to the chin, and that measurement should be about 4 inches.

2 When the latex head is thoroughly dry, remove it from the mold and trim off the neck ½ inch below the chin with strong, sharp scissors.

3 Use the paper pattern to cut out the head cover from the brown stockinette and mark the center line, top and bottom, with chalk or cut a little notch. Glue the fabric cover to the head as explained on page 36.

4 When the head is covered, the glue dry, and the stitching finished, fit the neck joint. Insert the disc with the central pin into the neck base. Gather the edge of the overhanging fabric with strong thread, and pull it tightly around the disc. Fasten off securely and then cover liberally with glue, rubbing it into the gathers; leave to dry.

The Face

1 Following the shape of the features, draw the outline on the doll's face with a soft pencil, then using acrylic or fabric paints, paint the whole white of the eyes.

2 While they are drying, you can paint the lips. On a brown-skinned child mix a brownish pink for the lips (not bright red).

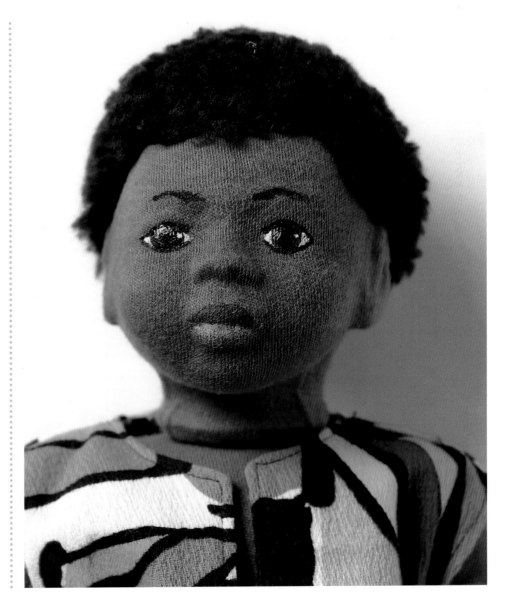

3 When the white is dry, paint a brown iris on each eye, making sure that the circle of the eye is cut off by upper and lower eyelids, otherwise the doll will have a staring expression.

4 Paint the pupil with black, and using a fine brush, outline the eye and paint short eyebrows.

5 Finally paint a little white spot in each eye to the right of the iris; this gives them a sparkle.

6 When all the paint is thoroughly dry, paint a clear acrylic gloss varnish on the eyes to give them extra shine (optional).

The Body

1 Pin the pattern pieces for the body front and body back on the wrong side of a single layer of the stockinette, and cut out. Stitch the dart at the base of the center front, and lightly gather the base of the center back.

2 Fold the remaining stockinette right sides together and place the templates for the arms and legs on it, making sure the crosswise arrows align with the maximum stretch of the fabric. If the stockinette is very stretchy, reinforce it by ironing on lightweight non-woven interfacing to the wrong side. Trace around the templates twice.

3 For the arms, stitch around them, twice, leaving an opening for stuffing. Cut them out and snip the cloth almost to the stitching, as indicated on the pattern, and turn them right side out. Lay the arms side by side, thumbs pointing outward, and place a disc (with

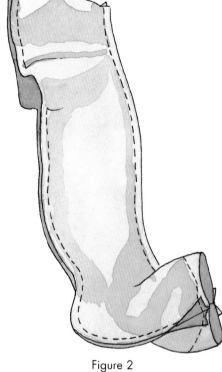

Figure 2

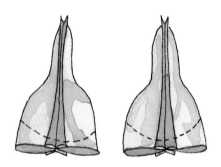

Figure 3

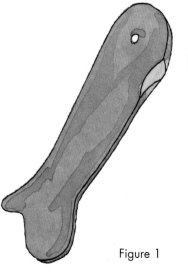

Figure 1

a central hole) at the top of each arm and mark the center. Remove the disc, cut a small hole through one layer of fabric, rub glue around it, and leave to dry (Figure 1).

4 For the legs, stitch the front and back seams leaving openings as indicated on the pattern (Figure 2). Place the front and back seams together at the toe and stitch across in a curve (Figure 3). Trim the seam and turn right side out.

Assembling, Jointing, and Stuffing

1 Place the seams together at the top of the legs, and stitch across. Pin the legs to the front body, and stitch to secure (Figure 4).

2 Place the body back on top of the body front (it will extend beyond the front at the top), sandwiching the legs inside, and stitch twice along the seam line. Now place the back and front top edges together and pin along the shoulder line and down the sides, taking care not to catch any part of the legs that should not be caught. The extra length of the back folds over to form a bottom, so that the doll will sit easily. Stitch along the seam line and curve it in at the bottom (Figure 5), remembering to leave a side opening (as marked on the back pattern) big enough to take the neck disc.

3 Snip the center of the shoulder seam, and rub glue around the cut to prevent the seam from coming undone. Check that the hole is big enough for the pin of the disc to pass through.

4 Turn the body right side out, by pulling the legs through the side opening. Place the

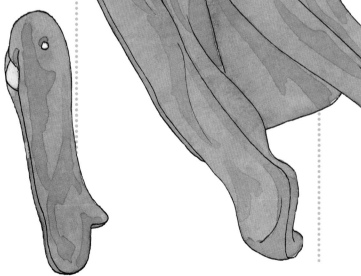

Figure 4

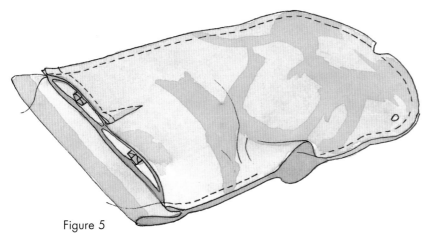

Figure 5

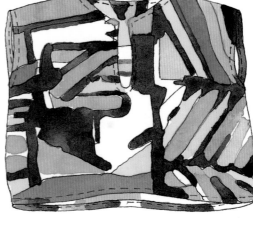

Figure 7

body front pattern on the body and mark the position where the arms will join. Snip a small hole, rub it with glue, and leave to dry.

5 Insert the head disc pin through the hole in the shoulder seam, and push the other half of the disc over the pin from inside the body; then press on the safety washer. You will find that a wooden cotton reel is useful for pushing the washer home as far as it will go.

6 Insert a disc into the top of each arm (make one right and one left arm) with the pin sticking through the hole. Now attach the arms to the body, making sure the thumbs are pointing forward. Push the disc with the hole and the safety washer on from the inside of the body.

7 Stuff each part very firmly, starting with the arms and legs, and then the body. It is important to stuff firmly around the neck and shoulders. Close the openings in the legs, arms, and body using ladder stitch (Figure 6).

8 You may like to define the fingers and toes by hand stitching three lines on the hands, and four loops on the feet.

The Wig

1 Pin the paper pattern on the wrong side of the fur fabric and cut out the wig. Pin the side and center back seams, check that it fits your doll's head, adjust if necessary, and stitch.

2 Rub glue around the inside of the wig, and press it onto the head firmly. As an extra precaution, sew the wig to the head around the edges with matching thread.

Making the Clothes

Shirt

1 Right sides together, fold the patterned cotton fabric in half, pin the paper patterns in place, and cut out as instructed.

2 Right sides together, pin and stitch the shirt front and back at the shoulder seams only, and then the shirt front and back facings in the same way. Lay the facing on the shirt, right sides together, and stitch around the neck and the front opening. Cut between the lines of stitching for the front opening as far as the notch. Snip into the corners, and

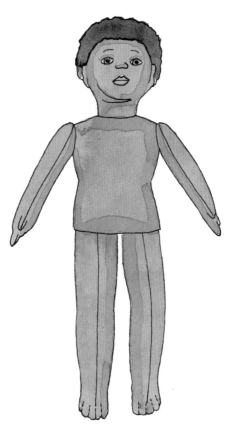

Figure 6

turn the facing to the inside. Top stitch the neck and front opening (Figure 7).

3 Fold the shirt at the shoulders, right sides together, and join the side seams. Turn up and stitch a narrow hem around the bottom of the shirt, and on the armhole edges.

Figure 8

Pants

1 Fold the fabric in half, pin the pants and pocket patterns in place, and cut out. On each pocket, make a hem at the top, fold in the other three sides, and pin in place to the pants back. Stitch around three sides.

2 Right sides together, sew the center back and the center front seams of the pants. Open up, refold, and stitch the underleg seam.

3 Fold over the top to make a casing (stitching the top and bottom of the hem) and leaving a gap to insert the elastic. Turn up the lower hems and stitch in place (Figure 8).

Pierrot

★ ★ ★

*P*ierrot is a dreamy figure, full of charm and tenderness—
a well-known and much-loved character of the Commedia dell'Arte, *a style of popular theater*
which originated in sixteenth century Italy. Its characters are just as popular today and include
Harlequin, Columbine, and Punchinello (Punch) as well as Pierrot. Pierrot's face is painted,
and decorated with fascinating gold or silver shapes, on stretch fabric over a buckram
mask fitted over the "inner head" of the body.

Materials

You will need
For a doll 20 inches tall

For the body
- ❖ 36 x 22 in white cotton stockinette (not too stretchy) for the body and face mask
- ❖ 36 x 22 in very fine woven cotton for lining (only needed if stockinette is very stretchy)
- ❖ 5 x 8 in thick, stiff non-woven fabric for neck support
- ❖ ⅓ lb high bulk polyester stuffing
- ❖ A buckram or papier-mâché mask for the face, 3½ in from top of forehead to chin. For how to make masks, see page 33
- ❖ White craft glue and a brush to apply it
- ❖ Acrylic fabric paints in red, white, black, brown, and an eye color such as blue, green, or violet, for painting the face

- ❖ Metallic fabric paints in gold or silver, and glitter paint, for decorating the face

For the clothes
- ❖ 36 x 20 in white satin or the color of your choice, for the tunic and pants
- ❖ 16 x 28 in netting for the ruffle in matching color
- ❖ 39 in narrow ribbon (⅛ in width), in matching or contrasting color
- ❖ 9 x 9 in black felt for the slipper shoes
- ❖ 9 x 9 in black or gray non-woven interlining
- ❖ Two large buttons or button formers, 1 in diameter
- ❖ 2 x 4 in black satin for buttons
- ❖ 12 x 4 in black stockinette for the skull cap
- ❖ 2 press studs, and a piece of narrow elastic

Making the Doll

The patterns and templates for this doll are on pages 185–87.

The Body

1 This doll is designed to be quite soft and flexible, so it is best to use a stockinette which is not too stretchy. If necessary, line the stockinette with the fine woven cotton fabric, and treat the two layers of fabric as one.

2 From the white stockinette cut a square 12 x 12 inches for the face mask, with the maximum stretch widthwise, and put to one side. For the body cut a rectangle 36 inches wide by 12 inches long and fold it in half so it becomes 18 inches wide.

3 Position the body, two arm, and two leg templates on the double fabric leaving enough space between for the addition of seam allowances afterward, and draw around. Do not cut out.

4 Machine stitch on the traced lines, leaving openings as indicated. Cut out, adding ¼ inch seam allowances all around. Trim the seams to ⅛ inch around the hands.

5 Open up the toe area, match seams in the center, and stitch across in a gentle curve to form the toes (Figure 1). Turn all the pieces right side out.

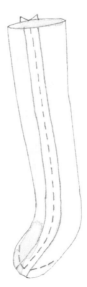

Figure 1

6 Stuff the arms and legs only as far as the elbow and knee joints shown on the templates. Run a gathering stitch with double thread along each arm and leg joint, to make flexible knees and elbows. Pull up and close (Figures 2a and 2b). Stuff the rest of the arms and legs up to 1 inch below the top edges.

Figure 2a

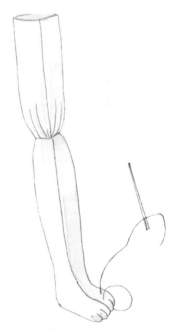

Figure 2b

7 At the top of the legs, bring the two seams together, matching at the center, so that the toes point forward; turn each top edge in, and close with ladder stitch. Do the same at the top of the arms, but keep the seams at the sides.

8 Stitch the fingers, by hand or machine. Make toes by stitching with "loop" stitches, and pull to indent (Figure 2b).

9 Prepare a neck support by making a tight roll with the thick non-woven fabric, and overstitch to secure.

10 Stuff the body to halfway up the chest, then fill the shoulders well, leaving space at the center top of the chest area, to position the neck support. This should extend through the neck to halfway into the head area. Stuff firmly around it to give the doll a firm neck and head. Close the opening at the top.

11 With the toes pointing forward, ladder-stitch the legs to the front body along a line ½ inch above the lower seam around the front and back of the top leg seams. This allows the doll to sit nicely. With the thumbs pointing forward, stitch the arms to the shoulders in the same way (Figure 3).

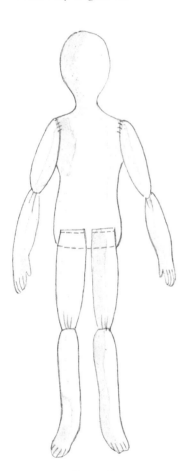

Figure 3

Making the Face

1 Make a mask face, 3½ inches long from top of forehead to chin, using the buckram or papier-mâché method explained on page 33. If possible, include ears on the sides of the face, as this gives a better shape to the head.

2 Place the paper pattern on the stockinette put aside earlier and cut out the face-cover. Using white craft glue, stick the fabric to the mask head as explained on page 35.

Painting the Face

1 Lightly mark the outlines of the eyes and mouth with a pencil.

2 Paint the whole eye shape white. When dry, mark the iris and paint it blue or any other eye color. Paint a lighter eye color on the lower left-hand corner of the iris.

3 Paint medium large black dots for the pupils in the center of the iris, and tiny white dots for highlights at the top right-hand edge of the pupils.

4 Paint the mouth red or pink, making the lower lip lighter than the top lip. Draw a fine brown line in the middle, following the curve of the upper lip. Draw further lip outlines if wanted.

5 Paint black lines around the eyes to emphasize them. Paint the eyebrows in

fancy, decorative shapes. Then, using metallic silver or gold fabric paints, proceed to paint shapes on the face to your own design, including eyeshadows. Add dots in glitter paint.

Attaching the Head to the Body

1 Turn up the fabric in the neck area of the mask. Place on the body front, neck covering the "inner head", and hold temporarily with a few pins.

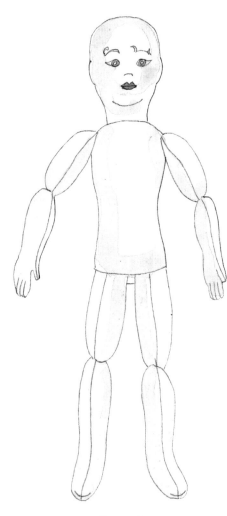

Figure 4

2 Following the instructions on page 35, stitch to close the fabric at the back, add extra stuffing to give the back of the head a good shape, and then close the top (Figure 4).

Making the Clothes

Tunic

1 Note: as satin frays easily it is advisable to cut the fabric with pinking shears if possible. Cut a 20 inch square of satin, fold it in half right sides together, and then fold again into a quarter square. Place the tunic pattern on top, matching the center body to one fold and the center sleeves to the two folds, with the neck on the center point. Pin, trace shape, and cut out (Figure 5).

Figure 5

2 Using the paper pattern, cut out the neck facing from satin. Right sides together, pin it to the tunic neck. Make a 3 inch slash at the center back of the tunic and facing—so the tunic will fit over the doll's head. Stitch ¼ inch from the neck edge, and around the back opening, stitching across the lower point. Carefully snip the seam allowances, turn the facing out, and press against tunic.

3 Hem the sleeves, and decorate near the edge with a row of machine embroidery, preferably using metallic silver or gold thread, or a shiny rayon thread.

4 Right sides together, pin and stitch the undersleeve and side seams, making sure the edges match. Turn right side out, make a hem on the lower edge, and decorate with a row of machine embroidery as for the sleeves.

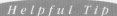

5 Sew the press studs on the back opening. Attach two large buttons at the front, using button formers covered with satin; or black plastic stem buttons (Figure 6), covered by placing inside a circle of satin about 1 inch wider in diameter than the button; gather around the edge, and enclose the button in it.

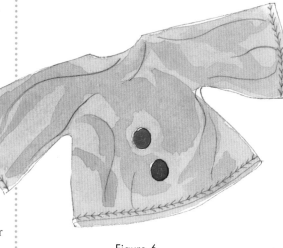

Figure 6

Pants

1 With the remaining fabric, fold the short sides to the center, right sides together, place the leg pattern on the folds to make two pant legs and cut out. Right sides together, stitch the center front and center back seams from waist to crotch.

2 Turn up the bottom hems and decorate with a row of machine embroidery as for the tunic. Right sides together, refold the pants, matching the center, and stitch the inner leg seam from one lower edge to the other.

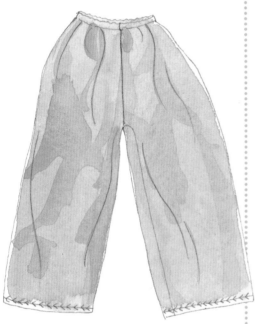

Figure 7

3 Make a casing at the waist by folding the fabric once a ¼ inch and a second time ½ inch, and stitching in place, leaving an opening. Measure the doll's waist and thread elastic through to fit (Figure 7).

Figure 8

Skull Cap

Fold the black stockinette in half, right sides together, place the pattern on the fold, and cut out. Open up, close the darts first, then stitch the center back seam. Hem the edge, and place on the doll's head (Figure 8).

Ruffle

1 Cut a rectangle of net fabric, 16 x 28 inches and fold in half lengthwise. Using a long needle and strong double thread, gather along the center of the two layers (Figure 9).

2 Fold along the gathering line and place the ruffle on the neck. Pull the gathers to fit, knot the ends, and tie securely. Decorate with the fine ribbon, by twice wrapping it round the neck and making a bow at the front.

Slipper Shoes

1 To make the slippers stronger, it is best to fuse fine, non-woven iron-on interlining, in gray or black, to one side of the black felt. Now fold the felt in half, interlining side out and the patterns on top. Cut out.

2 Right sides together, join the back seams of the shoe uppers; then fit and stitch the soles. Turn right side out. The slippers can be decorated with small pompoms of satin made from fabric left-over from the costume. Cut out two circles of satin, gather the outer edge, fill with a small amount of polyester filling, and draw up the thread. Stitch in place (Figure 10).

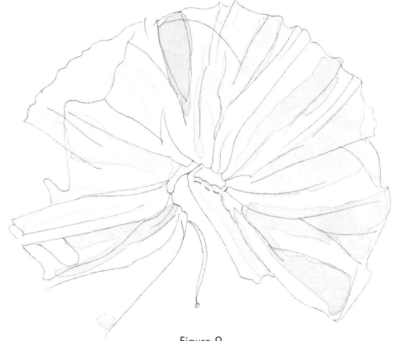

Figure 9

Figure 10

Pirate Princess
Marifran

★ ★ ★ ★

*H*ere is an adult-looking doll who would look good in a range of
interesting, fantasy costumes. Her fabric-covered mask face, with its prominent
cheek-bones, is painted in strong make-up colors. Her black pirate's outfit is enriched with a
princess's silk cape and with shiny mauve and gold trimmings. Her multi-colored hair is topped
with a pirate hat. She is ready to jump onto the deck of her ship and set sail on her
next adventure. In order to make the Pirate Princess, it is assumed that
the reader will have some dollmaking experience.

You will need
For a doll 22 inches tall

For the body
- ❖ 30 x 30 in flesh-colored, minimum stretch fabric, for the body
- ❖ 4 in long from head to chin latex mask with adult-looking features
- ❖ 18 x 12 in soft, open-weave fabric (optional) for the face lining
- ❖ 7 oz loose polyester stuffing
- ❖ Acrylic or fabric paints for the face, blue-green, pinky red, brown, black, white, purple, mauve, gold, and a fine brush
- ❖ Two buttons, strong carpet thread, and a long needle, for jointing the arms
- ❖ 9 x 9 in beige felt
- ❖ 2 oz multi-colored wefted artificial fiber hair (several wefts) or multi-colored yarn

For the clothes
- ❖ 16 x 24 in black satin for the pants
- ❖ 32 x 10 in patterned black viscose for the shirt, and 3 x 12 in shiny red/mauve fabric for the cuffs
- ❖ 3 small pieces of black Velcro™ or other fasteners
- ❖ 14 x 9 in cotton batik or other fancy print fabric for the vest, and the same amount of a plain matching fabric for the lining
- ❖ 24 x 22 in red/mauve silk or other fancy fabric for the cape and 48 in purple narrow ribbon
- ❖ 36 x 5 in deep yellow/gold organza or other transparent fabric for the waistband
- ❖ 10 x 10 in black felt for the hat, and a scrap of fancy fabric for decoration
- ❖ 12 x 8 in fine black gloving leather, or black felt, for the boots

Making the Doll

The patterns and templates for this doll are on pages 188–90.

The Face Mask

1 To make the face mask, see page 33. Cut one face cover from the minimum stretch fabric (stockinette) and one (optional) from soft, open-weave fabric, folded right sides together. Glue the fabric to the latex mask as explained on page 35 (Figures 1 and 2).

2 When the glue is dry, draw the features, see page 24.

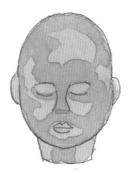

Figure 1

Painting the Face

Begin by painting the whites of the eyes. When they are dry, paint the irises blue-green, then the black pupil and white highlights. Above the eyes, paint purple eye shadow, and then black eyebrows and the line above the eye. Paint her lips a mauve/pink and, if you wish, stripes across her face and a gold star and black outline above her eyes.

The Body

1 Fold the stretch body fabric, right sides together, place the templates on the fabric and trace round them as instructed, remembering to make two arms and two legs.

2 Pin and stitch only the center seams of all the body pieces. Stitch around the arms and legs on the marked lines, leaving openings where indicated.

3 Cut out, adding ¼ inch seam allowances to the stitched center seams, and cutting on the marked line on the outside of the body pieces. Press center seams open.

4 Make the bust by running two short rows of gathering stitch along the lower edge of the upper body front where indicated. Pull up the gathers to fit the lower body edge. Right sides together, pin and stitch to make a complete body front. (For further details and illustrations on shaping this kind of body, see the Mermaid on page 94.)

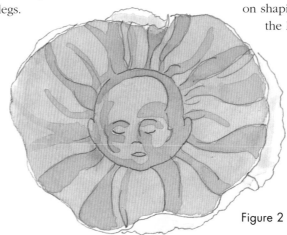
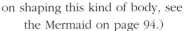

Figure 2

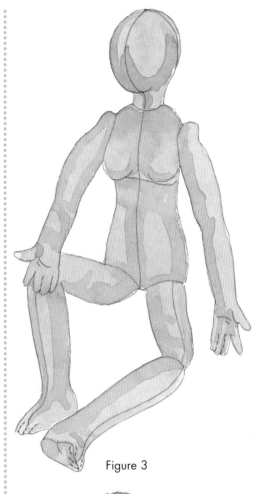

Figure 3

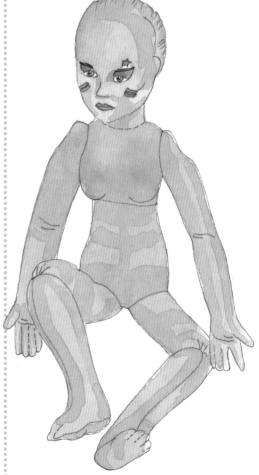

5 Right sides together, pin and stitch around the body front and back with a ¼ inch seam, leaving an opening at the top of the head.

6 Turn right side out, and stuff firmly, especially the neck and shoulders. Shape the bust nicely by molding the stuffing into the stretch fabric, and then fill the neck and head well. Close the opening.

7 For the arms, snip the seam between the fingers, and turn the arms right side out. Carefully, but firmly stuff the fingers and hands, then the rest of the arm, and close the opening. Stitch the remaining fingers.

8 For the legs, place the material right sides together, insert the soles into the feet, pin, and stitch. Turn the legs right side out.

9 Stuff the legs up to the knee only, then gather to form a flexible knee joint, and continue stuffing to just about 1 inch from the top. Turn the top edges in and ladder stitch closed.

10 To soft-sculpt the feet, stitch lines for toes, and then stitch from side to side to indent the heels.

Assembling the Doll

1 Attach the legs to the front body, 1 inch up from the lower seam, and ladder stitch in place along the front and the back of the legs.

2 Joint the arms with buttons (Figure 3), following the instructions on page 21.

3 Attach the face mask to the body and finish at the back (Figure 4) as explained on page 35.

Figure 4

The Hair

Prepare the hair, but attach it to the doll after putting on the clothes.

Make a "skull cap" in beige felt as described on page 29. If you are using wefted artificial hair (Figure 5), attach the wefts to it as on page 29, but if you are using multicolored yarn, make that into wefts and proceed as for artificial hair, see page 26.

Figure 5

Making the Clothes

Pants

1 For the pants, fold the black satin widthwise in half, right sides together, pin the patterns in place, and cut to obtain two backs and two fronts. Right sides together, stitch the front crotch seam and the back crotch seam. Stitch the front and back darts.

2 Place the back and front right sides together, and stitch the side seams, leaving the top 2 inches open. Match, pin, and stitch the underleg seam. Make narrow hems on the lower edges of the legs, on the waist, and along the two open sides. Attach small pieces of black Velcro™ to the waist opening so that the front overlaps the back (Figure 6).

Shirt

1 For the shirt, fold the fabric widthwise in half, right sides together, pin the pattern pieces in place, and cut out the front, backs, and sleeves. Right sides together, join the front to the backs at the shoulders. Gather the top of the sleeves, fit and stitch into the armholes while still flat.

2 To make the cuffs, cut two pieces, each 6 x 3 inches, from the red/mauve shiny fabric. Then gather the lower edge of the sleeves to fit one strip of fabric. Wrong sides together, stitch across. Fold the back over the front of the shirt, pin, and stitch the underarm seams. Fold

Figure 6

each cuff in half, turn up and hem in place on the inside sleeve. Turn the shirt right side out.

3 For the neck band, cut a strip of fabric 7 x 1½ inches and stitch one long side to the neck edge, right sides together. Turn twice toward the inside and hem. Fold in the back opening edges and hem. Attach three fasteners or pieces of Velcro™ to the back of the shirt (Figure 7).

Figure 7

Vest

1 To make the vest, place the fancy fabric and lining, right sides together, and then the complete template on top. Draw around, pin, and stitch on the marked line, leaving an opening in the lower back (Figure 8). Cut out, trim the corners, snip into the curves and turn right side out. Press carefully and close the opening. Overlap shoulders and stitch (Figure 9).

2 Put the shirt and pants on the doll. Wrap the waistband fabric around the waist, tie at the front, toward one side. Put on the vest.

Cape

For the cape, make narrow hems on all four edges of the 24 x 22 inch piece of fabric. Place around the doll's shoulders, and wrap doubled purple ribbon around the neck, leaving a 3 inch collar above the neck. Tie at the back.

part of the boot. Repeat for the other boot. Turn the boots right side out and put on the doll (Figure 10).

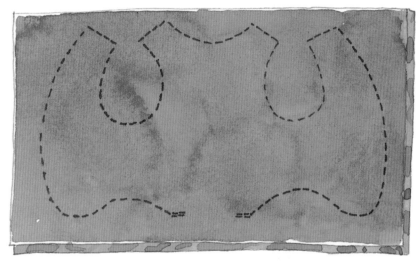

Figure 8

Boots

To make the boots, cut out the boot sides and the soles from the gloving leather or felt, as instructed. Place two matching boot sides, right sides together, and stitch the back seam and the front curved seam. Insert the sole in the lower

Figure 10

Hat

1 For the hat, fold the black felt in half, position the hat template and trace around it. Stitch the long curved side and cut out the hat, adding a ¼ inch seam allowance. Turn right side out, and decorate the front with a gathered circle of gold organza or other fancy fabric (Figure 11).

2 Now attach her hair, stitching the skull cap to the doll as on page 29. Place the hat on top at a jaunty angle to finish.

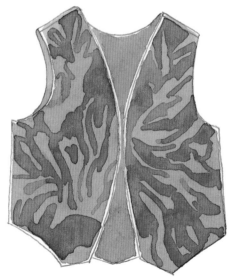

Figure 9

Figure 11

BASIC DOLLS

Scale 70% Note: for all patterns and templates at a scale of 70%, enlarge on a photocopier at 142% to trace at full size

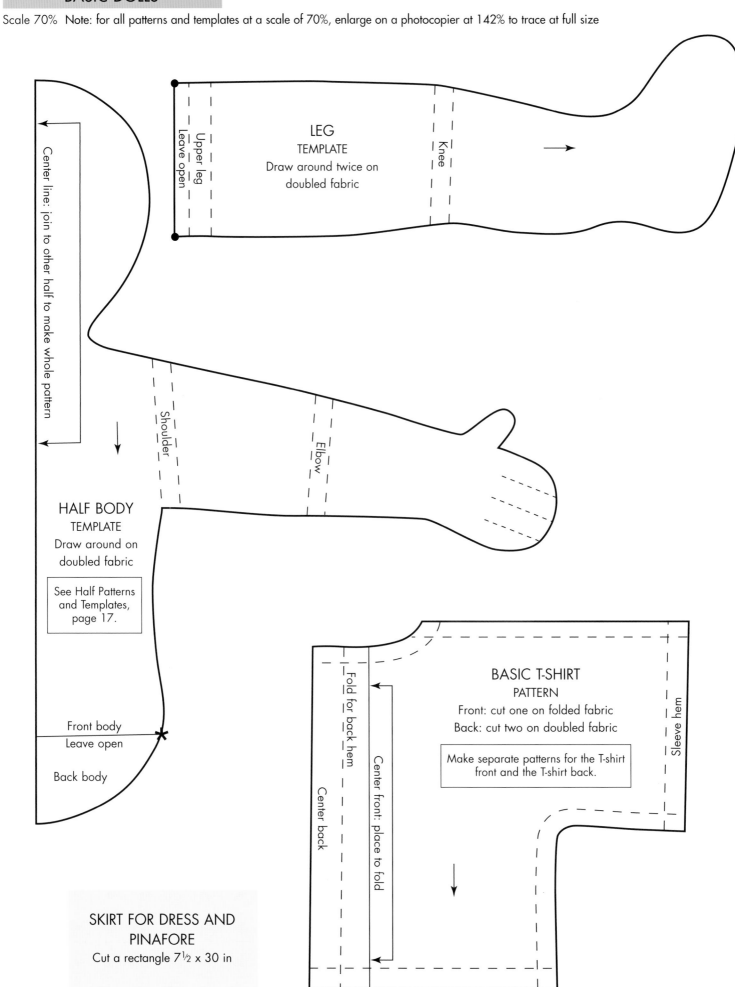

Center line: join to other half to make whole pattern

Upper leg
Leave open

LEG
TEMPLATE
Draw around twice on doubled fabric

Knee

Shoulder

Elbow

HALF BODY
TEMPLATE
Draw around on doubled fabric

See Half Patterns and Templates, page 17.

Front body
Leave open

Back body

Fold for back hem

Center back

Center front: place to fold

BASIC T-SHIRT
PATTERN
Front: cut one on folded fabric
Back: cut two on doubled fabric

Make separate patterns for the T-shirt front and the T-shirt back.

Sleeve hem

SKIRT FOR DRESS AND PINAFORE
Cut a rectangle 7½ x 30 in

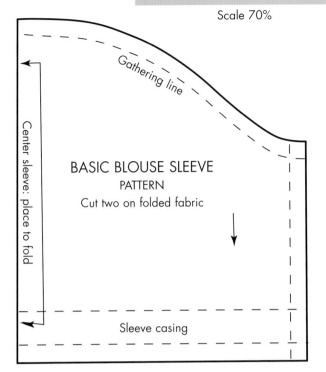

BASIC BLOUSE SLEEVE
PATTERN
Cut two on folded fabric

Gathering line

Center sleeve: place to fold

Sleeve casing

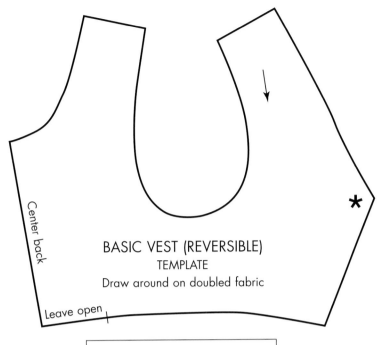

BASIC VEST (REVERSIBLE)
TEMPLATE
Draw around on doubled fabric

Center back

Leave open

BASIC VEST TEMPLATE

Trace the vest template twice, cut out, reverse one on the center line and join together with sticky tape. See Reversing Patterns, page 18.

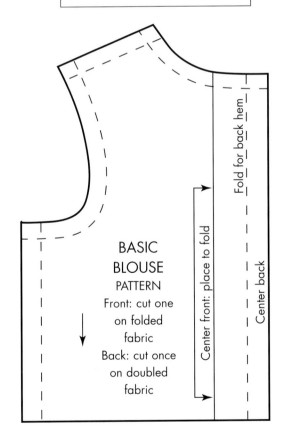

BASIC
BLOUSE
PATTERN
Front: cut one on folded fabric
Back: cut once on doubled fabric

Fold for back hem

Center front: place to fold

Center back

BASIC BLOUSE PATTERN

Make pattern once using the lines for the front and a second time using the lines for the back

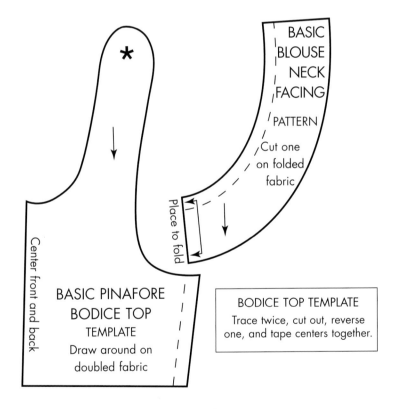

BASIC PINAFORE
BODICE TOP
TEMPLATE
Draw around on doubled fabric

Center front and back

BASIC
BLOUSE
NECK
FACING
PATTERN
Cut one on folded fabric

Place to fold

BODICE TOP TEMPLATE

Trace twice, cut out, reverse one, and tape centers together.

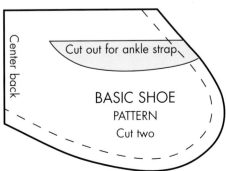

Center back

Cut out for ankle strap

BASIC SHOE
PATTERN
Cut two

BASIC SHOE PATTERN

Trace the shoe pattern twice, cut out, reverse one at the center back and tape together. See Reversing Patterns, page 18.

BASIC DOLLS

Scale 70%

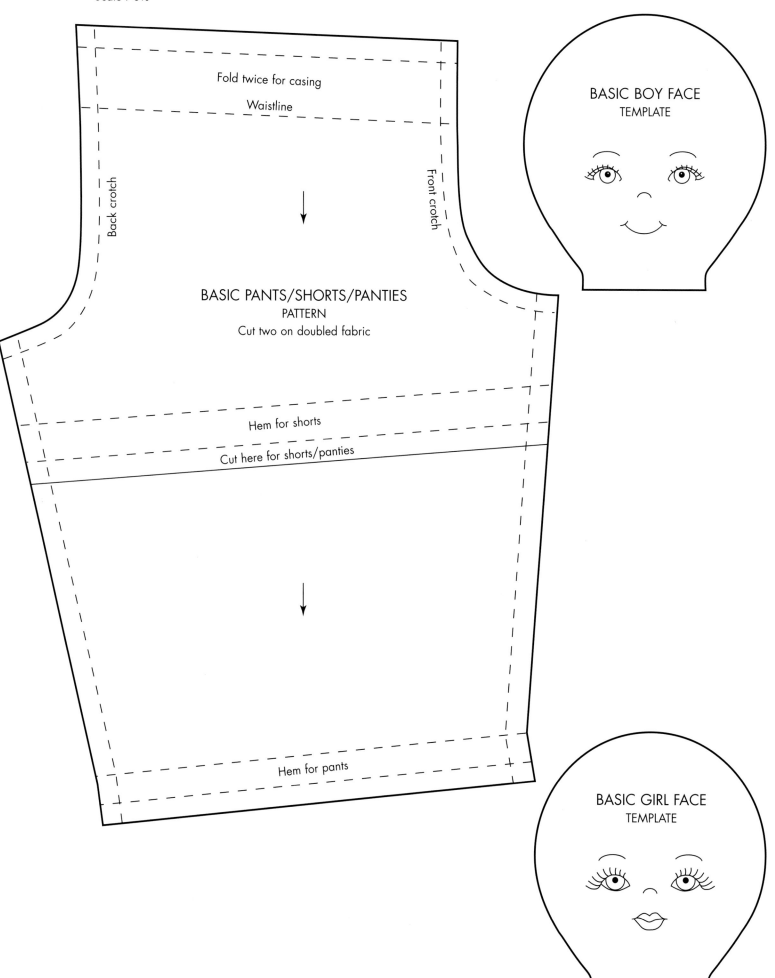

Fold twice for casing

Waistline

Back crotch

Front crotch

BASIC PANTS/SHORTS/PANTIES
PATTERN
Cut two on doubled fabric

Hem for shorts

Cut here for shorts/panties

Hem for pants

BASIC BOY FACE
TEMPLATE

BASIC GIRL FACE
TEMPLATE

FOLK ART DOLL
Scale 100%

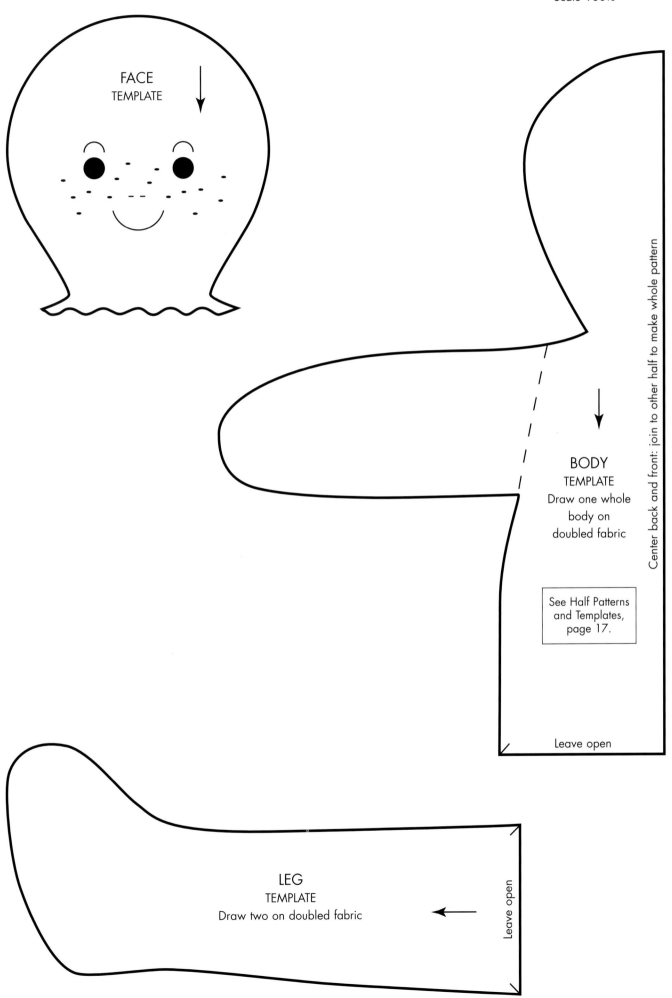

FACE
TEMPLATE

BODY
TEMPLATE
Draw one whole
body on
doubled fabric

See Half Patterns
and Templates,
page 17.

Center back and front: join to other half to make whole pattern

Leave open

LEG
TEMPLATE
Draw two on doubled fabric

Leave open

TRADITIONAL DOLL

Scale 70%

FACE
PATTERN
Cut one in single fabric

Dart

Leave open

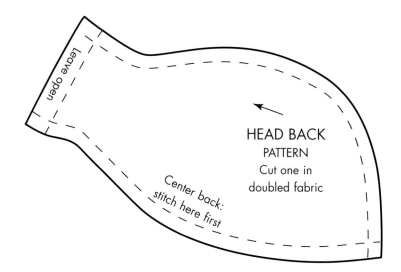

Leave open

HEAD BACK
PATTERN
Cut one in doubled fabric

Center back: stitch here first

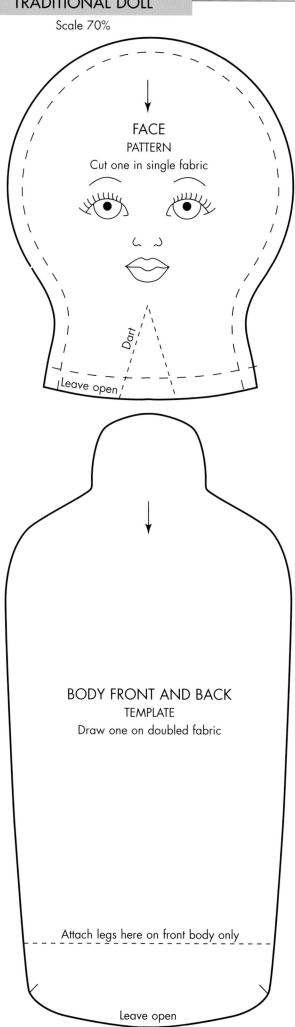

BODY FRONT AND BACK
TEMPLATE
Draw one on doubled fabric

Attach legs here on front body only

Leave open

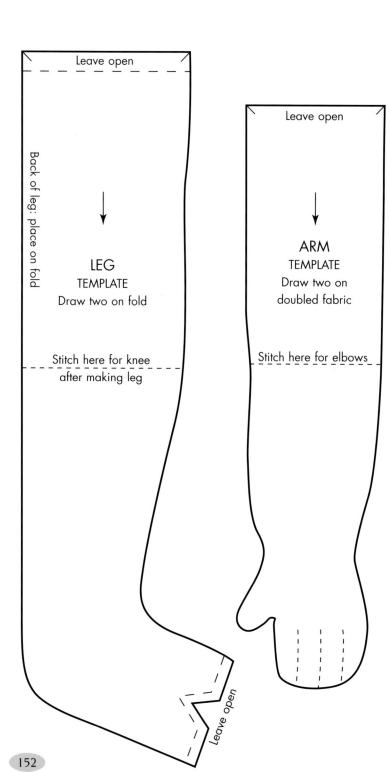

Leave open

Back of leg: place on fold

LEG
TEMPLATE
Draw two on fold

Stitch here for knee
after making leg

Leave open

Leave open

ARM
TEMPLATE
Draw two on doubled fabric

Stitch here for elbows

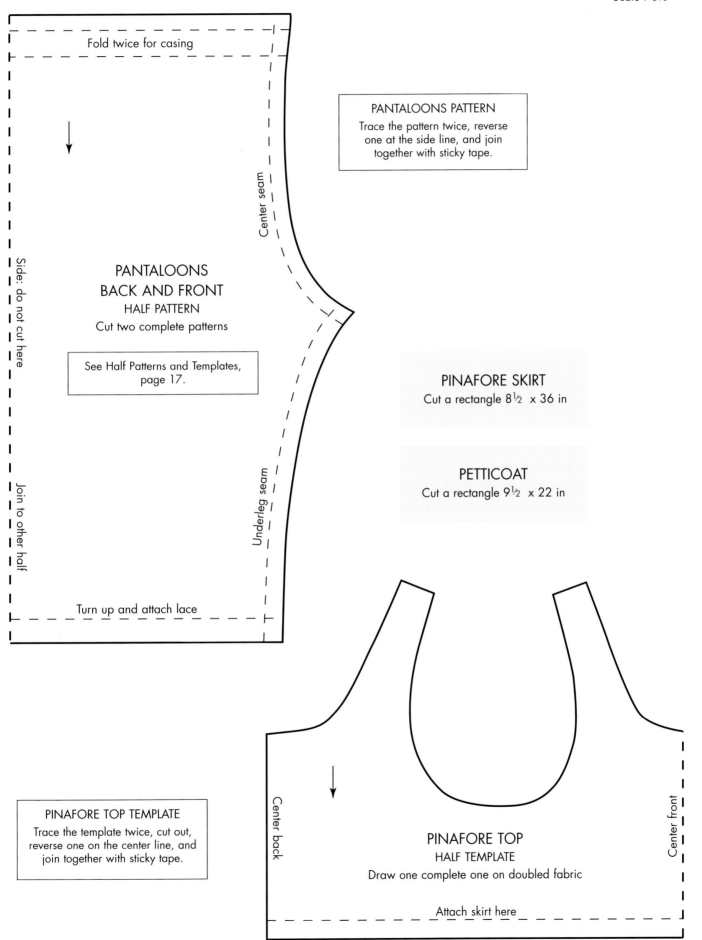

Fold twice for casing

Side: do not cut here

Join to other half

PANTALOONS
BACK AND FRONT
HALF PATTERN
Cut two complete patterns

See Half Patterns and Templates,
page 17.

Center seam

Underleg seam

Turn up and attach lace

PANTALOONS PATTERN
Trace the pattern twice, reverse
one at the side line, and join
together with sticky tape.

PINAFORE SKIRT
Cut a rectangle 8½ x 36 in

PETTICOAT
Cut a rectangle 9½ x 22 in

PINAFORE TOP TEMPLATE
Trace the template twice, cut out,
reverse one on the center line, and
join together with sticky tape.

Center back

Center front

PINAFORE TOP
HALF TEMPLATE
Draw one complete one on doubled fabric

Attach skirt here

TRADITIONAL DOLL
Scale 70%

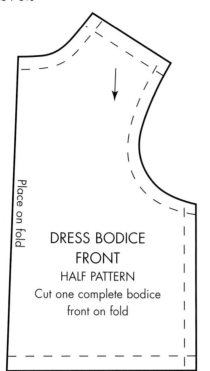

DRESS BODICE FRONT
HALF PATTERN
Cut one complete bodice front on fold

Place on fold

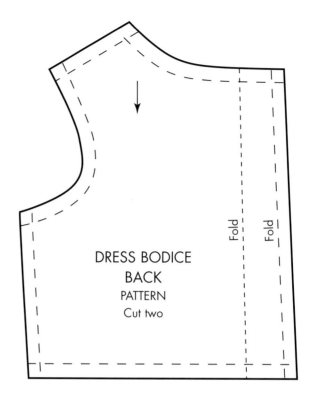

DRESS BODICE BACK
PATTERN
Cut two

Fold

Fold

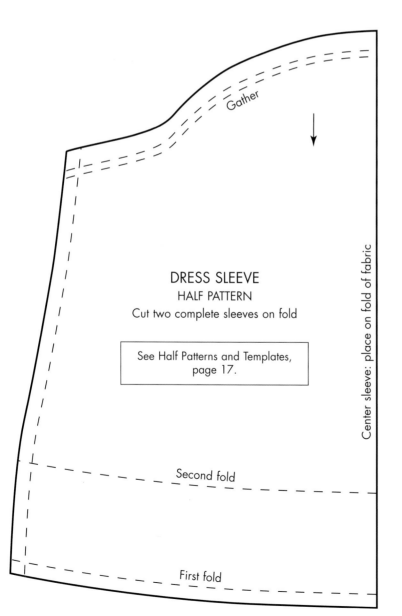

Gather

DRESS SLEEVE
HALF PATTERN
Cut two complete sleeves on fold

See Half Patterns and Templates, page 17.

Center sleeve: place on fold of fabric

Second fold

First fold

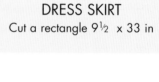

DRESS SKIRT
Cut a rectangle 9½ x 33 in

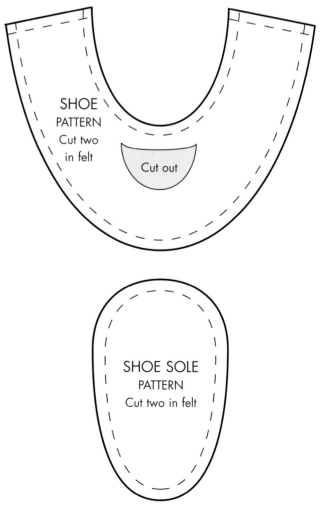

SHOE PATTERN
Cut two in felt

Cut out

SHOE SOLE PATTERN
Cut two in felt

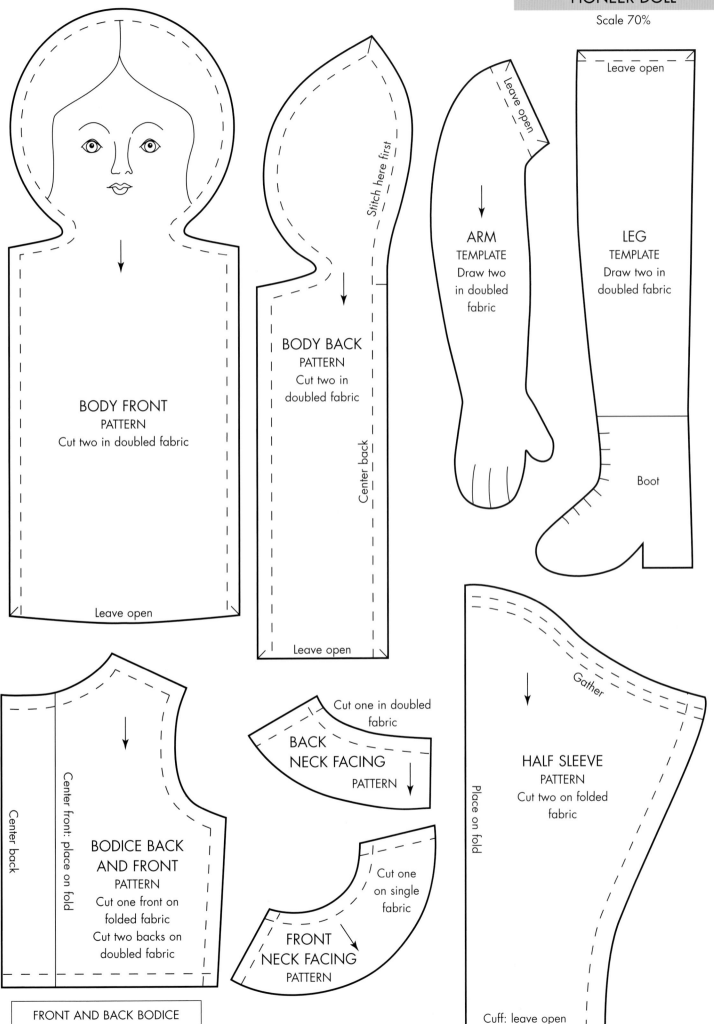

PIONEER DOLL

Scale 70%

BODY FRONT
PATTERN
Cut two in doubled fabric

Leave open

BODY BACK
PATTERN
Cut two in
doubled fabric

Stitch here first

Center back

Leave open

ARM
TEMPLATE
Draw two
in doubled
fabric

Leave open

LEG
TEMPLATE
Draw two in
doubled fabric

Leave open

Boot

BODICE BACK
AND FRONT
PATTERN
Cut one front on
folded fabric
Cut two backs on
doubled fabric

Center back

Center front: place on fold

Cut one in doubled
fabric

BACK
NECK FACING
PATTERN

Cut one
on single
fabric

FRONT
NECK FACING
PATTERN

Gather

HALF SLEEVE
PATTERN
Cut two on folded
fabric

Place on fold

Cuff: leave open

FRONT AND BACK BODICE
Make one pattern for the front
bodice and one for the back.

155

SPRING DOLL

Scale 70%

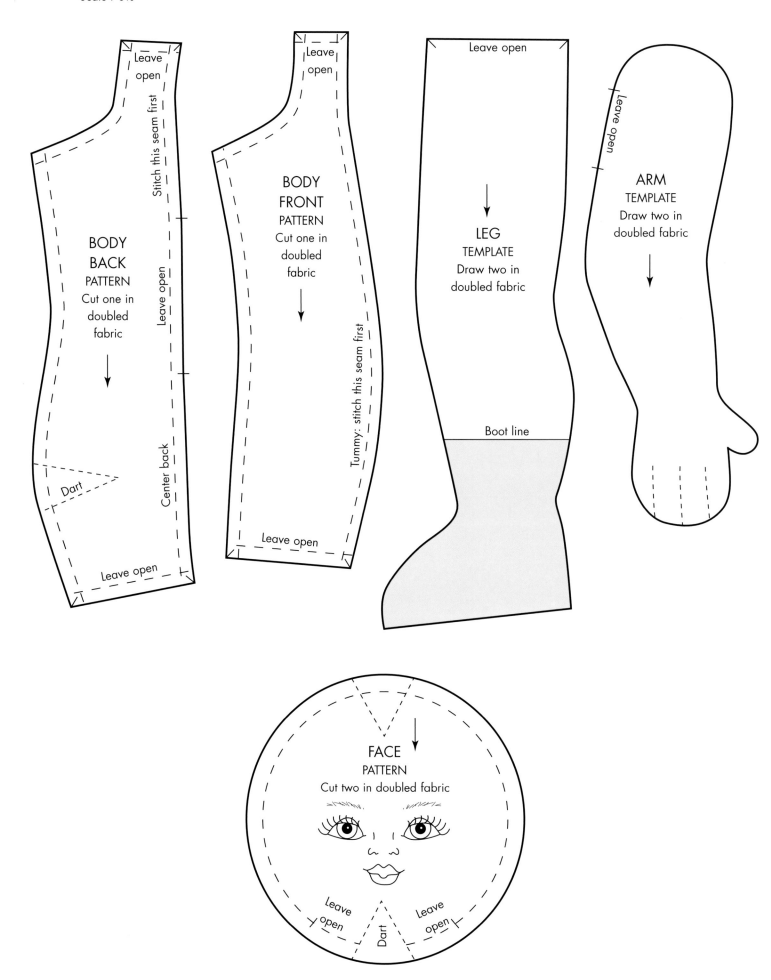

BODY BACK PATTERN
Cut one in doubled fabric

Leave open

Stitch this seam first

Leave open

Center back

Dart

Leave open

BODY FRONT PATTERN
Cut one in doubled fabric

Leave open

Tummy: stitch this seam first

Leave open

LEG TEMPLATE
Draw two in doubled fabric

Leave open

Boot line

ARM TEMPLATE
Draw two in doubled fabric

Leave open

FACE PATTERN
Cut two in doubled fabric

Leave open

Dart

Leave open

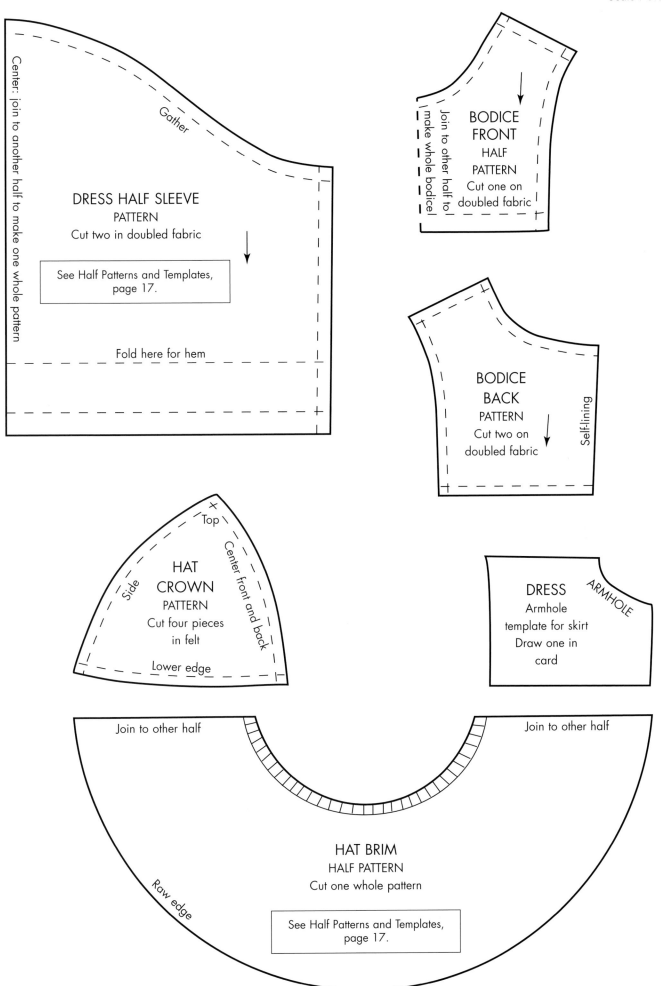

Center: join to another half to make one whole pattern

Gather

DRESS HALF SLEEVE
PATTERN
Cut two in doubled fabric

See Half Patterns and Templates,
page 17.

Fold here for hem

Join to other half to make whole bodice

BODICE
FRONT
HALF
PATTERN
Cut one on
doubled fabric

BODICE
BACK
PATTERN
Cut two on
doubled fabric

Self-lining

Top

Side

Center front and back

HAT
CROWN
PATTERN
Cut four pieces
in felt

Lower edge

DRESS
Armhole
template for skirt
Draw one in
card

ARMHOLE

Join to other half

Join to other half

HAT BRIM
HALF PATTERN
Cut one whole pattern

See Half Patterns and Templates,
page 17.

Raw edge

TODDLER DOLL

Scale 70%

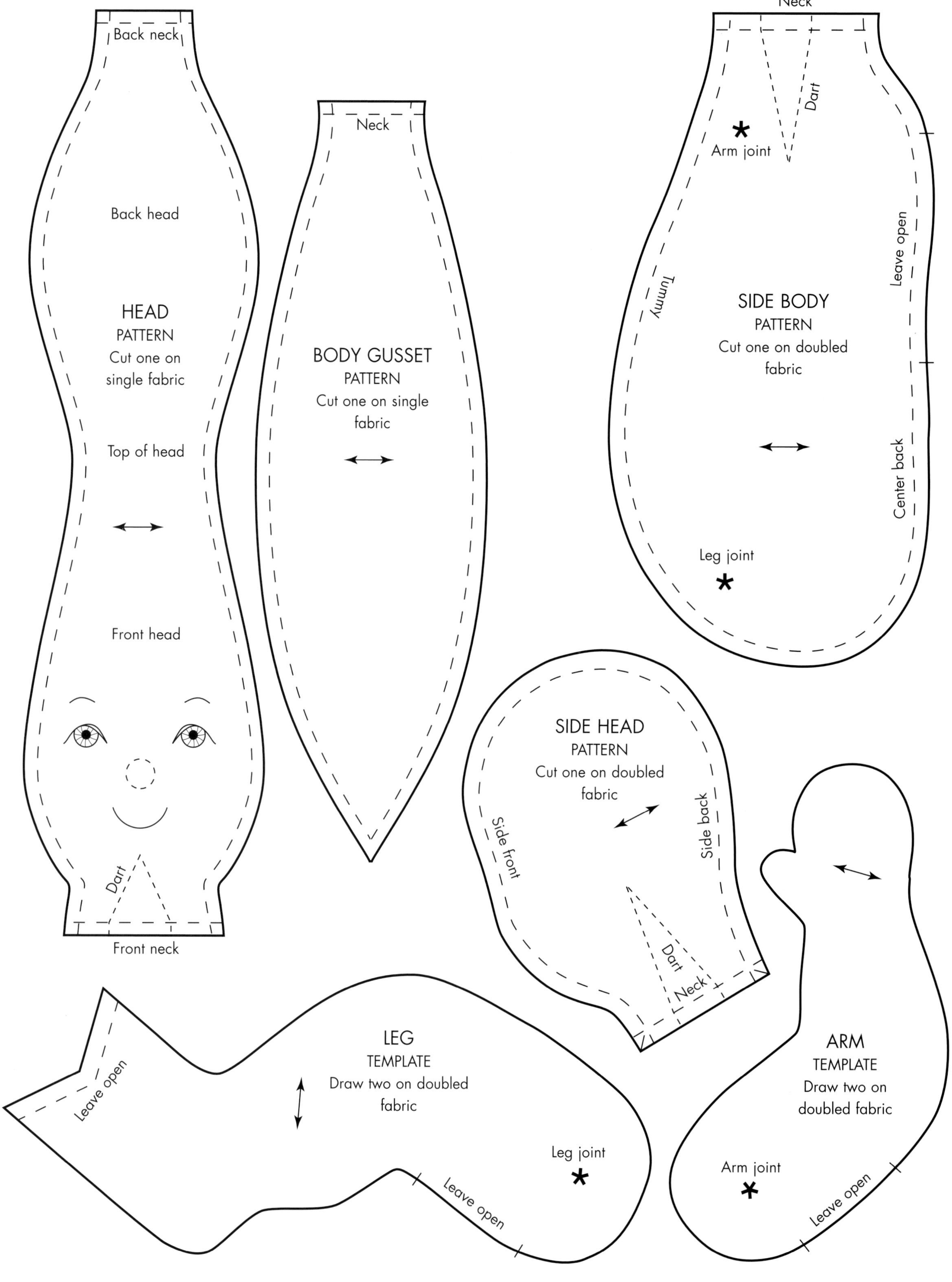

Back neck

Back head

HEAD
PATTERN
Cut one on
single fabric

Top of head

←→

Front head

Dart

Front neck

Neck

BODY GUSSET
PATTERN
Cut one on single
fabric

←→

Neck

Dart

Arm joint *

Tummy

SIDE BODY
PATTERN
Cut one on doubled
fabric

←→

Leave open

Center back

Leg joint
*

SIDE HEAD
PATTERN
Cut one on doubled
fabric ←→

Side front

Side back

Dart

Neck

←→

Leave open

LEG
TEMPLATE
Draw two on doubled
fabric

↕

Leg joint
*

Leave open

Leave open

ARM
TEMPLATE
Draw two on
doubled fabric

Arm joint
✱

Leave open

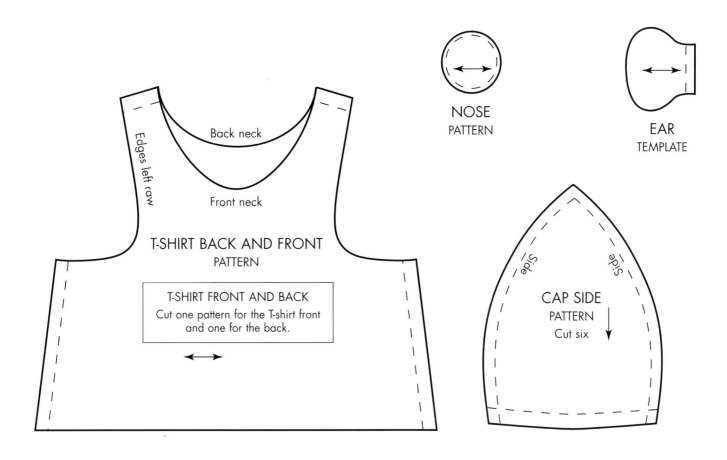

NOSE
PATTERN

EAR
TEMPLATE

Back neck

Front neck

Edges left raw

T-SHIRT BACK AND FRONT
PATTERN

T-SHIRT FRONT AND BACK
Cut one pattern for the T-shirt front
and one for the back.

Side

Side

CAP SIDE
PATTERN
Cut six

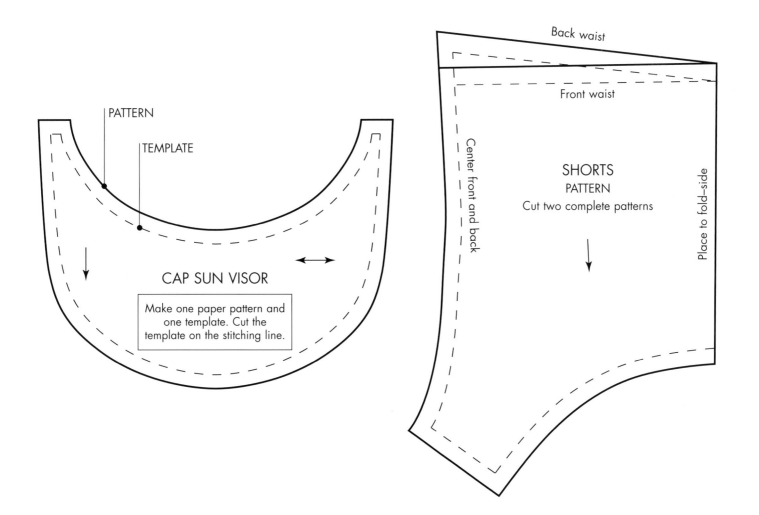

PATTERN

TEMPLATE

CAP SUN VISOR

Make one paper pattern and
one template. Cut the
template on the stitching line.

Back waist

Front waist

Center front and back

SHORTS
PATTERN
Cut two complete patterns

Place to fold-side

DECORATIVE STRING DOLL
Scale 100%

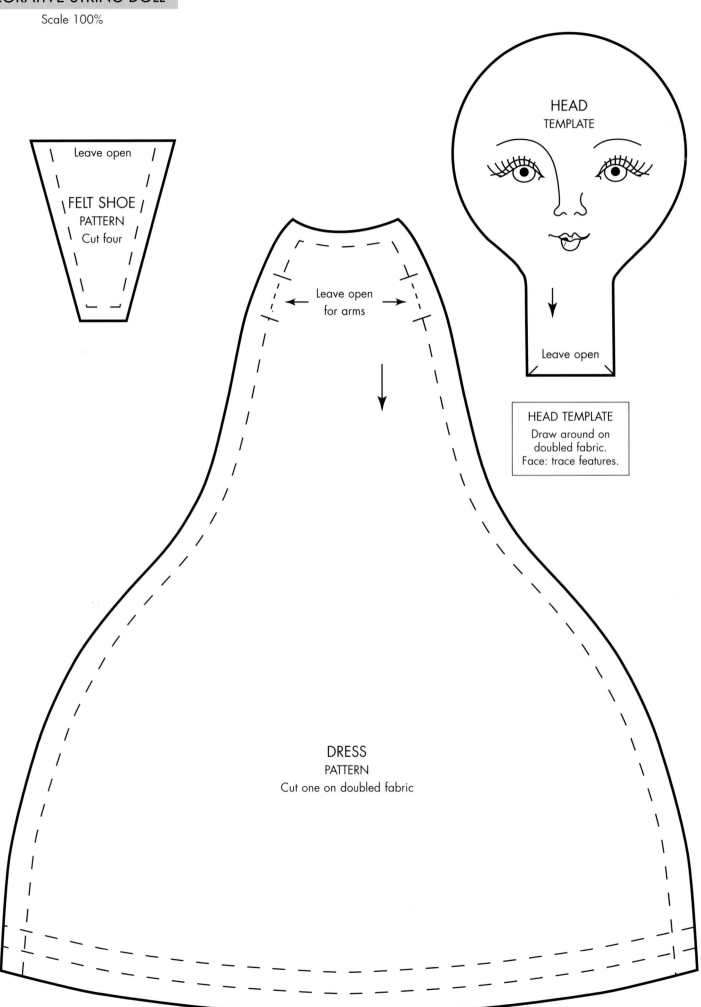

Leave open

FELT SHOE
PATTERN
Cut four

Leave open
for arms

HEAD
TEMPLATE

Leave open

HEAD TEMPLATE
Draw around on
doubled fabric.
Face: trace features.

DRESS
PATTERN
Cut one on doubled fabric

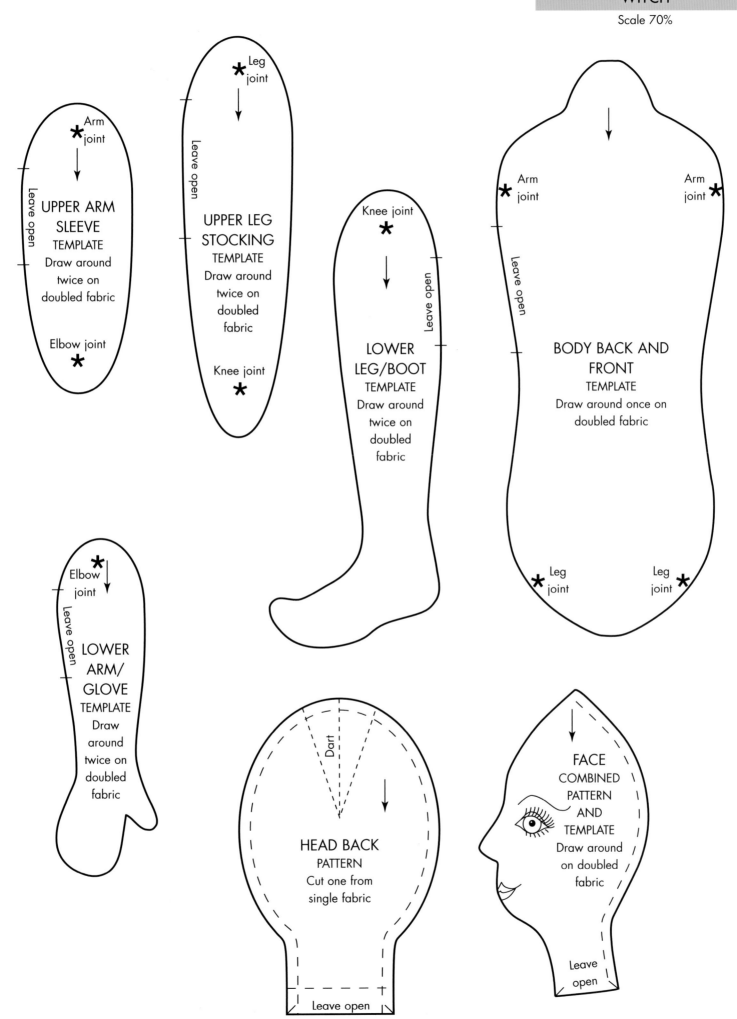

Arm joint
✱

UPPER ARM
SLEEVE
TEMPLATE
Draw around
twice on
doubled fabric

Leave open

Elbow joint
✱

Leg joint
✱

Leave open

UPPER LEG
STOCKING
TEMPLATE
Draw around
twice on
doubled
fabric

Knee joint
✱

Knee joint
✱

Leave open

LOWER
LEG/BOOT
TEMPLATE
Draw around
twice on
doubled
fabric

Arm
joint
✱

Arm
joint
✱

Leave open

BODY BACK AND
FRONT
TEMPLATE
Draw around once on
doubled fabric

Leg
joint
✱

Leg
joint
✱

Elbow
joint
✱

Leave open

LOWER
ARM/
GLOVE
TEMPLATE
Draw
around
twice on
doubled
fabric

Dart

HEAD BACK
PATTERN
Cut one from
single fabric

Leave open

FACE
COMBINED
PATTERN
AND
TEMPLATE
Draw around
on doubled
fabric

Leave
open

WITCH
Scale 70%

Cut here for
back collar

Cut here for
front collar

Fold up twice for hem

Cut here to separate sleeve from dress

DRESS FRONT AND BACK
PATTERN
Front: cut once on doubled fabric
Back: cut once on doubled fabric

Center back and front

Cut one pattern for the
dress front and one for
the back.

Fold up twice for hem

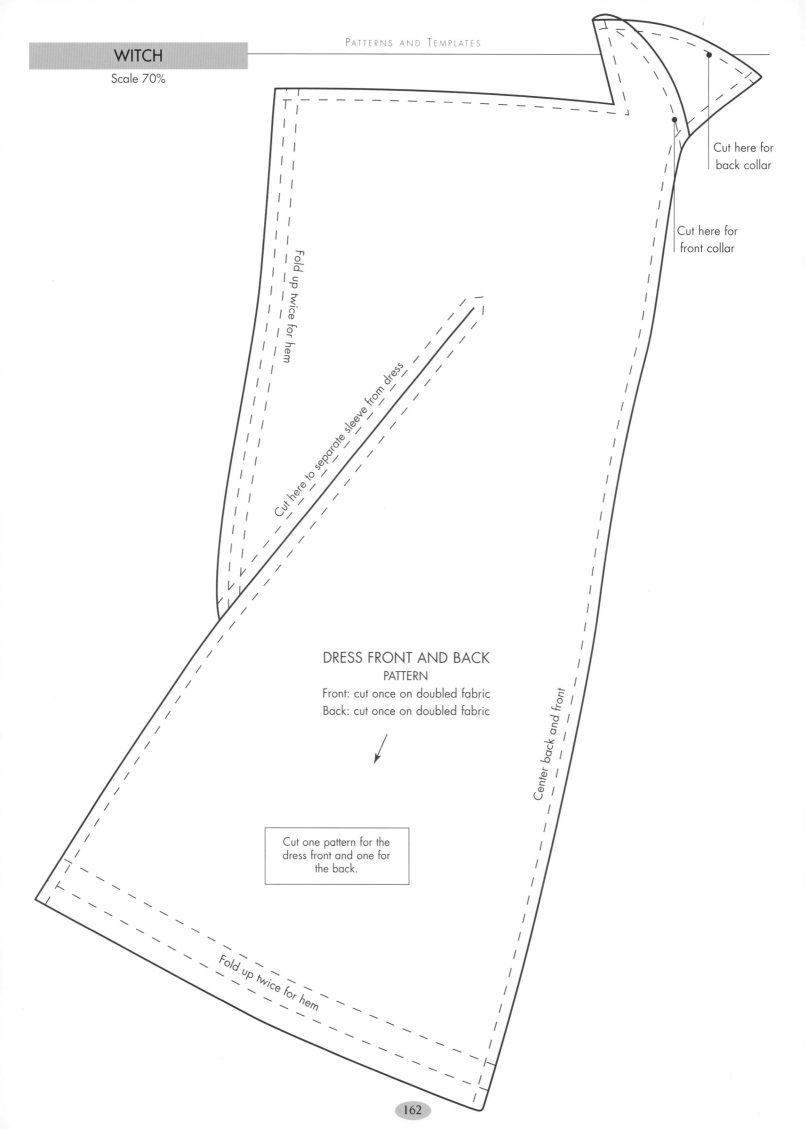

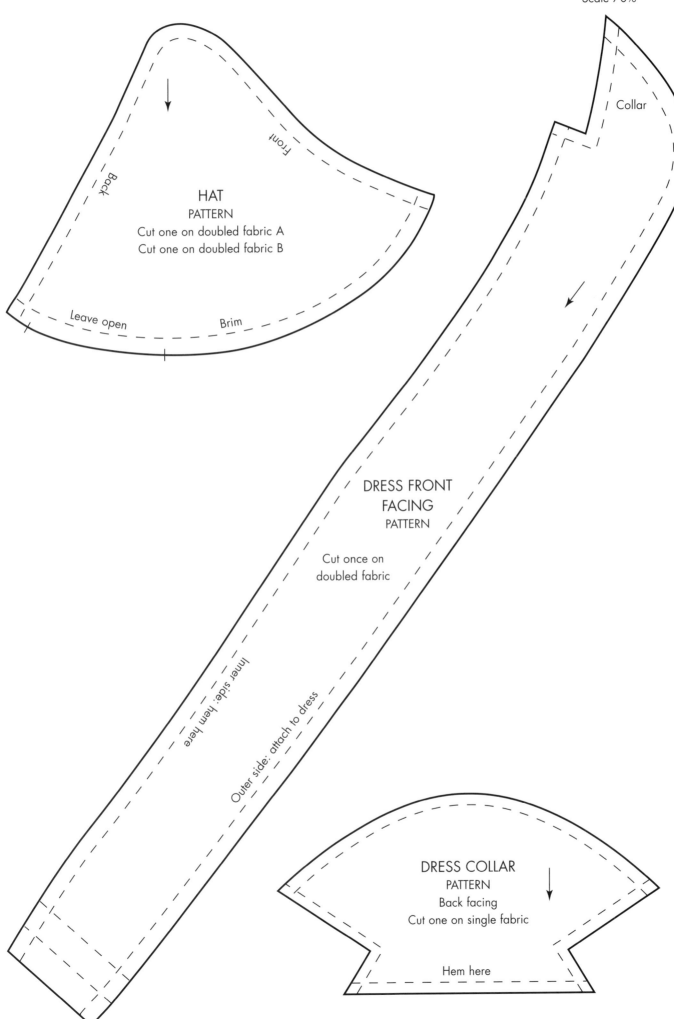

Collar

HAT
PATTERN
Cut one on doubled fabric A
Cut one on doubled fabric B

Back

Front

Leave open

Brim

DRESS FRONT
FACING
PATTERN

Cut once on
doubled fabric

Inner side: hem here

Outer side: attach to dress

DRESS COLLAR
PATTERN
Back facing
Cut one on single fabric

Hem here

ANGEL

Scale 70%

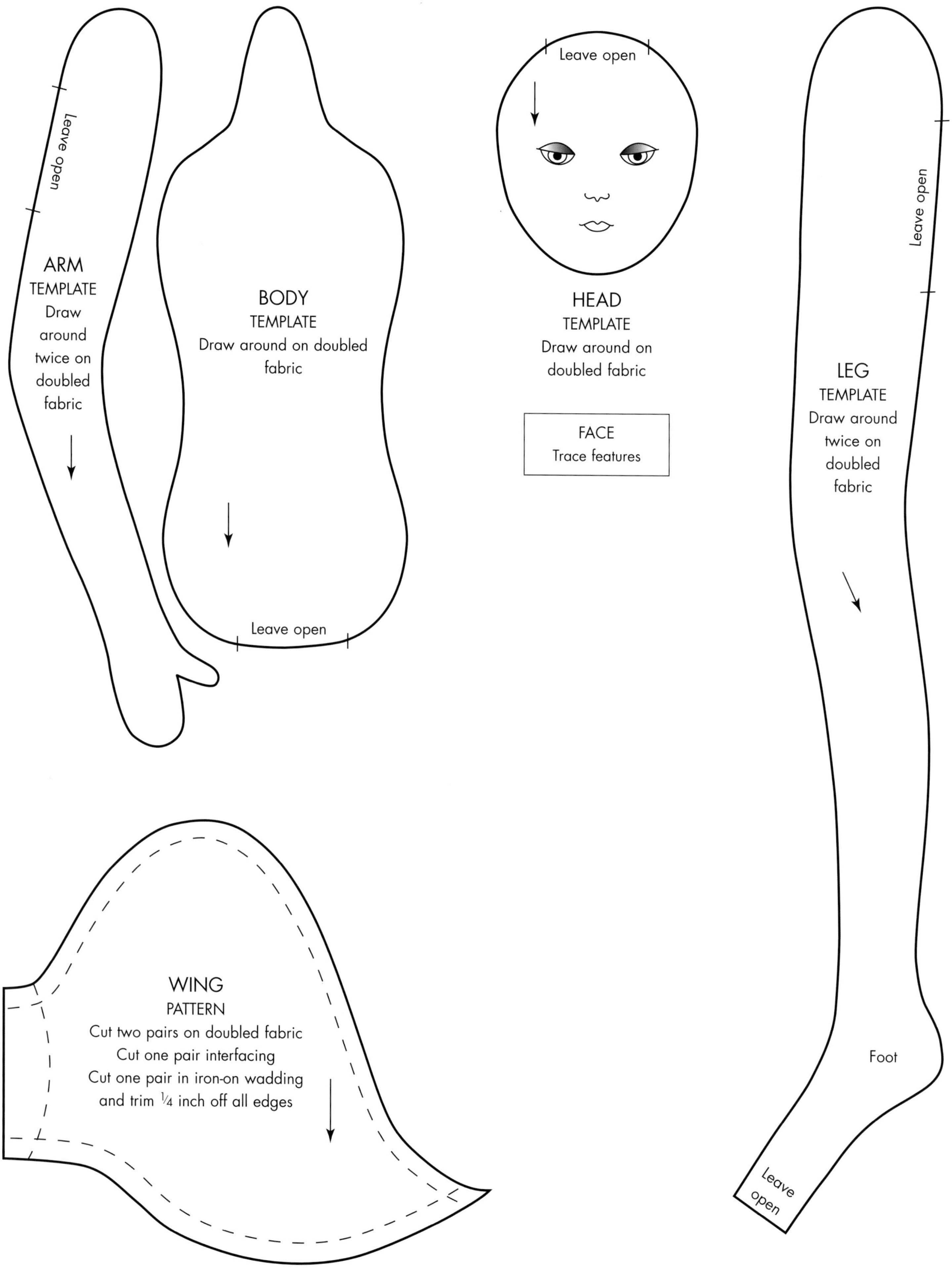

ARM
TEMPLATE
Draw around twice on doubled fabric

Leave open

BODY
TEMPLATE
Draw around on doubled fabric

Leave open

HEAD
TEMPLATE
Draw around on doubled fabric

Leave open

FACE
Trace features

LEG
TEMPLATE
Draw around twice on doubled fabric

Leave open

Foot

Leave open

WING
PATTERN
Cut two pairs on doubled fabric
Cut one pair interfacing
Cut one pair in iron-on wadding
and trim 1/4 inch off all edges

164

Scale 70%

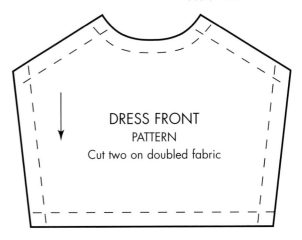

DRESS FRONT
PATTERN
Cut two on doubled fabric

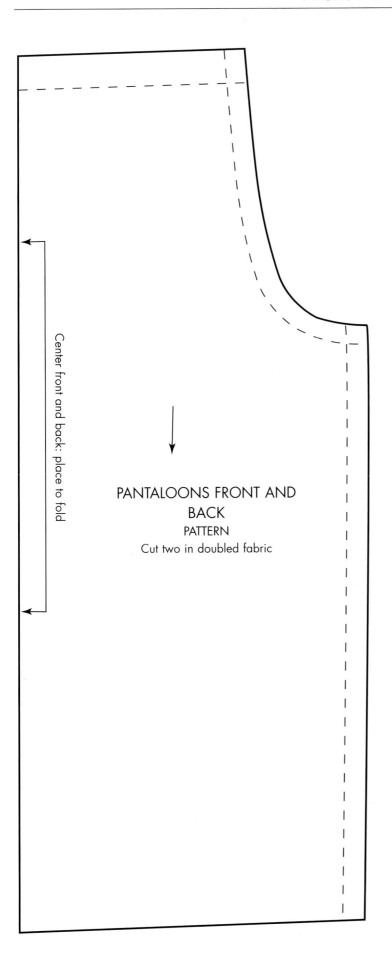

Center front and back: place to fold

PANTALOONS FRONT AND BACK
PATTERN
Cut two in doubled fabric

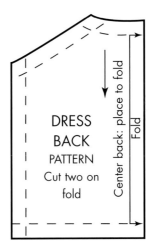

DRESS BACK
PATTERN
Cut two on fold

Center back: place to fold

Fold

OVERDRESS FRONT AND BACK
PATTERN
For front and back: cut two on doubled fabric

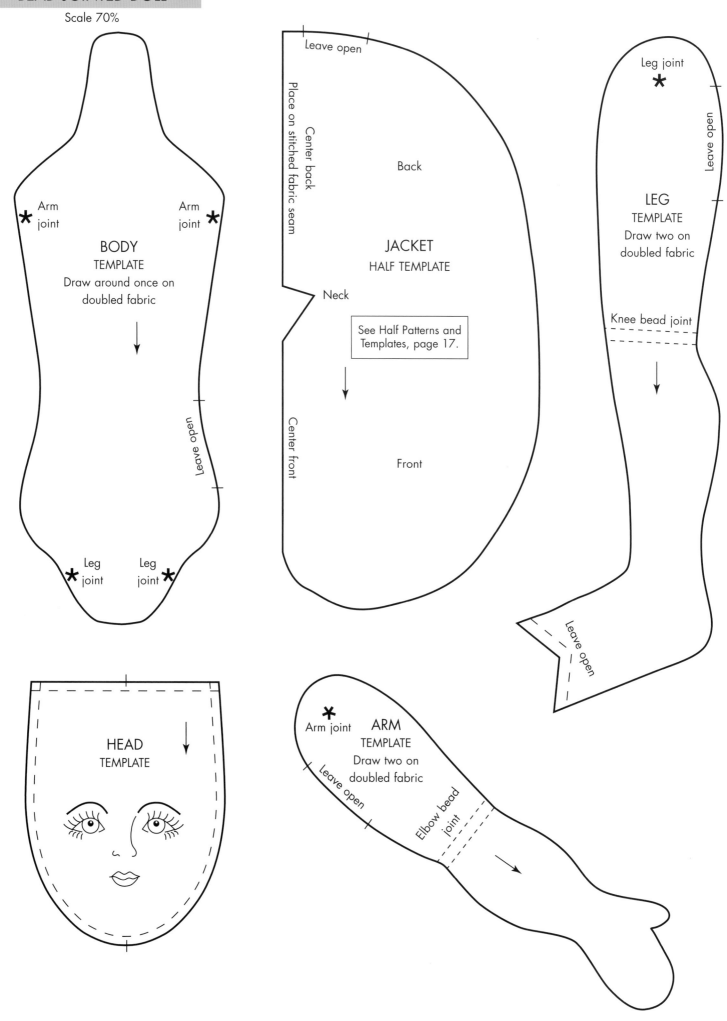

Scale 70%

Leave open

Place on stitched fabric seam

Center back

Back

JACKET
HALF TEMPLATE

Neck

See Half Patterns and
Templates, page 17.

Center front

Front

Leg joint

✱

Leave open

LEG
TEMPLATE
Draw two on
doubled fabric

Knee bead joint

Leave open

Arm
joint ✱

Arm
joint ✱

BODY
TEMPLATE
Draw around once on
doubled fabric

Leave open

Leg
joint ✱

Leg
joint ✱

HEAD
TEMPLATE

✱
Arm joint

ARM
TEMPLATE
Draw two on
doubled fabric

Leave open

Elbow bead
joint

MERMAID

Scale 70%

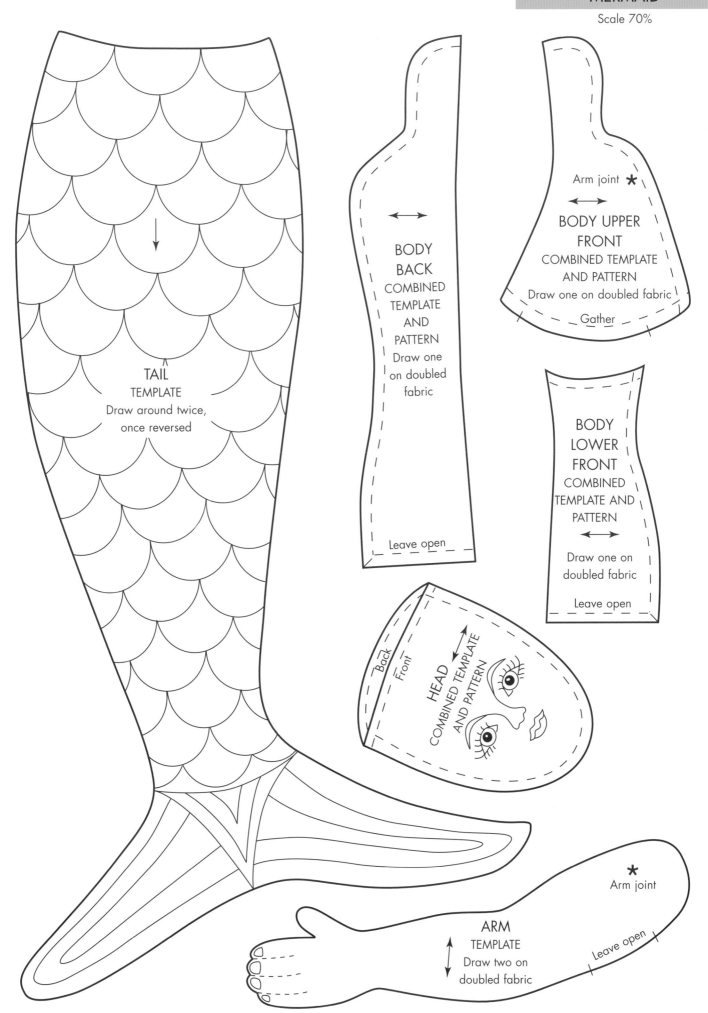

TAIL
TEMPLATE
Draw around twice,
once reversed

**BODY
BACK**
COMBINED
TEMPLATE
AND
PATTERN
Draw one
on doubled
fabric

Leave open

Arm joint ✱

**BODY UPPER
FRONT**
COMBINED TEMPLATE
AND PATTERN
Draw one on doubled fabric

Gather

**BODY
LOWER
FRONT**
COMBINED
TEMPLATE AND
PATTERN

Draw one on
doubled fabric

Leave open

Back
Front

HEAD
COMBINED TEMPLATE
AND PATTERN

✱
Arm joint

ARM
TEMPLATE
Draw two on
doubled fabric

Leave open

ROSE FAIRY

Scale 70%

HEAD, ARM, AND LEG
TEMPLATES
Leave open between dots
when stitching.

Elbow joint

Shoulder joint

Leave open

Leave open

Elbow
joint

LOWER ARM
TEMPLATE
Draw around twice
on doubled fabric

UPPER ARM
TEMPLATE
Draw around twice
on doubled fabric

HEAD AND FACE
TEMPLATE
Draw around on doubled fabric

**BODY FRONT
AND BACK**
TEMPLATE
Draw around on
doubled fabric

Hip joint

Knee
joint

Leave open

Leave open

Knee joint

UPPER LEG
TEMPLATE
Draw around twice
on doubled fabric

LOWER LEG
TEMPLATE
Draw around twice
on doubled fabric

WING
TEMPLATES

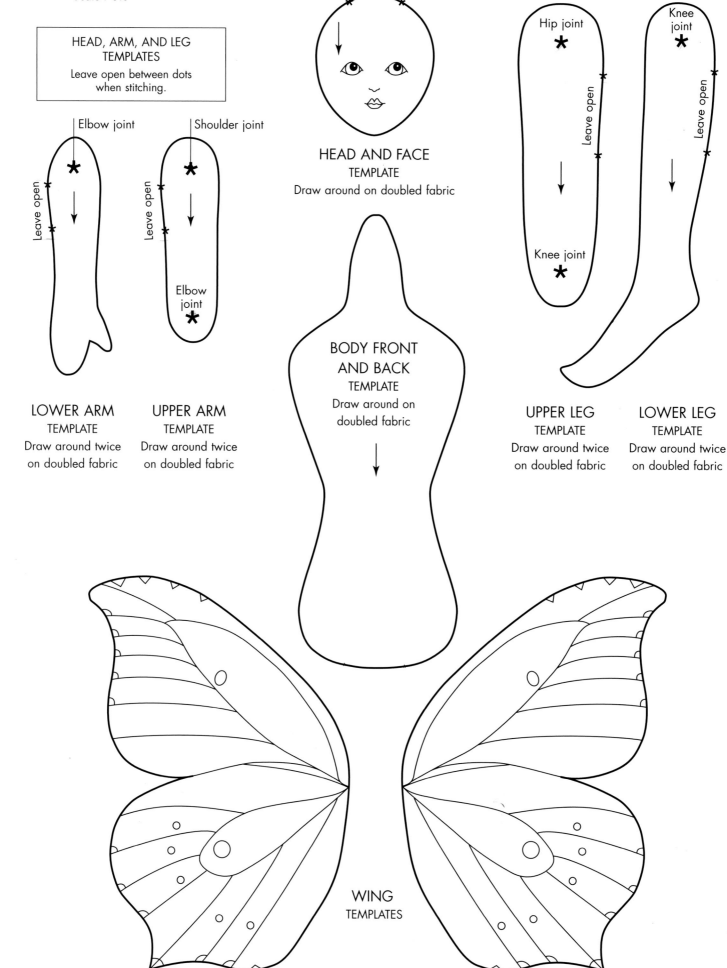

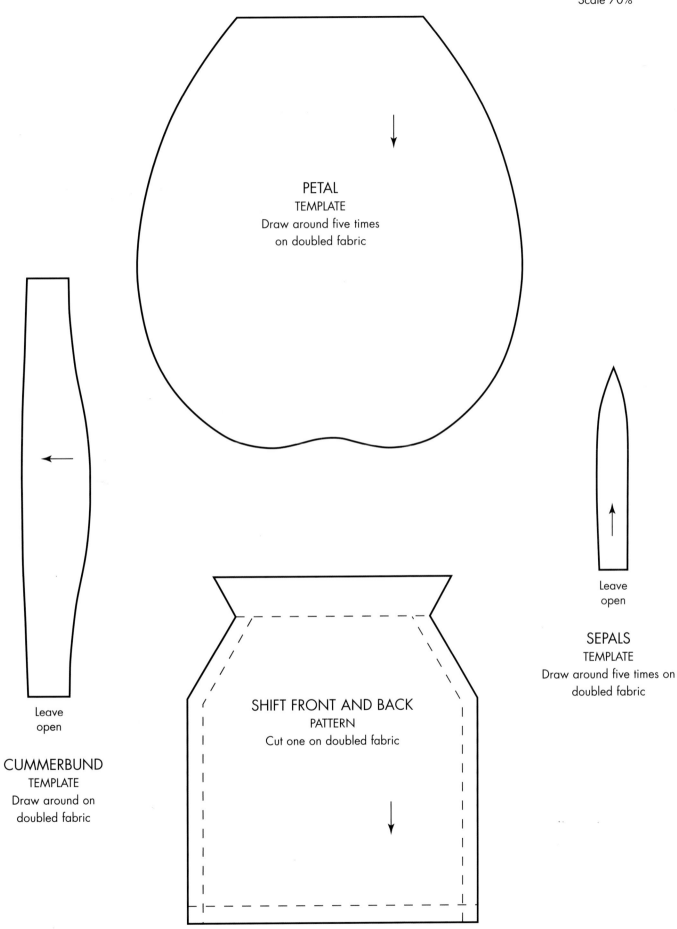

PETAL
TEMPLATE
Draw around five times
on doubled fabric

SEPALS
TEMPLATE
Draw around five times on
doubled fabric

Leave
open

CUMMERBUND
TEMPLATE
Draw around on
doubled fabric

Leave
open

SHIFT FRONT AND BACK
PATTERN
Cut one on doubled fabric

ROSE FAIRY

Scale 70%

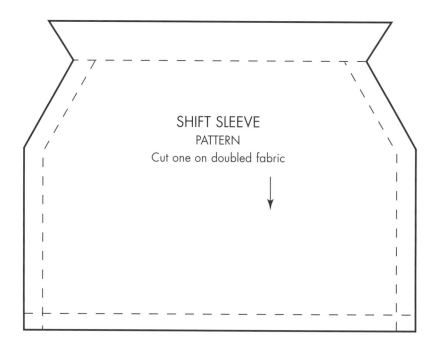

SHIFT SLEEVE
PATTERN
Cut one on doubled fabric

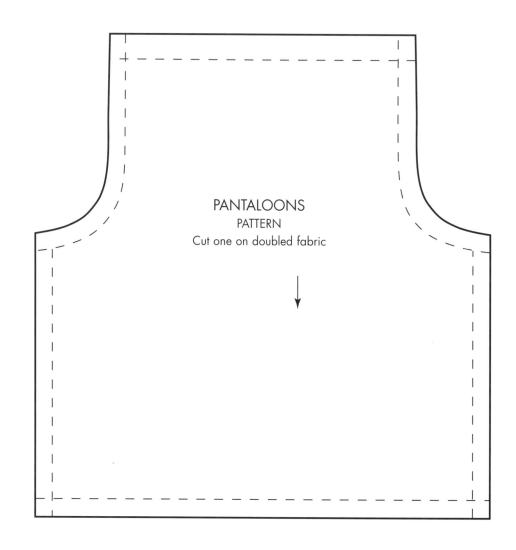

PANTALOONS
PATTERN
Cut one on doubled fabric

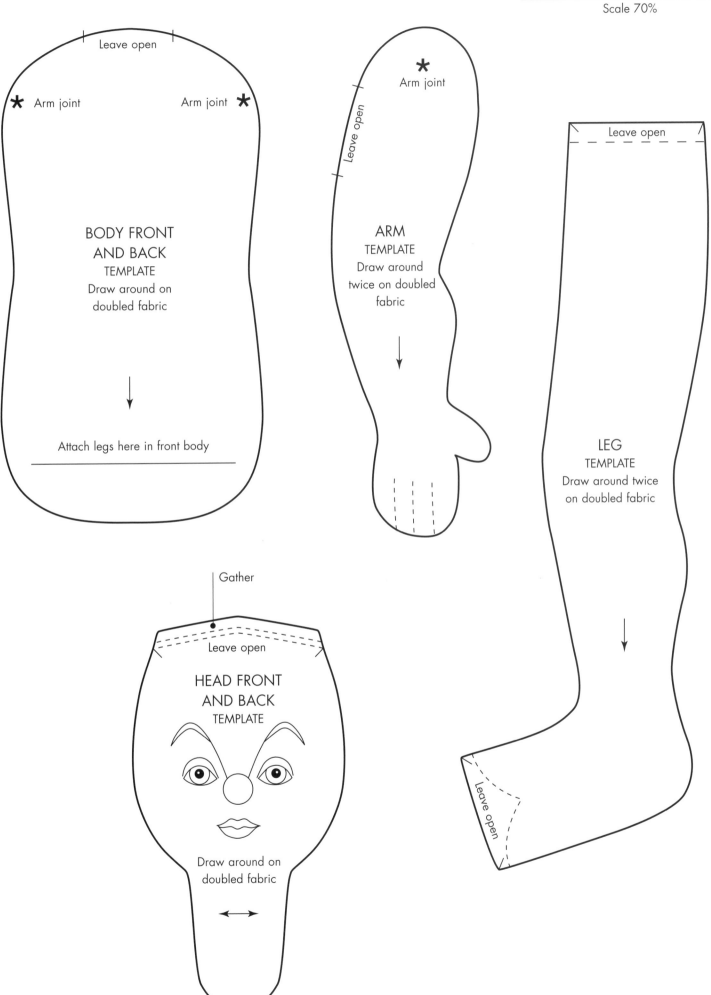

Leave open

* Arm joint   Arm joint *

BODY FRONT
AND BACK
TEMPLATE
Draw around on
doubled fabric

Attach legs here in front body

Leave open

* Arm joint

ARM
TEMPLATE
Draw around
twice on doubled
fabric

Leave open

LEG
TEMPLATE
Draw around twice
on doubled fabric

Leave open

Gather

Leave open

HEAD FRONT
AND BACK
TEMPLATE

Draw around on
doubled fabric

CLOWN

Scale 70%

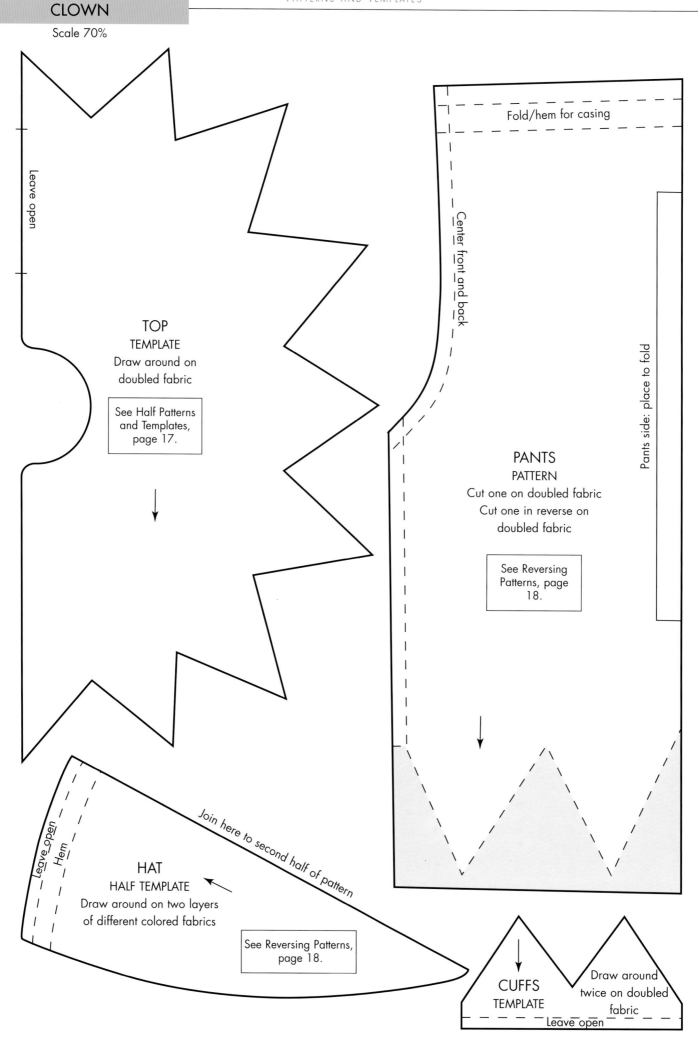

Leave open

TOP
TEMPLATE
Draw around on
doubled fabric

See Half Patterns
and Templates,
page 17.

Fold/hem for casing

Center front and back

Pants side: place to fold

PANTS
PATTERN
Cut one on doubled fabric
Cut one in reverse on
doubled fabric

See Reversing
Patterns, page
18.

Leave open
Hem

Join here to second half of pattern

HAT
HALF TEMPLATE
Draw around on two layers
of different colored fabrics

See Reversing Patterns,
page 18.

CUFFS
TEMPLATE

Draw around
twice on doubled
fabric

Leave open

SANTA

Scale 70%

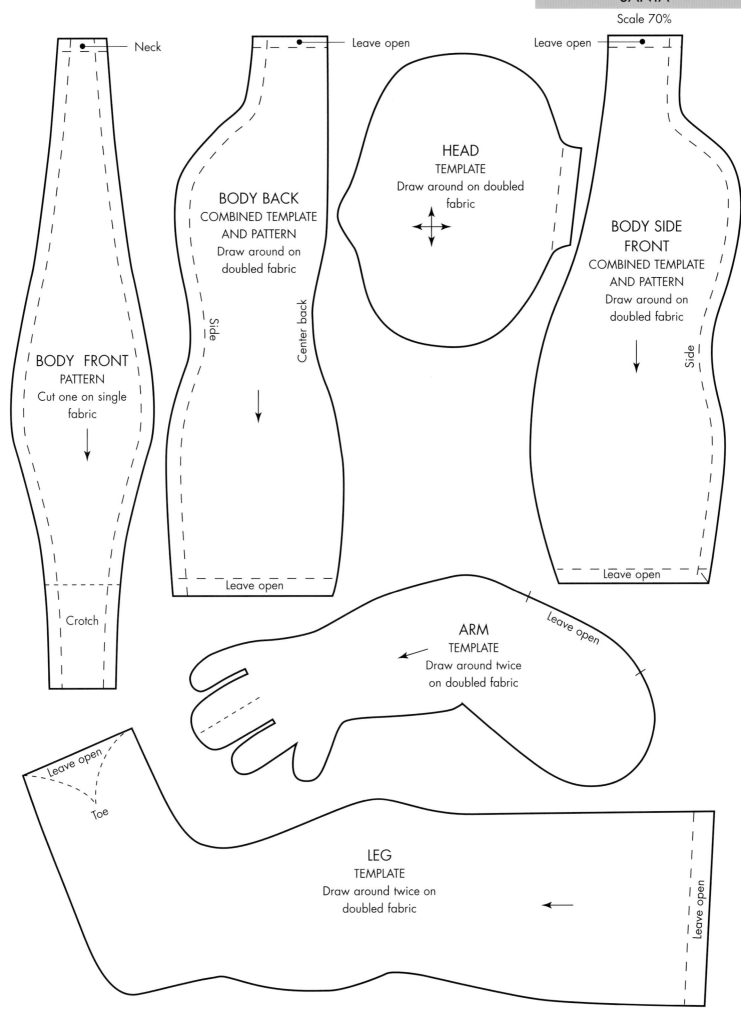

Neck

Leave open

Leave open

HEAD
TEMPLATE
Draw around on doubled fabric

BODY BACK
COMBINED TEMPLATE AND PATTERN
Draw around on doubled fabric

Side

Center back

BODY SIDE FRONT
COMBINED TEMPLATE AND PATTERN
Draw around on doubled fabric

Side

BODY FRONT
PATTERN
Cut one on single fabric

Leave open

Leave open

Crotch

ARM
TEMPLATE
Draw around twice on doubled fabric

Leave open

Leave open

Toe

LEG
TEMPLATE
Draw around twice on doubled fabric

Leave open

SANTA
Scale 70%

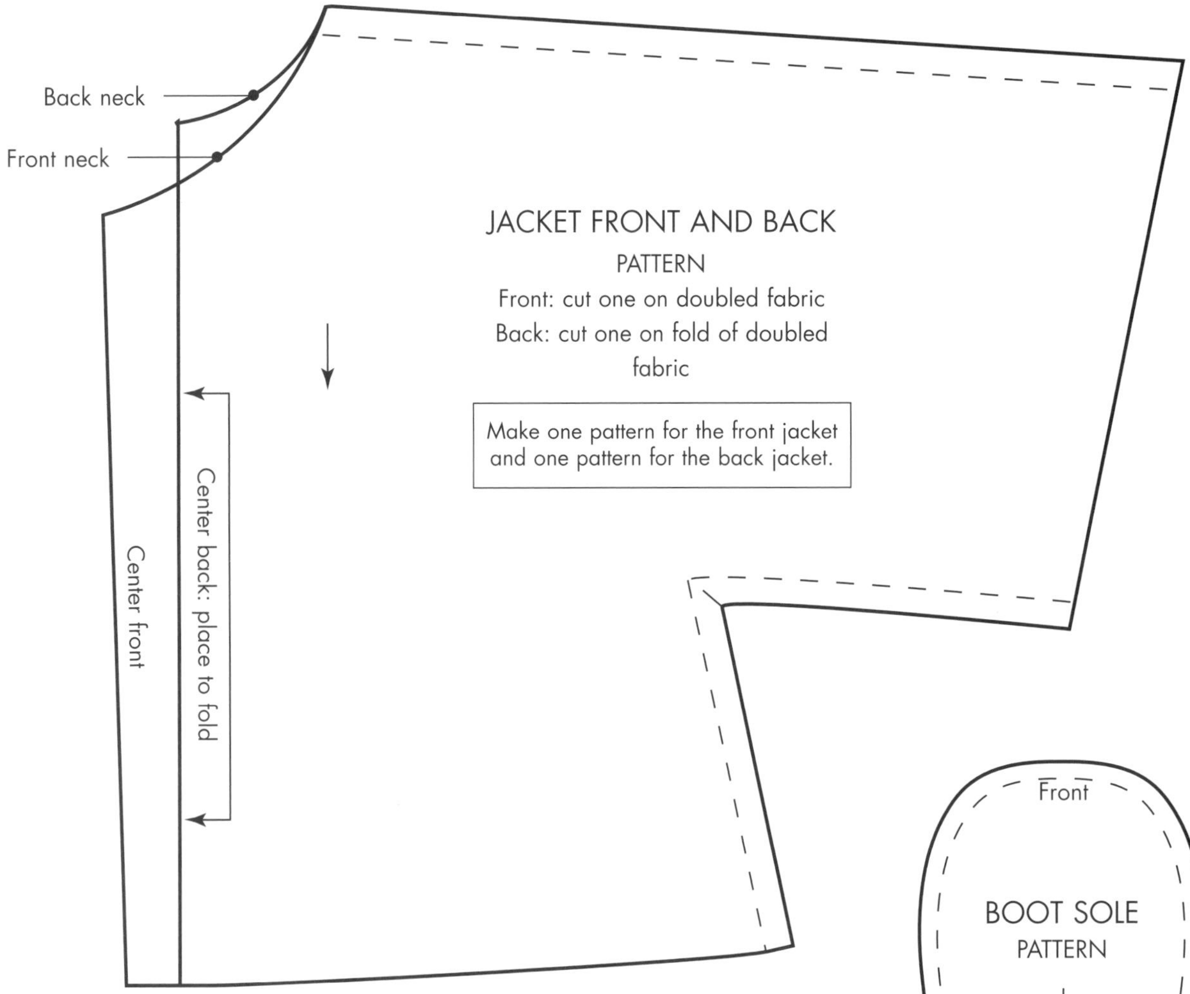

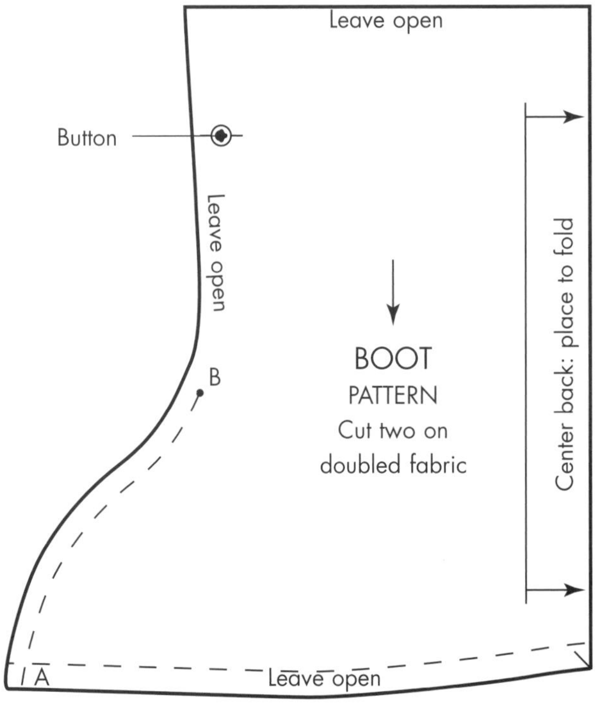

JACKET FRONT AND BACK
PATTERN
Front: cut one on doubled fabric
Back: cut one on fold of doubled fabric

Make one pattern for the front jacket and one pattern for the back jacket.

Back neck

Front neck

Center back: place to fold

Center front

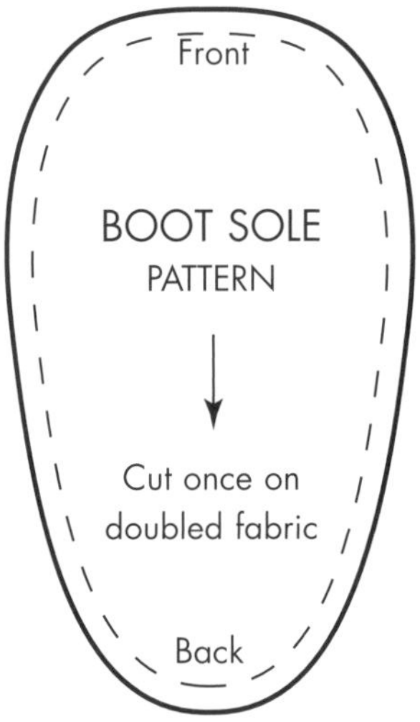

BOOT SOLE
PATTERN

Front

Cut once on doubled fabric

Back

Leave open

Button

Leave open

B

BOOT
PATTERN
Cut two on doubled fabric

Center back: place to fold

A

Leave open

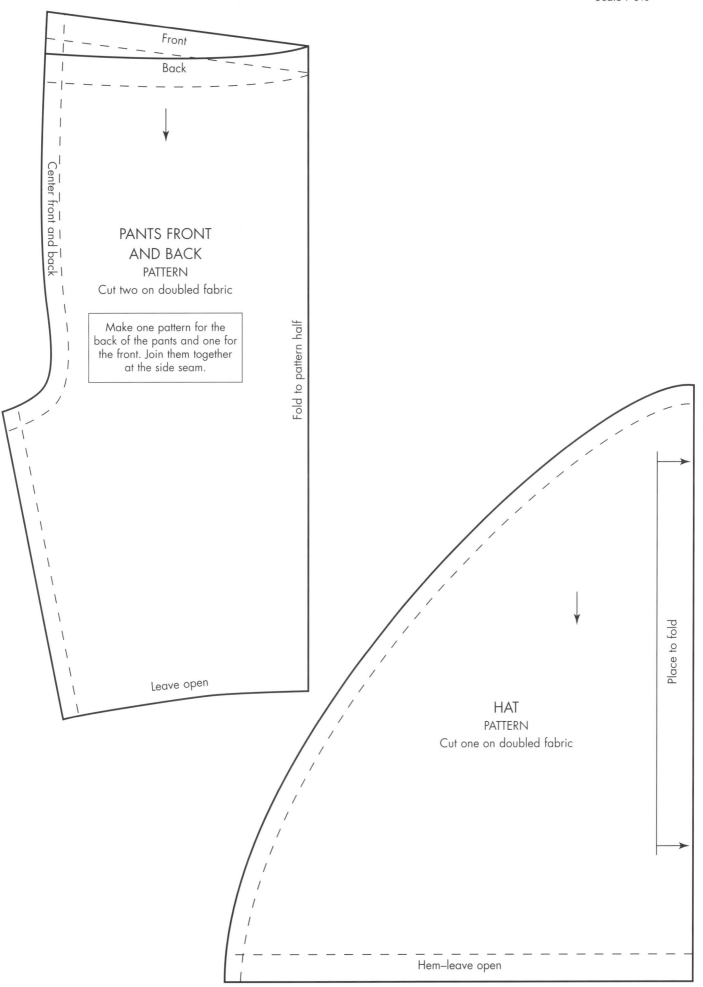

Front

Back

Center front and back

PANTS FRONT
AND BACK
PATTERN
Cut two on doubled fabric

Make one pattern for the
back of the pants and one for
the front. Join them together
at the side seam.

Fold to pattern half

Leave open

Place to fold

HAT
PATTERN
Cut one on doubled fabric

Hem–leave open

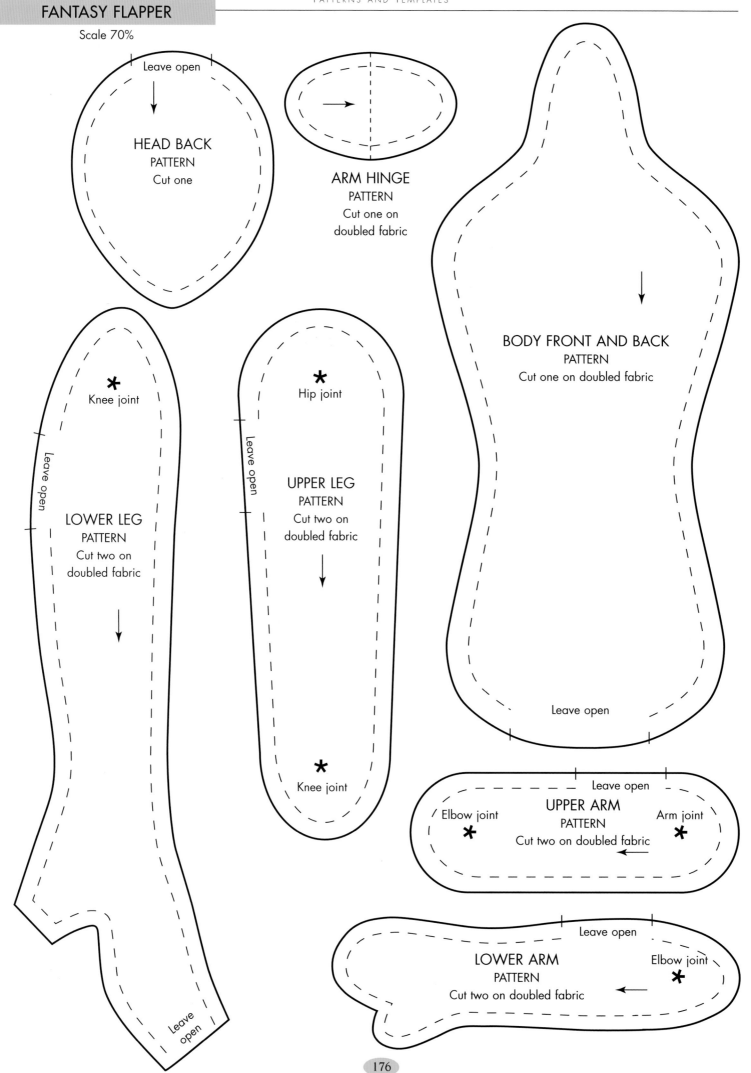

FANTASY FLAPPER

Scale 70%

Leave open

HEAD BACK
PATTERN
Cut one

ARM HINGE
PATTERN
Cut one on
doubled fabric

BODY FRONT AND BACK
PATTERN
Cut one on doubled fabric

Leave open

*
Knee joint

Leave open

LOWER LEG
PATTERN
Cut two on
doubled fabric

Leave
open

*
Hip joint

Leave open

UPPER LEG
PATTERN
Cut two on
doubled fabric

*
Knee joint

Leave open

Elbow joint
*

UPPER ARM
PATTERN
Cut two on doubled fabric

Arm joint
*

Leave open

LOWER ARM
PATTERN
Cut two on doubled fabric

Elbow joint
*

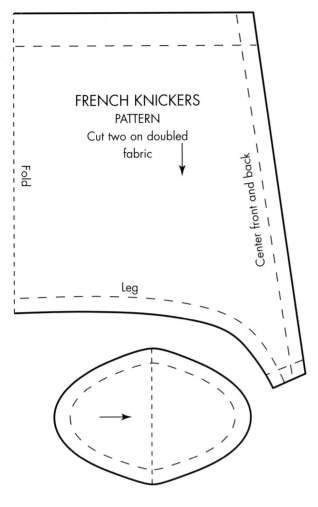

FRENCH KNICKERS
PATTERN
Cut two on doubled fabric

Fold

Center front and back

Leg

FACE
TEMPLATE

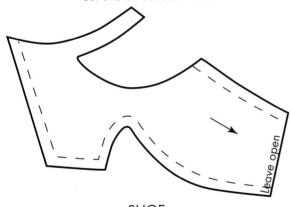

LEG HINGE
PATTERN
Cut one on doubled fabric

Leave open

SHOE
PATTERN
Cut two on bonding web
Cut two in reverse on bonding web

SHOE
Iron adhesive webbing to wrong side
before cutting out two pairs.

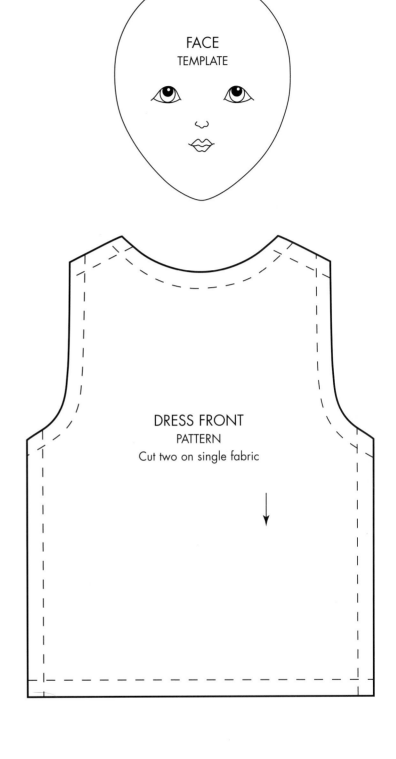

DRESS FRONT
PATTERN
Cut two on single fabric

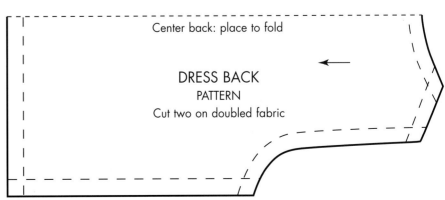

Center back: place to fold

DRESS BACK
PATTERN
Cut two on doubled fabric

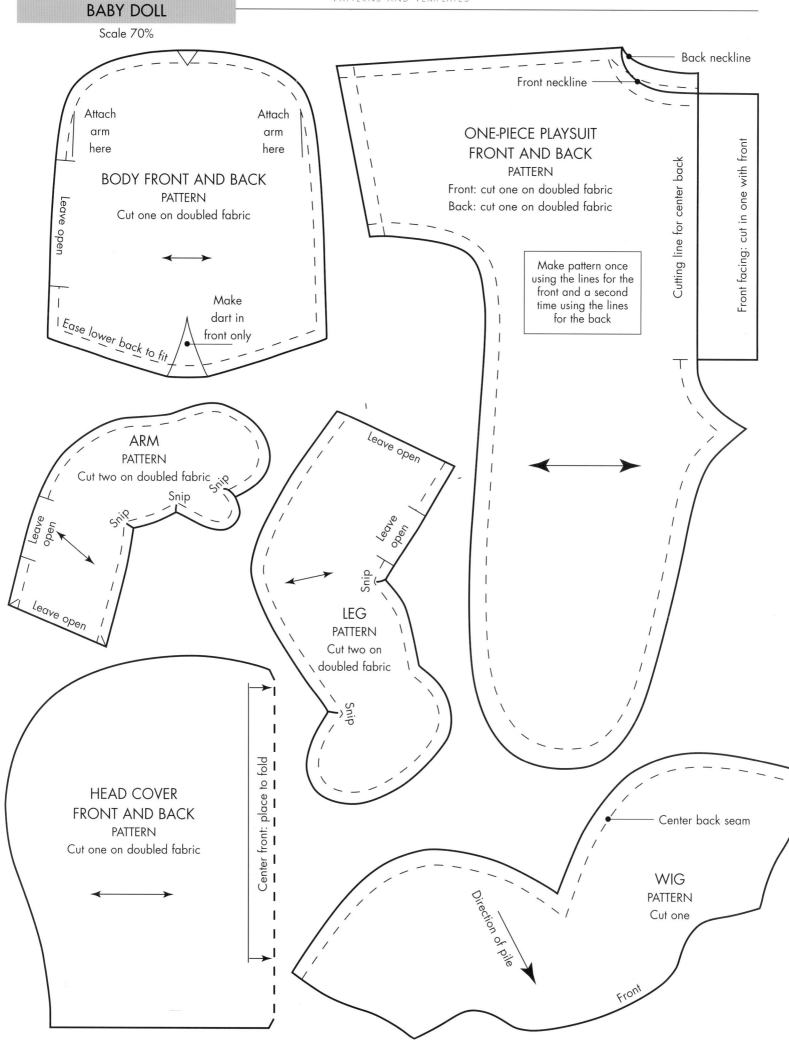

BABY DOLL
Scale 70%

BODY FRONT AND BACK
PATTERN
Cut one on doubled fabric

Attach arm here

Attach arm here

Leave open

Ease lower back to fit

Make dart in front only

ONE-PIECE PLAYSUIT FRONT AND BACK
PATTERN
Front: cut one on doubled fabric
Back: cut one on doubled fabric

Back neckline

Front neckline

Cutting line for center back

Front facing: cut in one with front

Make pattern once using the lines for the front and a second time using the lines for the back

ARM
PATTERN
Cut two on doubled fabric

Snip
Snip
Snip

Leave open
Leave open

LEG
PATTERN
Cut two on doubled fabric

Leave open
Leave open
Snip
Snip

HEAD COVER FRONT AND BACK
PATTERN
Cut one on doubled fabric

Center front: place to fold

WIG
PATTERN
Cut one

Center back seam

Direction of pile

Front

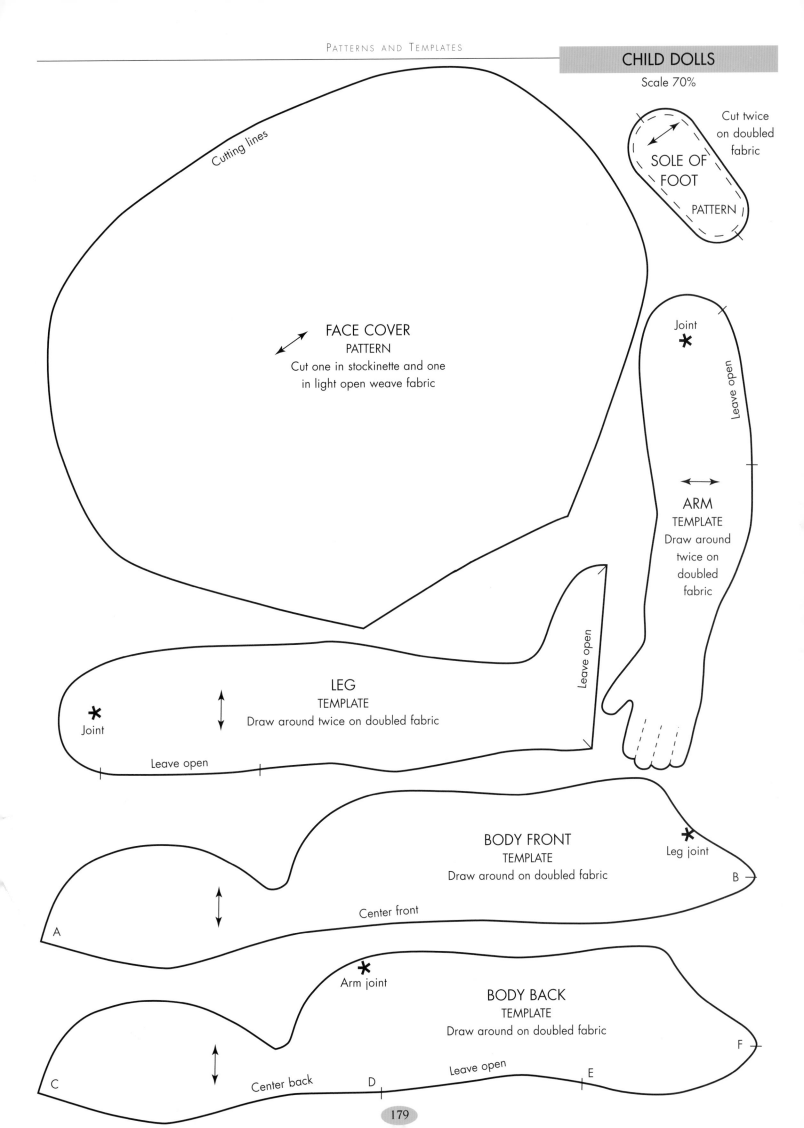

CHILD DOLLS

Scale 70%

Cutting lines

Cut twice
on doubled
fabric

SOLE OF
FOOT

PATTERN

FACE COVER
PATTERN
Cut one in stockinette and one
in light open weave fabric

Joint

✱

Leave open

ARM
TEMPLATE
Draw around
twice on
doubled
fabric

LEG
TEMPLATE
Draw around twice on doubled fabric

✱
Joint

Leave open

Leave open

BODY FRONT
TEMPLATE
Draw around on doubled fabric

✱
Leg joint

B

A

Center front

✱
Arm joint

BODY BACK
TEMPLATE
Draw around on doubled fabric

F

C

Center back   D   Leave open   E

179

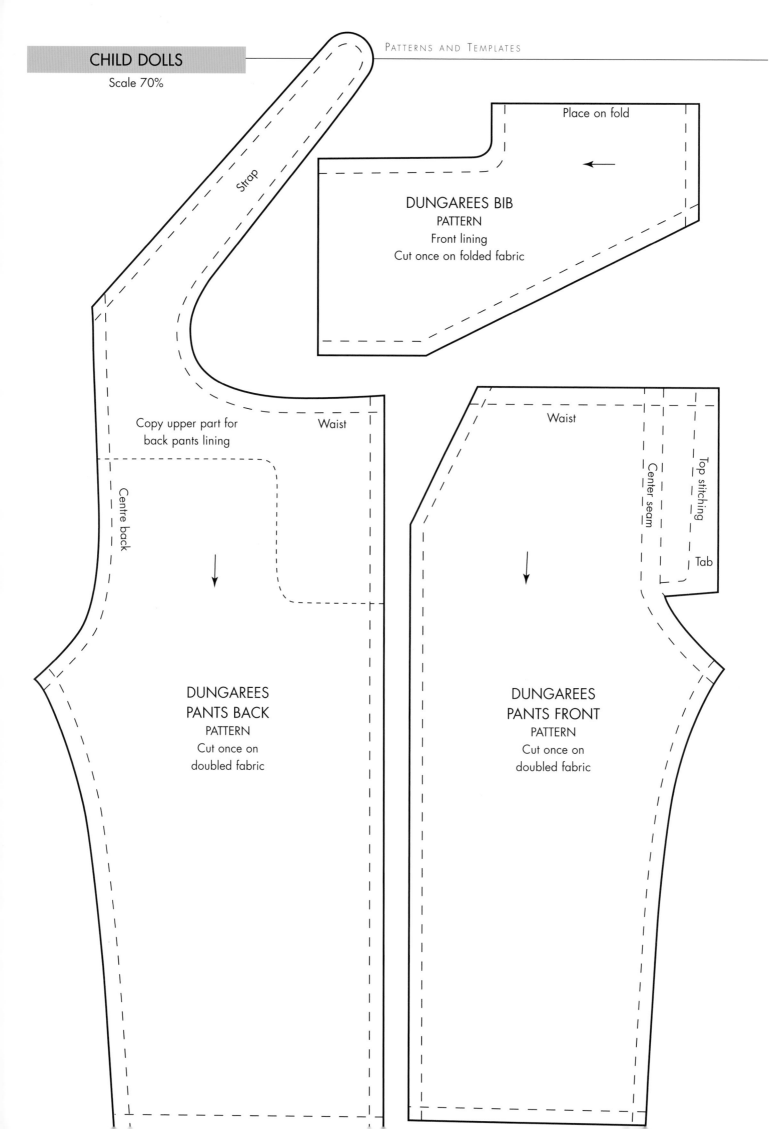

CHILD DOLLS

Scale 70%

Strap

DUNGAREES BIB
PATTERN
Front lining
Cut once on folded fabric

Place on fold

Copy upper part for
back pants lining

Waist

Centre back

DUNGAREES
PANTS BACK
PATTERN
Cut once on
doubled fabric

Waist

Center seam

Top stitching

Tab

DUNGAREES
PANTS FRONT
PATTERN
Cut once on
doubled fabric

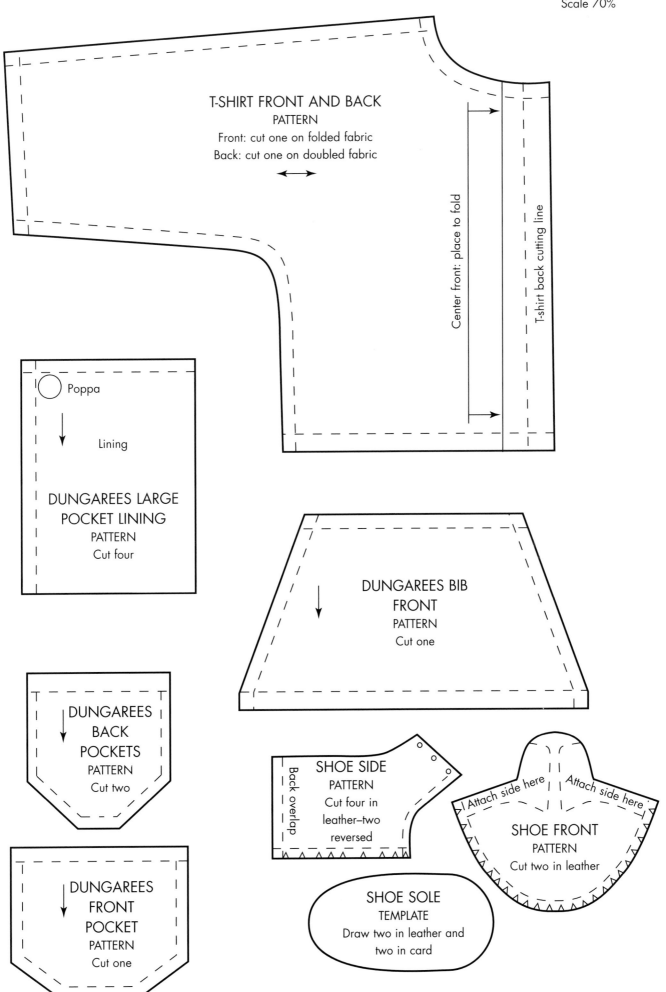

T-SHIRT FRONT AND BACK
PATTERN
Front: cut one on folded fabric
Back: cut one on doubled fabric

Center front: place to fold

T-shirt back cutting line

○ Poppa

Lining

**DUNGAREES LARGE
POCKET LINING**
PATTERN
Cut four

**DUNGAREES BIB
FRONT**
PATTERN
Cut one

**DUNGAREES
BACK
POCKETS**
PATTERN
Cut two

Back overlap

SHOE SIDE
PATTERN
Cut four in
leather—two
reversed

Attach side here   Attach side here

SHOE FRONT
PATTERN
Cut two in leather

**DUNGAREES
FRONT
POCKET**
PATTERN
Cut one

SHOE SOLE
TEMPLATE
Draw two in leather and
two in card

AFRICAN BOY

Scale 70%

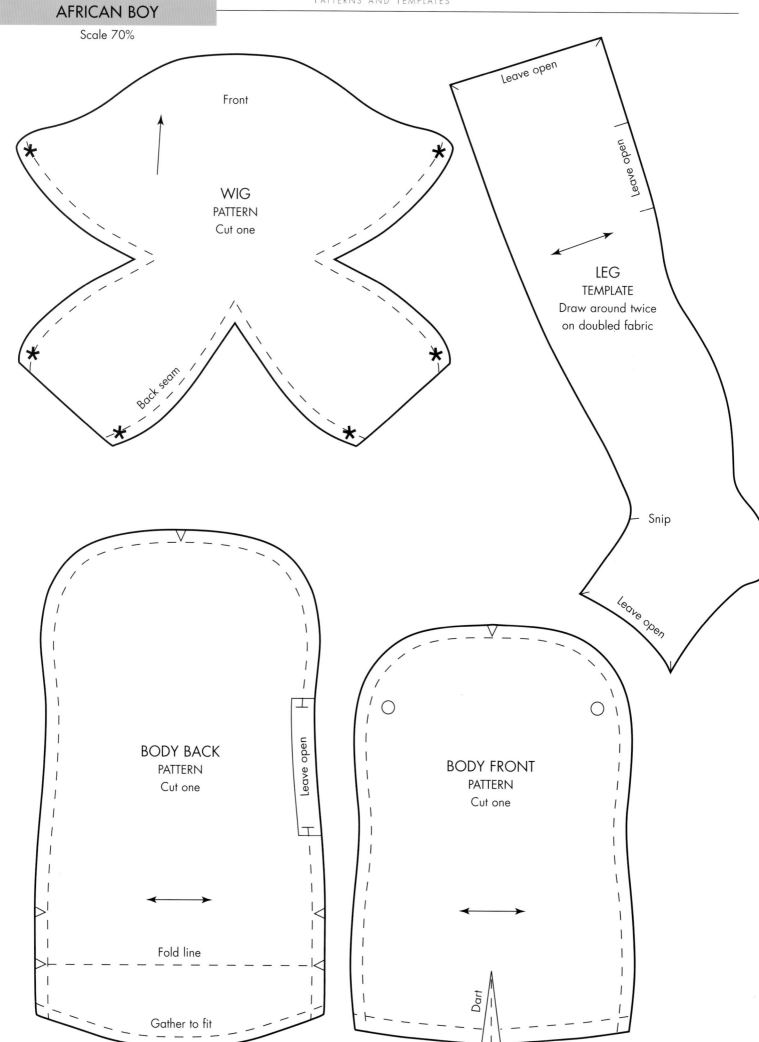

WIG
PATTERN
Cut one

Front

Back seam

LEG
TEMPLATE
Draw around twice
on doubled fabric

Leave open

Leave open

Snip

Leave open

BODY BACK
PATTERN
Cut one

Leave open

Fold line

Gather to fit

BODY FRONT
PATTERN
Cut one

Dart

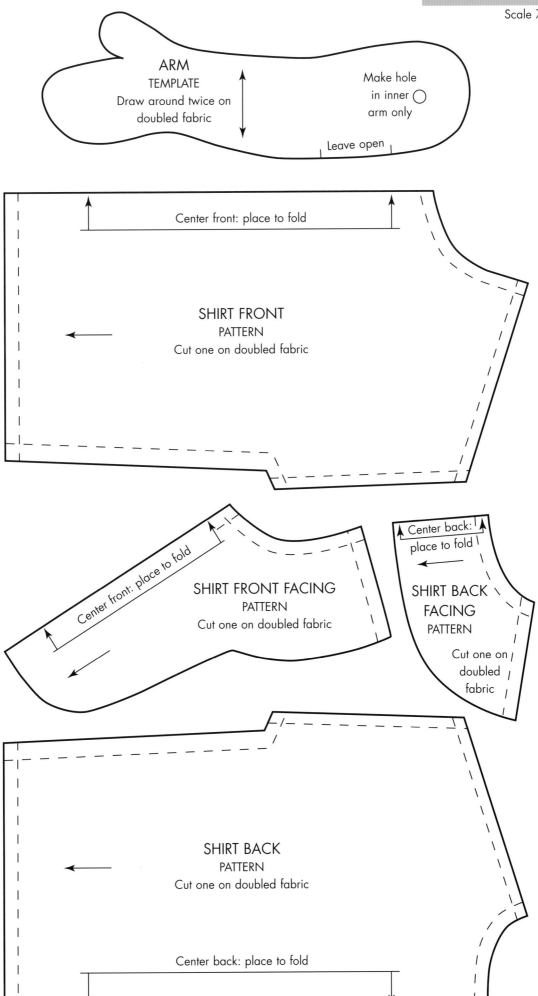

ARM
TEMPLATE
Draw around twice on
doubled fabric

Make hole
in inner
arm only

Leave open

Center front: place to fold

SHIRT FRONT
PATTERN
Cut one on doubled fabric

Center front: place to fold

SHIRT FRONT FACING
PATTERN
Cut one on doubled fabric

Center back:
place to fold

SHIRT BACK
FACING
PATTERN

Cut one on
doubled
fabric

SHIRT BACK
PATTERN
Cut one on doubled fabric

Center back: place to fold

AFRICAN BOY

Scale 70%

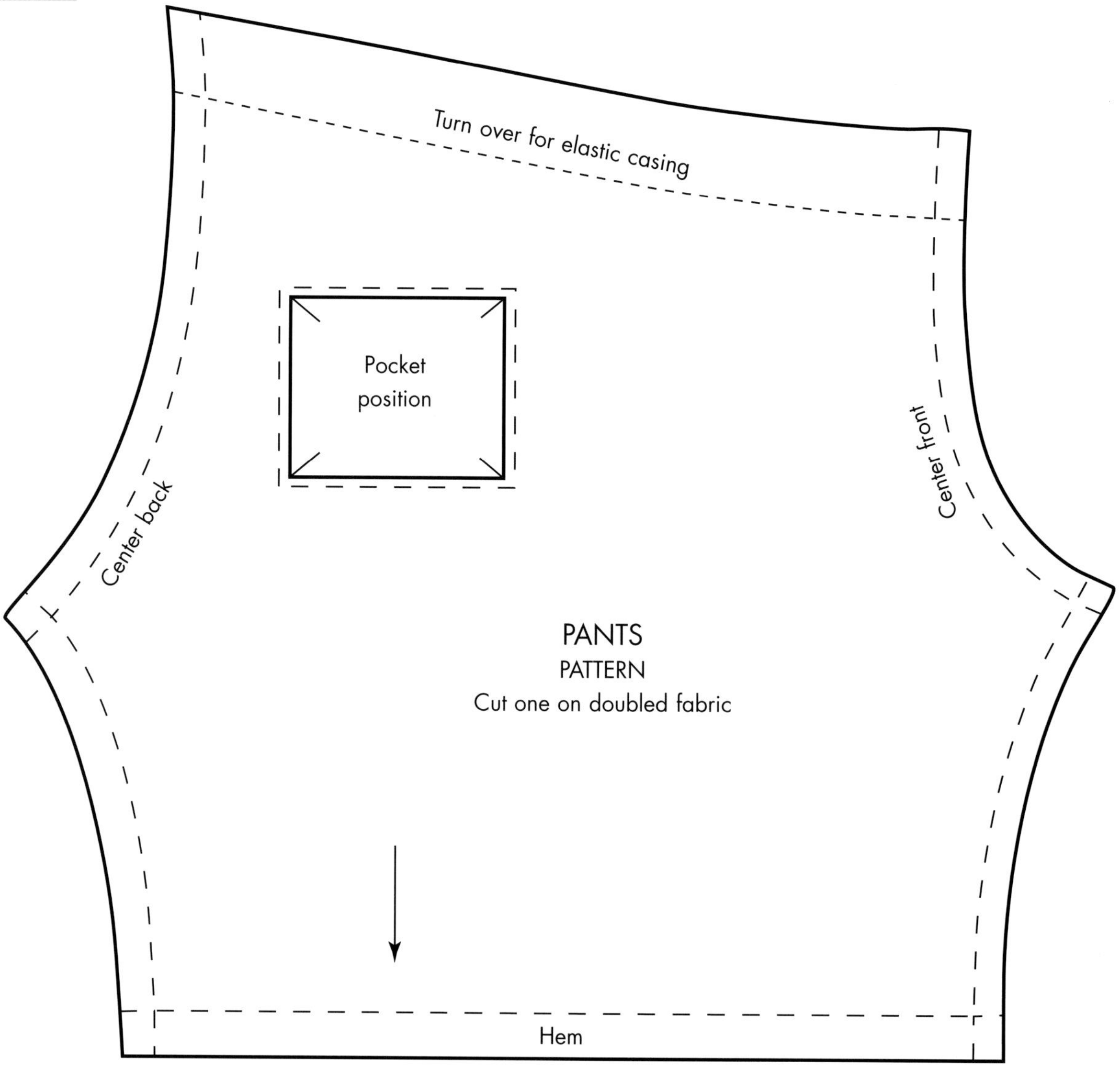

Turn over for elastic casing

Center back

Center front

Pocket position

PANTS
PATTERN
Cut one on doubled fabric

Hem

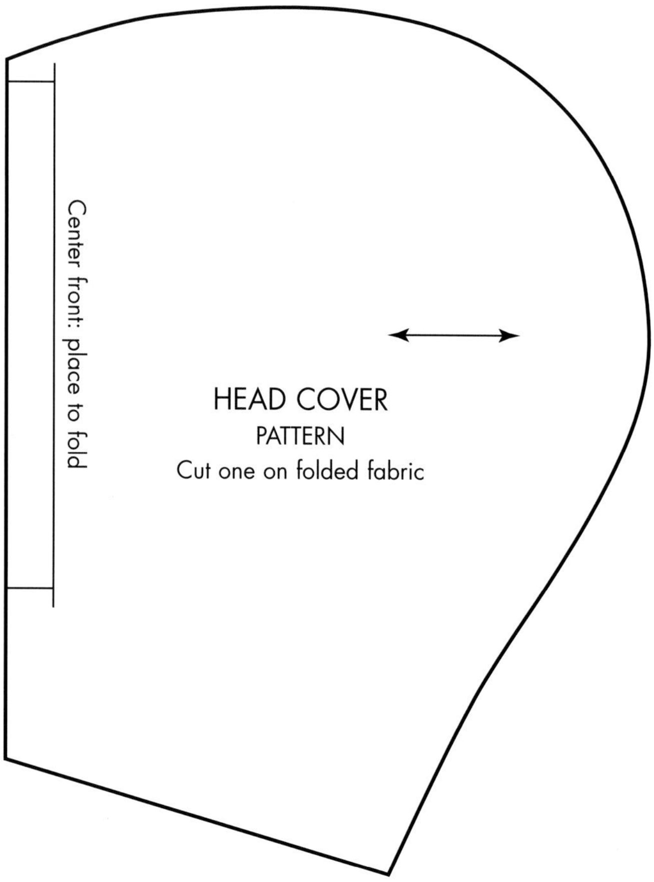

Center front: place to fold

HEAD COVER
PATTERN
Cut one on folded fabric

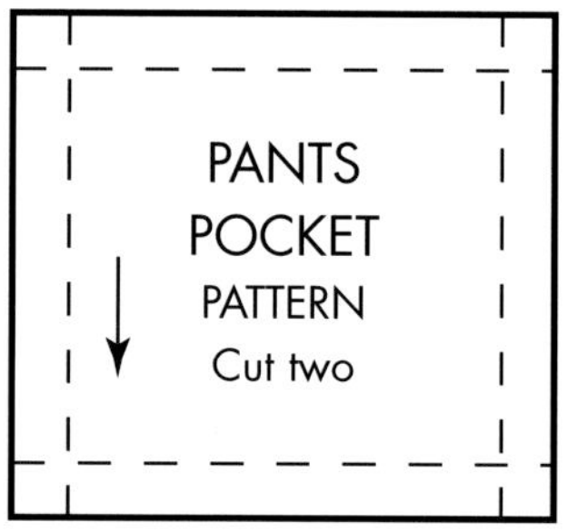

PANTS POCKET
PATTERN
Cut two

PIERROT

Scale 70%

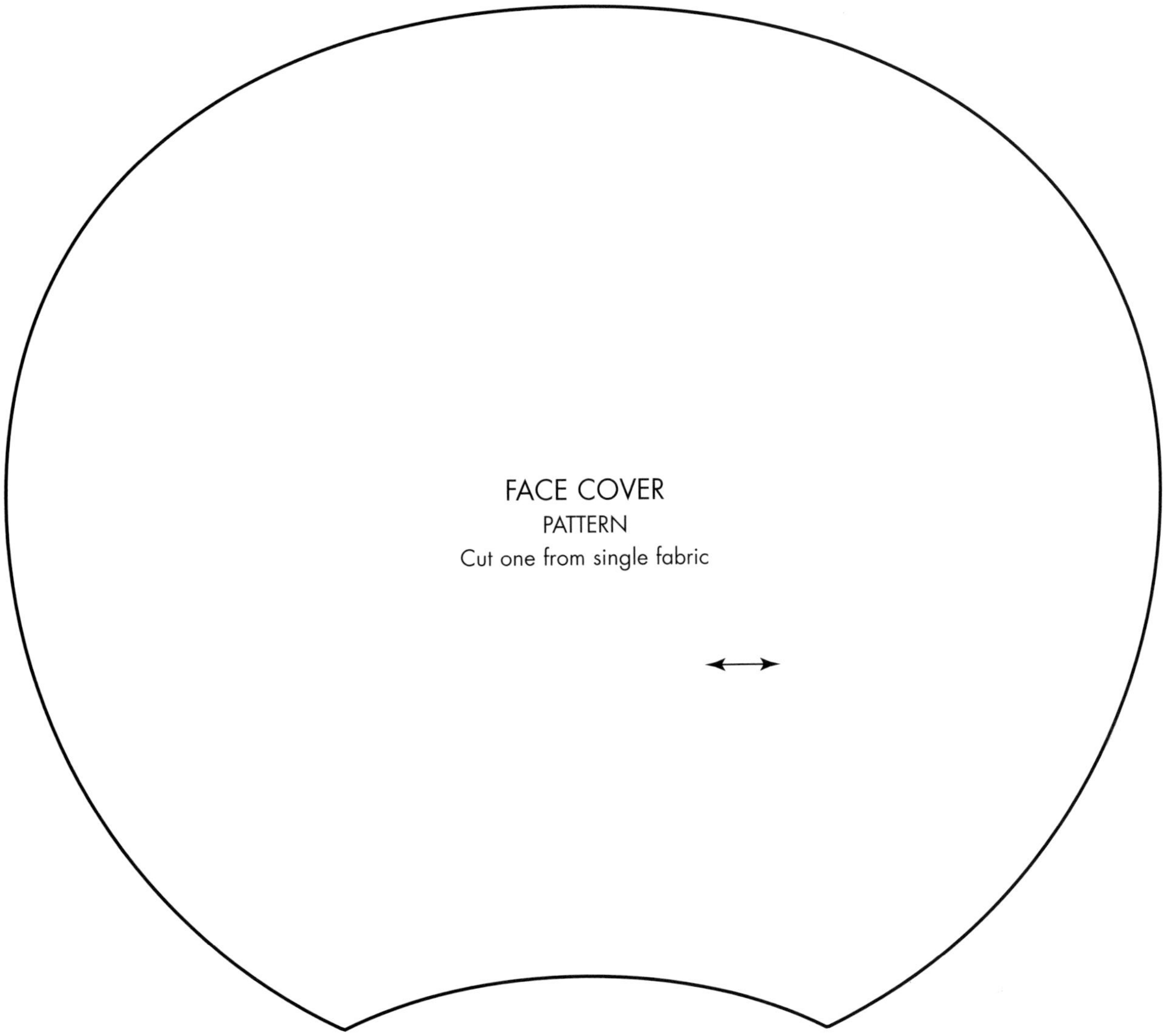
FACE COVER
PATTERN
Cut one from single fabric

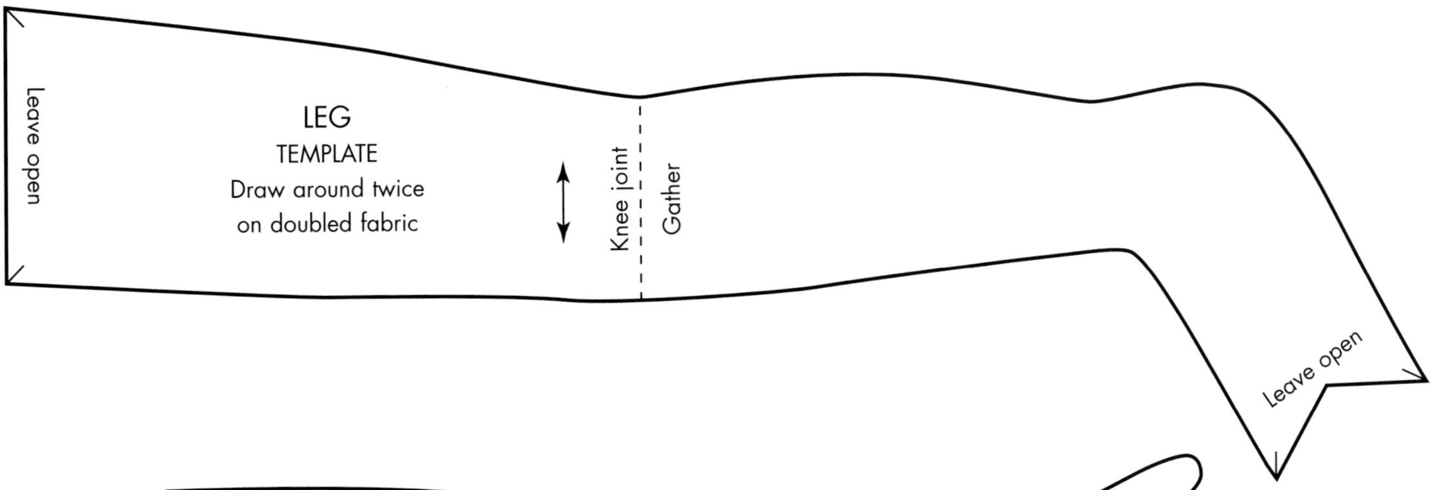
Leave open
LEG
TEMPLATE
Draw around twice
on doubled fabric
Knee joint
Gather
Leave open

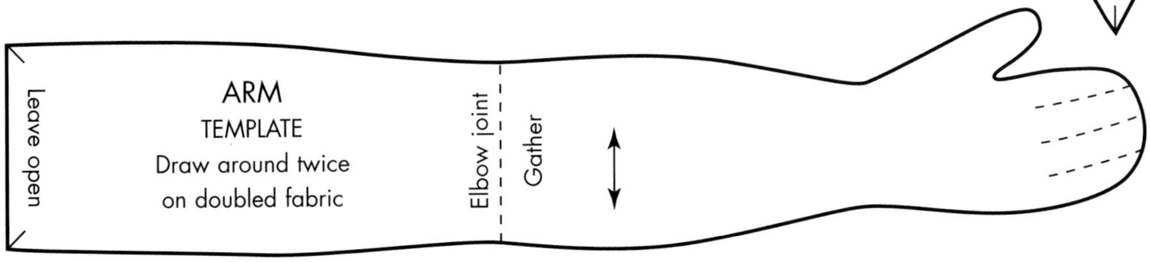
Leave open
ARM
TEMPLATE
Draw around twice
on doubled fabric
Elbow joint
Gather

PIERROT

Scale 70%

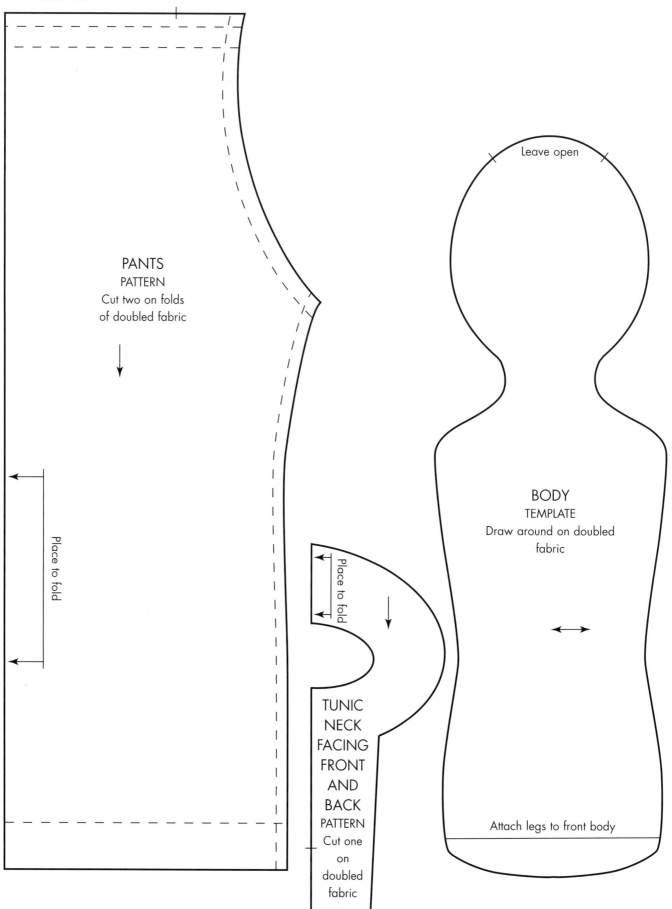

PANTS
PATTERN
Cut two on folds
of doubled fabric

Place to fold

Place to fold

TUNIC
NECK
FACING
FRONT
AND
BACK
PATTERN
Cut one
on
doubled
fabric

Leave open

BODY
TEMPLATE
Draw around on doubled
fabric

Attach legs to front body

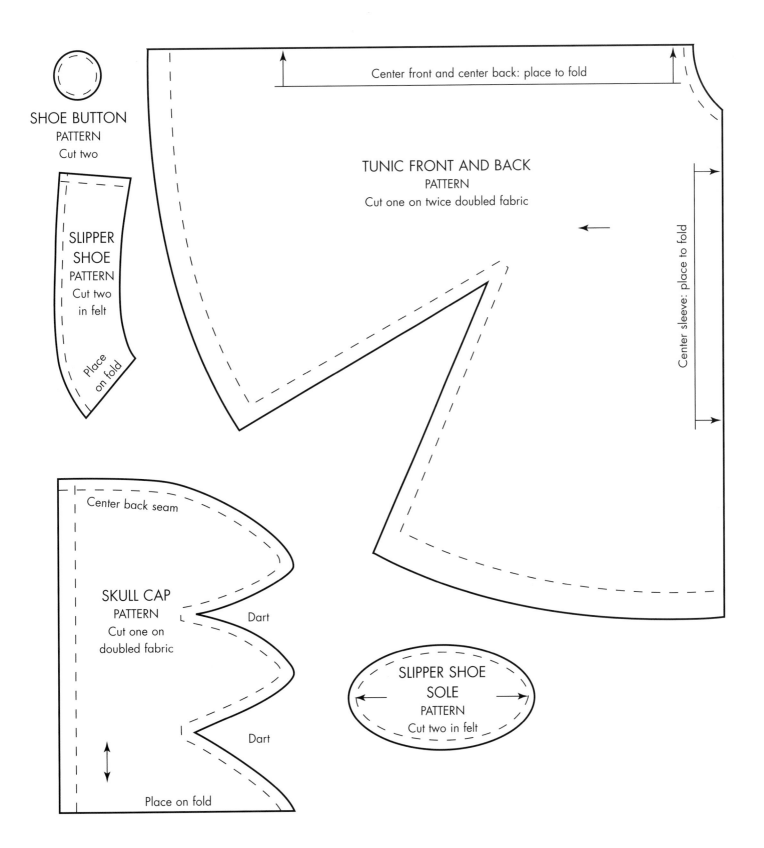

SHOE BUTTON
PATTERN
Cut two

SLIPPER SHOE
PATTERN
Cut two in felt

Place on fold

Center front and center back: place to fold

TUNIC FRONT AND BACK
PATTERN
Cut one on twice doubled fabric

Center sleeve: place to fold

Center back seam

SKULL CAP
PATTERN
Cut one on doubled fabric

Dart

Dart

Place on fold

SLIPPER SHOE SOLE
PATTERN
Cut two in felt

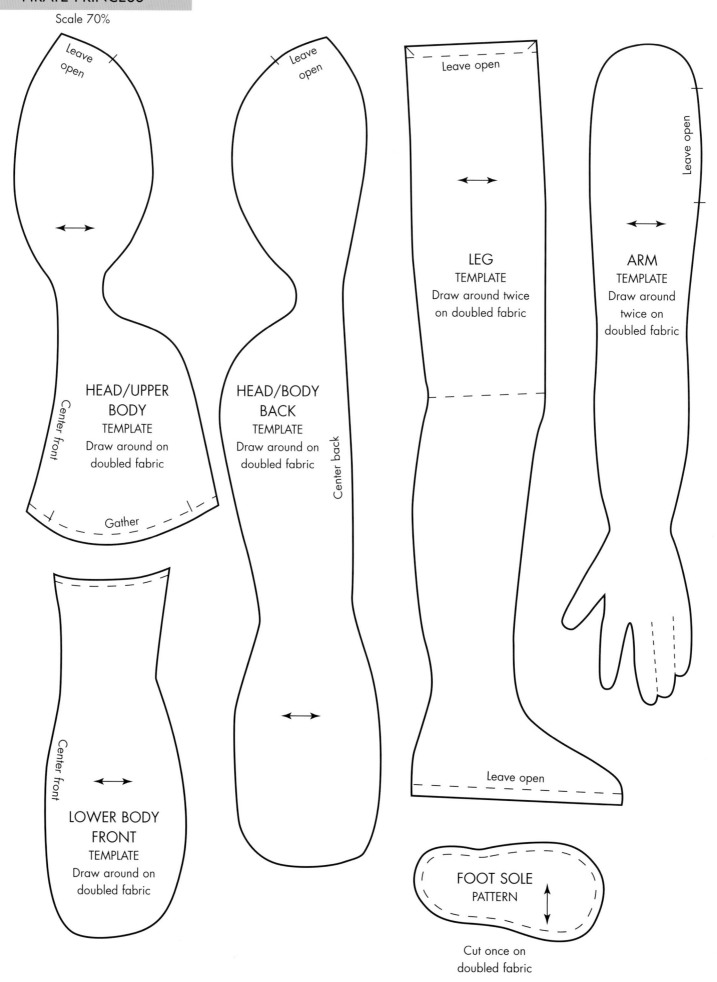

PIRATE PRINCESS

Scale 70%

Leave open

HEAD/UPPER BODY
TEMPLATE
Draw around on doubled fabric

Center front

Gather

LOWER BODY FRONT
TEMPLATE
Draw around on doubled fabric

Center front

Leave open

HEAD/BODY BACK
TEMPLATE
Draw around on doubled fabric

Center back

LEG
TEMPLATE
Draw around twice on doubled fabric

Leave open

Leave open

ARM
TEMPLATE
Draw around twice on doubled fabric

Leave open

FOOT SOLE
PATTERN

Cut once on doubled fabric

PIRATE PRINCESS

Scale 70%

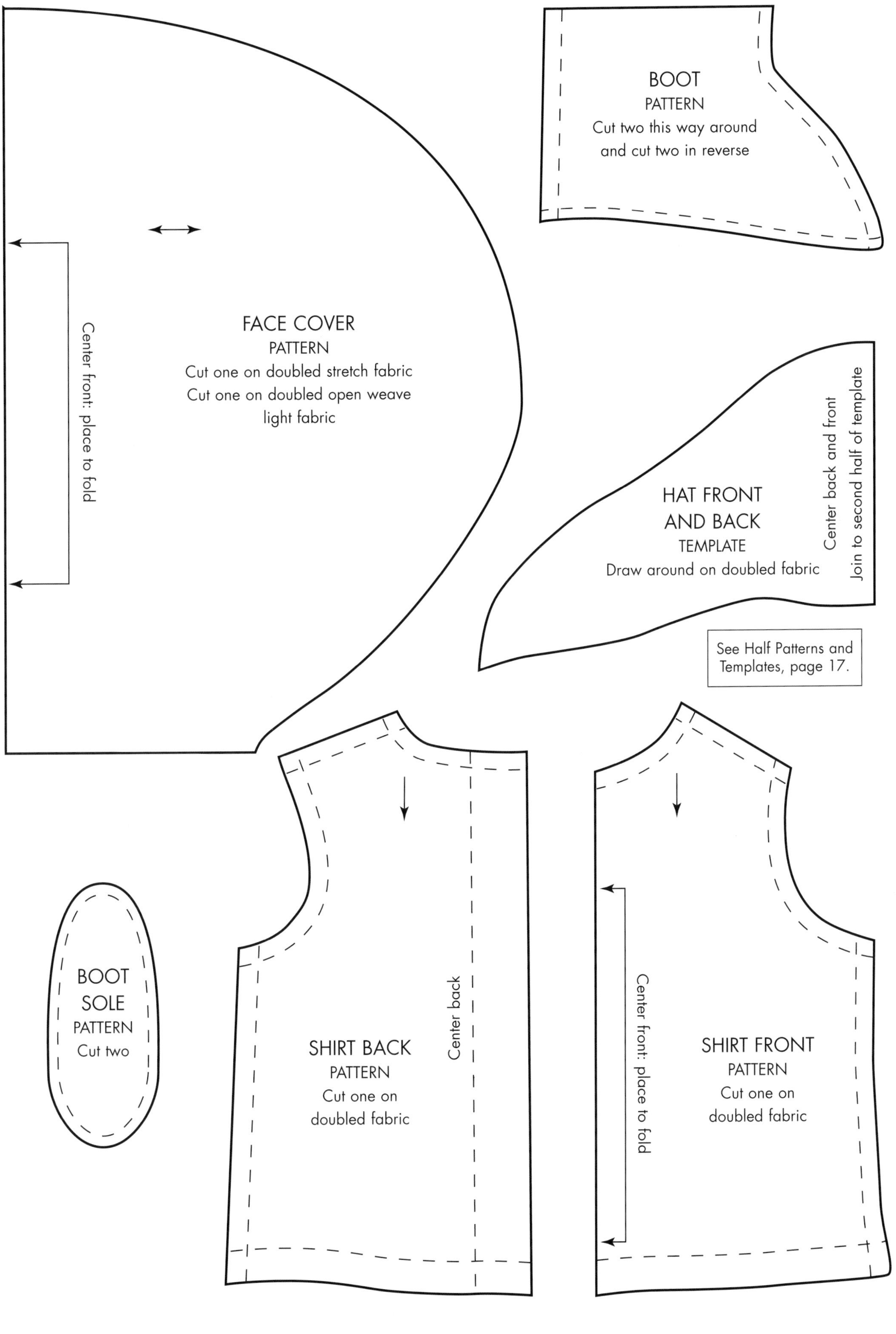
BOOT
PATTERN
Cut two this way around
and cut two in reverse
FACE COVER
PATTERN
Cut one on doubled stretch fabric
Cut one on doubled open weave
light fabric
Center front: place to fold
HAT FRONT
AND BACK
TEMPLATE
Draw around on doubled fabric
Center back and front
Join to second half of template
See Half Patterns and Templates, page 17.
BOOT
SOLE
PATTERN
Cut two
SHIRT BACK
PATTERN
Cut one on
doubled fabric
Center back
SHIRT FRONT
PATTERN
Cut one on
doubled fabric
Center front: place to fold

PIRATE PRINCESS

Scale 70%

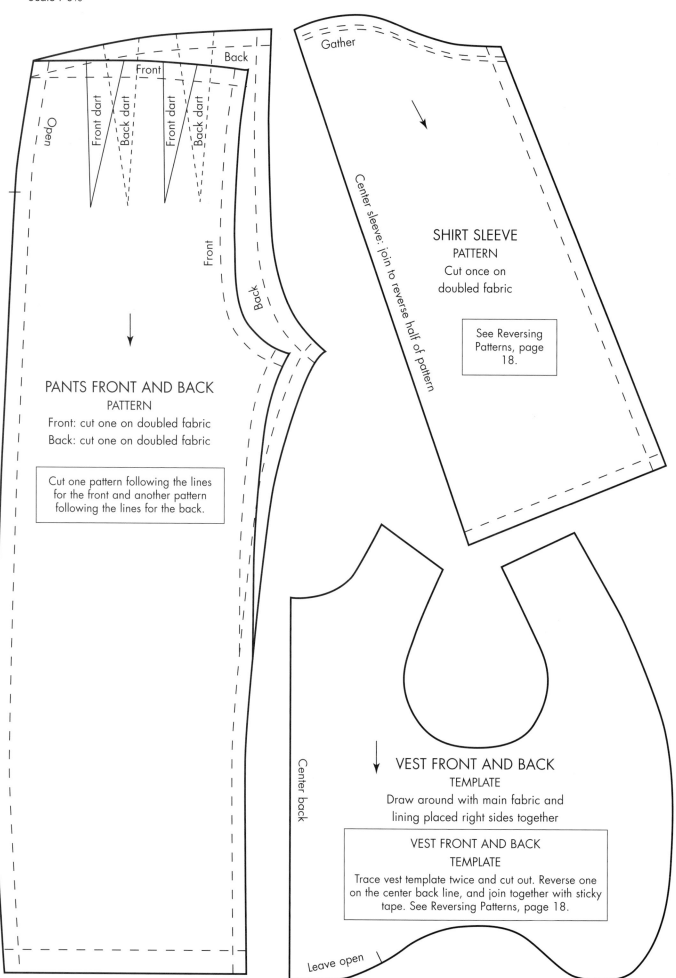

Open

Front dart **Back dart** **Front dart** **Back dart**

Front **Back**

Front

PANTS FRONT AND BACK
PATTERN
Front: cut one on doubled fabric
Back: cut one on doubled fabric

Cut one pattern following the lines
for the front and another pattern
following the lines for the back.

Back

Gather

Center sleeve: join to reverse half of pattern

SHIRT SLEEVE
PATTERN
Cut once on
doubled fabric

See Reversing
Patterns, page
18.

Center back

VEST FRONT AND BACK
TEMPLATE
Draw around with main fabric and
lining placed right sides together

VEST FRONT AND BACK
TEMPLATE
Trace vest template twice and cut out. Reverse one
on the center back line, and join together with sticky
tape. See Reversing Patterns, page 18.

Leave open

Resources

General craft stores and fabric stores sell most of the materials required for doll making.

All suppliers mentioned here offer a mail order service, unless otherwise stated.

Suppliers

CR's Crafts
Box 8-TD81
Leland, IA 50453

Sells everything you need to create dolls.

Kemper Doll Supplies
13595 12th Street
Chino, California 91710
Tel: 1–800 388 5367/(1-909) 627 6191
Fax: (1-909) 627 4008

Doll supplies, free catalog.

One & Only Creations
P.O. Box 2730
Napa, CA 94558
Tel: 1–800 262 6768
Fax: (1-916) 663 4541

Quality doll making supplies, free catalog.

Powell Sheep Co.
P.O. Box 183
Ramona, CA 92065

Mohair, wool, rovings, and yarns for doll hair and Santa's beards. They can be contacted for price lists and samples.

Putnam Company Inc.
P.O. Box 310
Walworth, WI 53184
Tel: 1–800 338 4776

Sell many kinds of polyester filling.

Sisters & Daughters, Inc.
1001 Cooper Pt Rd SW
Suite 140-168
Olympia, WA 98502
Fax: (1-360) 705 1228

Cloth doll making supplies.

Tallina's Doll Supplies Inc.
15791 S.E. Hwy 224
Clackamas, OR 97015

Doll supplies.

Publications

The Cloth Doll "The Voice of Cloth Doll Making Worldwide"
Beswick Publishing
8700 S.W. 26th Avenue
Suite Q
Portland, OR 97219-4033
Tel: (1-503) 244 3539
Fax: (1-503) 244 2370

Magazine published quarterly.

Contemporary Doll Collector
Scott Publications
30595 Eight Mile
Livonia, MI 48152-1798
Tel: 1–800 458 8237/(1-248) 477 6650
Fax: (1-248) 477 6795

Magazine published quarterly.

Soft Dolls and Animals
For details see *Contemporary Doll Collector.*

Index

Acknowledgments

The author wishes to acknowledge and thank the following people for their contributions to the book:

Hilarie Berzins for the Angel, Rose Fairy, and Fantasy Flapper doll projects.

Hilarie is a talented doll maker who has developed her design skills in her spare time as a computer programmer. Three years ago she returned to her first love and began making original cloth dolls, specializing in period fantasy dolls.

Helene McLeod for the Baby Doll and African Doll projects.

Helene, a doll artist of long standing, has a strong interest in the real, wider world with its rich variety of people and lifestyles. This is reflected in her dolls, which she makes in porcelain, papier mâché and wood, as well as in fabric.